5.36

PR11 22 69

Essay Index

PROBLEMS OF THE MODERN ECONOMY

Defense, Science, and Public Policy

PROBLEMS OF THE MODERN ECONOMY

General Editor: EDMUND S. PHELPS, *University of Pennsylvania*

Each volume in this series presents
prominent positions in the debate of
an important issue of economic policy

Defense, Science,
and
Public Policy

Edited by

EDWIN MANSFIELD

WHARTON SCHOOL,
UNIVERSITY OF PENNSYLVANIA

Essay Index

NEW YORK

W · W · NORTON & COMPANY · INC ·

Contents

PART FOUR: Basic Research, Civilian Technology, and Public Policy

Introduction

EVEN A CURSORY GLANCE at the daily newspaper shows that the American economy is influenced in a very important way by the nation's defense requirements. In 1967, estimated expenditures on national defense totaled about $70 billion—or about 60 per cent of the federal administrative budget. In part, this was due to the Vietnamese war, but even before our role in Vietnam became so extensive, national defense accounted for a large percentage of the federal budget as well as of the gross national product. For example, in 1963 military expenditures were over $50 billion—or over 50 per cent of the federal administrative budget and almost 10 per cent of the nation's gross national product.

Defense spending is of great significance to society not only because of its sheer size and its importance to the existence of our nation and to the preservation of our freedom and institutions. It is also of fundamental importance because of its close relationship with science and technology. Defense and space programs utilize a major share of the scientific and engineering talent in the United States, and play a large role in shaping the course of scientific and technological advance here and abroad. The closeness of the relationship between defense and science (and technology) is by no means new. For example, Archimedes designed fortifications and engines of war to help Syracuse keep at bay the Romans in the third century B.C. For better or worse, defense, science, and technology have always been intertwined.

This book considers a number of central public policy issues in the interrelated areas of defense and science, some of the major questions being: What are the effects of large defense expenditures on our economy and on our international economic relations? To what extent are large defense expenditures necessary for prosperity? To what extent are they a political danger? What are the advantages of the program budgeting and cost-effectiveness techniques introduced by former Secretary of Defense McNamara? What are their disadvantages? How efficient have we been in developing new weapons? What steps can be taken to improve our efficiency? What role should the government play in the support of basic research and civilian technology? How should the federal research and development budget be allocated? In view of the size and importance of the resources devoted to national defense and science, these questions are of the greatest significance—and in many cases they are as difficult as they are important.

Both defense and science are extremely complex areas of government concern. The nature of some of the public policy issues in these areas is discussed in the introductory essay by Jerome Wiesner, formerly Science Adviser to Presidents Kennedy and Johnson and now Provost at Massachusetts Institute of Technology. In his view, we are at a crossroads. After the tremendous changes in military technology during the 1950's, progress in defense technology will be more modest, thus allowing us to turn our attention and resources to nondefense needs and opportunities. This belief is not shared by all observers, as evidenced by Baldwin's article in Part Two of this book. Wiesner also distinguishes between "science in policy" problems and "policy in science" problems, the former being problems of applying science and technology to affect our capabilities for government action, the latter being problems of optimizing the impact of federal policy on science.

DEFENSE AND THE ECONOMY

Before evaluating the impact of defense spending on the economy, it is important to understand the general problem of nuclear war as it exists today, and the kinds of strategic forces which it involves. Secretary of Defense McNamara provides a brief description of this nation's objectives and capabilities, as well as an assessment of the size and character of the threat from the Soviet Union and Red China. He states that our nuclear forces should have two basic capabilities: "(1) To deter deliberate nuclear attack . . . by maintaining, continuously, a highly reliable ability to inflict an unacceptable degree of damage upon any . . . aggressor . . . even after absorbing a surprise first strike. (2) In the event such a war nevertheless occurred, to limit damage to

our population and industrial capacity." Included in this article is
a reference to the controversy over the deployment of antiballistic
missile defense systems. Also included is a table showing the size
of United States and Soviet intercontinental strategic nuclear
forces.[1]

We have already noted that defense expenditures are a large
percentage—about 60 per cent in 1967—of the federal administrative budget. What does this money go for? Murray Weidenbaum describes the changes over time in the size and composition
of defense expenditures and the industries and regions primarily
involved. In 1964 about 26 per cent of all these expenditures went
for the procurement of weapons systems, 18 per cent went for
research and development, 3 per cent went for construction, and
53 per cent went for operating expenses. About 50 per cent of
defense contract awards went to the aircraft industry, about 25
per cent went to the electronic industry. Six states depend on defense and space work for at least 10 per cent of personal income
—Virginia, Utah, Washington, California, Alaska, and Hawaii.
Weidenbaum notes that defense and space programs have a particularly important effect on the allocation of the nation's scientific
and engineering talent, and he discusses the effects of military
research and development on civilian technology.

What are the effects of these large expenditures on the economy? According to some observers, it is only the stimulus of
defense spending that has kept the U. S. economy from returning
to the mass unemployment of the thirties. According to another
view, defense has not been an economic burden because the resources devoted to it would have been wasted on trivia and status
symbols. In the next article, James Tobin dismisses both of these
views and discusses the nature of the real economic burden of
our defense effort. He also points out that the revolution in military technology has had dramatic effects on our international
economic relations. "The dollar has been serving as an international currency, and the United States has been the world's
banker. These functions will be shared more and more with
Europe, and more and more internationalized. In this, as in other

1. However, according to some military experts, these estimates overstate
the true ratio of U.S. to Soviet forces. See "Pentagon Concern on Lack of
Missile Defense Grows," *The New York Times,* May 21, 1967.

respects, the military revolution has brought the United States down to earth, subject to the same burdens, frustrations, and problems as the ordinary run of mortal nations."

The next article contains the famous passage from Dwight D. Eisenhower's last address to the nation as President, in which he stressed some other possible effects of these large defense expenditures. "In the councils of government we must guard against th acquisition of unwarranted influence, whether sought or unsought, by the military-industrial complex. The potential for the disastrous rise of misplaced power exists and will persist." It seems unlikely that a conspiracy actually exists, but the pressures of the "military-industrial complex" are nonetheless real and important. Adam Yarmolinsky, formerly a prominent Defense Department official, believes that the "pressures can still be resisted, and there is every reason to believe that they will be. But it is unreasonable to expect any Secretary of Defense to resist them alone, or supported only by a few people within the Department who are entirely his own men."

DECISION MAKING IN THE DEPARTMENT OF DEFENSE

A great many important innovations and reforms have been made in the management of the military establishment since the appointment of Robert McNamara as Secretary of Defense. One of the most significant innovations is the system of program budgeting, which has subsequently been extended by President Johnson to other parts of the federal government. David Novick describes the new program budgeting procedure and explains its advantages over earlier methods. The new procedure has two principal aims: to allow analysis of total force structures for all of the services in terms of common objectives and to project the financial requirements of the proposed force structure over a period of years. The new planning-programming-budgeting system consists of five elements: "(1) A program structure in terms of missions, forces, weapon and support systems. (2) The analytical comparisons of alternatives. (3) A continually updated five-year force structure and financial program. (4) Related year-round decision-making on new programs and changes. (5) Progress reporting to test the validity and administration of the plan."

Despite their apparent advantages, the new management tech-

niques introduced by McNamara have been the center of consider-
erable controversy. Some critics feel that the judgment of military
officers has been unduly downgraded, that there is too much centralization of decision-making in the Department of Defense, and
that the new cost-effectiveness techniques have held back the
development of new weapons. Hanson Baldwin presents this
point of view. In his opinion, "Mr. McNamara's 'whiz kids,' complete with slide rules and computers, brushed aside the factor of
professional judgment or scientific hunch when they took office
and their emphasis upon 'perfection on paper' and the cost part
of the cost-effectiveness formula has definitely slowed the pace
of military development." In particular, he criticizes the institution of the "project definition phase" of projects and the attitude,
expressed in Wiesner's introductory essay, that the revolution in
military technology is slowing down. He favors a return to "competition in hardware rather than competition on paper."

Charles Hitch, former Comptroller of the Department of Defense, presents the case for the new programming and cost-
effectiveness techniques. He begins by assailing the suspicion
that "cost-effectiveness studies put 'dollars before national security,' or will result in our going to war with 'cut-rate, cut-quality,
cheapest-to-buy weapons'." He points out that, "although our
national security objectives . . . reflect essentially the composite
values of the American people, the choice of a particular military
strategy or military objective cannot be divorced from the cost
of achieving it." He goes on to state that "economic choice is a
way of looking at problems and does not necessarily depend on
the use of any analytic aids or computational devices." As for the
charge that the role of the military men has been downgraded,
he argues that their role is actually greater now; formerly "the
plans they produced, because they were divorced from budget
realities, were largely ignored . . ." As for the charge that cost-
effectiveness studies act as too sharp a brake in the innovation
process, he says that it is only in advanced development that costs
and possible benefits begin to be considered.

MILITARY RESEARCH AND DEVELOPMENT

Realizing that any nation that falls significantly behind in military technology will be at the mercy of a more innovative foe,

the great powers have spent enormous amounts on military research and development, precipitating several revolutions in technology in the past twenty-five years. Most important have been the successful development and improvement of fission and fusion bombs, although significant achievements have also occurred in delivery vehicles, guidance techniques, radar and other areas. In view of the importance of military research and development, we must look at various issues concerning the adequacy and efficiency of our programs.

Based on a long series of studies of military development projects, economists at the RAND Corporation, led by Burton Klein, have made a number of suggestions regarding military development policy. Klein, in his paper, argues that it is important that the government devote a very significant proportion of its military R and D expenditures to activities falling outside the major weapons systems programs, i.e., to basic research, exploratory development, and advanced development.[2] By developing in this way a large menu of technology, we can hope to buy at a relatively low price the capability to adapt our weapons systems to the actual strategic situation in a short period of time. In carrying out weapons systems programs, Klein suggests that a frankly experimental approach be adopted. He believes that requirements for systems should be stated initially in broad terms, that flexibility should be maintained, and that decisions on the best set of compromises be postponed until there is a reasonable basis for making them.

In the following paper, Carl Kaysen, the new director of the Institute of Advanced Study, argues that, to a greater extent, military research and development should be divorced from production, and performed in nonprofit research institutes and government laboratories, which in his view are better suited than business firms to carrry out this task. If development can be separated from production, it will be possible to reap the benefits from competition at the development stage and from a freer

2. Research includes all effort toward increased knowledge of natural phenomena and toward the solution of problems having no clear military application. Exploratory development includes all efforts to resolve specific military problems short of major development projects. Advanced development includes all projects that have moved into development of hardware for experimental or operational tests.

choice of suppliers and contract instruments at the production stage. This, of course, is a very controversial proposal. Paul Cherington's paper is an attempt to rebut Kaysen's arguments. According to Cherington, Kaysen underestimates the difficulty of the integration task and the costs involved in separating development from production, the latter costs being high because there are considerable overlap and similarity between development and production and because learning is transferred between them. Cherington also claims that competitive pressures and the ability to obtain superior personnel are good reasons for relying primarily on business firms to carry out military research and development.

In the final article in this section, Merton Peck and Frederick Scherer summarize the conclusions of their major study of the weapons acquisition process. Based on experience in military research and development up to the early sixties, they conclude that, although technical performance, reliability, and development time have been at least reasonably satisfactory, there has been a notable failure to hold development and production costs to reasonable levels. In part this has been due to inadequate attention being given to the efficient use of technical and other manpower and to the development of increments of performance that were not worth their cost. More fundamentally it has been due to the greater emphasis that the services placed on time and quality considerations than on cost reduction. Moreover, cost-plus contracts provided little incentive to reduce costs. During the sixties, as we have seen, Secretary McNamara emphasized cost reduction to a greater extent than was formerly the case.

BASIC RESEARCH, CIVILIAN TECHNOLOGY, AND PUBLIC POLICY

In recent years many observers have expressed concern over the adequacy of our national science policies. There has been considerable uneasiness regarding the very heavy concentration of the nation's scientific resources on military and space work, some, like President Eisenhower, fearing that public policy may become the captive of a scientific elite, allied with military and industrial power, others being concerned that other high-priority fields, like transportation and housing, are being deprived of research and development resources. Questions also have been raised concerning the extent to which the government should support basic research, the efficiency of various government research and development programs, and the effectiveness of the federal decision making process concerning research and development programs.

Don Price, dean of the Graduate School of Public Administration at Harvard University, points out that during the early sixties it was evident "that science had become something close to an *establishment*, in the old and proper sense of that word: a set of institutions supported by tax funds, but largely on faith, and without direct responsibility to political control." In more recent years there is evidence of a growing friction between the scientific establishment and the Congress. More fundamentally, as Price says, science seems to be having a number of major effects on our political institutions, some of the results being the blurring of the distinction between the public and private sectors, a new order of complexity in the administration of public affairs, and the upsetting of our system of checks and balances.

William Carey, Executive Assistant Director of the Bureau of the Budget, describes the issues confronting the federal budget-makers in deciding how much money to allocate for various fields of science. In the following articles, Carl Kaysen and Harry Johnson try to come to grips with what is perhaps the most difficult question in this area: How much should the federal government spend for basic research in various areas? As Kaysen points out, the fruits of basic research are so uncertain and so difficult for a firm to appropriate that, without government support, there is almost sure to be an underinvestment in basic research. When it comes to deciding on a particular amount to spend, he concludes that no precise calculations can be made, expenditure on basic research being essentially an overhead item.

After summarizing some of the relevant economic literature regarding the relationship between the advance of knowledge and the rate of economic growth, Johnson concludes that economics "would require allocating resources among scientific fields so as to equalize the prospective social rates of return from marginal

expenditures on each field, and fixing the total of resources allocated to basic research at the level yielding a marginal rate of return on all investment in basic research comparable to what is
earned on other forms of investment . . ." He recognizes that
the information required to carry out these calculations is not
available, but he thinks that the principles may nonetheless be
of use. He is less inclined than Kaysen to use rule-of-thumb procedures based on the situation in the recent past.

In the United States, as well as many other countries, there has
been a great deal of attention paid to the "technology gap" and
the "brain drain." Indeed, these subjects have been extremely
fashionable in the mid-sixties. In the next article, Vice President
Humphrey discusses ways of closing the gap and voices the popular concern regarding the brain drain. In contrast, Richard Morse
claims that "if there is some gap between the U. S. and Europe
to which Europeans should direct their attention, it is not the
technological gap, but rather a *management gap.*" Harry Johnson
analyzes the sorts of losses incurred by a country when there is an
emigration of highly trained people, and suggests that they may
not be as great as is popularly assumed.

In the following paper, Richard Nelson discusses the effects of
various allocations of research and development resources, the
types of criteria that are relevant in choosing among alternative
allocations, and the role of the market and of public policy in
assuring that the actual allocation is as close as possible to the
optimum. He concludes that, "aside from the fields of defense
and space, it is likely that we are relying too much on the workings of private incentives as stimulated by the market to generate
R and D relevant to the public sector . . . [and that] the
federal government has not as yet recognized adequately the role
that it must play in helping to allocate private sector R and D
effectively in those instances where the market does not work
well."

In the concluding article, the editor discusses various aspects
of public policy concerning civilian technology—the alleged underinvestment in research and development in transportation,
housing, and pollution control, as well as in various industries like
textiles and machine tools, the State Technical Services Act, the
use of performance-based federal procurement, proposed changes

in the National Science Foundation, various problems in coordinating the vast number of federal R and D programs, and the procedures by which the federal R and D budget is allocated. With respect to the allocation procedures, he concludes that: "Although it is generally acknowledged that somewhat more coordination would be a good thing, . . . most observers [are] impressed with the difficulties involved in direct allocation of R and D resources . . . Nonetheless, it seems likely that more attempt will be made in the future to compare the costs and benefits of various kinds of research and development. However, it does not seem likely, or desirable, that the government will attempt to program science and technology on the basis of a totally integrated science and technology budget."

Prologue

The Scientific Revolution and Public Policy

JEROME WIESNER

Jerome Wiesner was Science Adviser to Presidents Kennedy and Johnson. Presently he is the Provost of Massachusetts Institute of Technology. This article, adapted from his testimony before the House Subcommittee on Science, Research, and Development, appears in his book, Where Science and Politics Meet, *published in 1965.*

The dimensions of detail and subtlety of concept in our scientific efforts are constantly multiplying and the most characteristic feature of these activities, the one that clearly predominates, is the law of change. From year to year, knowledge advances at such a rate that men and institutions, not the least of which must be the government, are challenged to adjust their perspectives to meet newly discovered needs and opportunities. On the one hand, technology is the servant of our social purposes and must respond to new demands and changing priorities based on considerations of economic growth or public health or military strategy. On the other hand, science itself sets out to achieve new understanding through exploration and analysis, so that what was not known yesterday becomes a working hypothesis today and an everyday product tomorrow.

Even categorization of scientific activities becomes steadily obsolete. One branch of nuclear physics becomes a part of astronomy. A whole new branch of astronomy—radioastronomy—grows into a major discipline within a few years, and with the laser, optics suddenly becomes a branch of communications engineering. A relatively young aspect of physics—magnetic resonance—takes

1

a new place as an important tool of biology. The electronic computer opens up new vistas in biology and medicine.

Esoteric research projects, meanwhile, which may have seemed subjects for idle curiosity a few years ago, have become the basis of major scientific applications. Studies of the mating habits of insects lead to a wholly new method of pest control, and examination of the migration and feeding habits of so-called trash fish contributes to understanding and avoiding sources of interference in the detection of submarines by underwater sound. Hitherto useless and highly abstract branches of pure mathematics underlie the design of electronic computers. And, at many frontiers of technology, the divisions among the classical disciplines of engineering grow obsolete and meaningless.

While this characteristic of constant change continued to dominate scientific activities, we may have reached a point of relative stability in that aspect of our technology—the development of weapons for military purposes—which has stimulated much of our scientific progress over the last ten years. The lesson of this revolutionary technical advance is clear: our leadership and our security in an uncertain world require spirited efforts to expand our knowledge and assume a stance of energetic readiness to turn new knowledge to practical ends.

At the beginning of the nineteen fifties, many of our wisest men did not foresee the wholly new military potentialities of developments in rocket propulsion, guidance, communications, and nuclear technology: the overall consequences of new technologies are always difficult to imagine, although there is danger, too, in assuming that everything new is superior. Now we have reached a state of extensive exploitation of these revolutionary advances, largely spurred by the need to keep well ahead of Soviet progress in the same technical areas. In most respects we are the strongest nation in the world, economically, technologically—in agriculture, medicine and in military capabilities—and in education and science. We cannot rest with these achievements. While I believe that our best security comes from effective limitation of armaments, I do not think that we can afford to relax the technical efforts which provide the basis of our security until such effective controls are well underway. Although the scientific-military revolution has stabilized, we must continue the process of refining past achievements in the military area and probing for new possibilities.

But security consists of more than armaments. It means good relations with others, a strong economy, and a healthy people, and science contributes in a major way to all these objectives. Ten years ago there was a close relationship between military-oriented research and development and civilian needs, and military efforts could—and did—make major contributions to the progress of most of our science and technology. Weapons research and development can no longer pace our progress to the same extent, and new and more conscious ways of insuring long-range scientific and technological advances are now required. At the same time, there are urgent needs for the application of knowledge to develop substitutes for familiar shortages, to confront pollution in our environment created by industrial and urban life, to meet foreign economic competition, and to adjust imbalances in our economy created by technology itself.

Today we are trying to understand the new implications and possibilities of all these changing needs and opportunities in science, just as we once wrestled primarily with military problems. Our chief concern in the government, in the broadest sense, is to bring this understanding of technology to bear on the collective needs of our people. It is a process that must combine the skills of the statesman, the scientific expert, the engineer, and the entrepreneur or industrialist, and it is a task that demands a major effort and the utmost imagination of all concerned.

Though the role of science in public affairs resists exact definition, we can set forth some broad categories that describe the ways in which scientific considerations affect decisions. One aspect might be called "science in policy," seeking to understand how knowledge of nature and technique affect possibilities for governmental action. The clearest example of this interaction is in the field of defense, where the technical performance of weapons systems has direct bearing on our ability to carry out our national policies and on the choice of policies we consider tenable. At the same time, we must be concerned with a policy for the support of science itself, with a conscious and purposeful effort to continue the development of a healthy scientific enterprise and to maximize the productivity of our human and material resources.

An appraisal of the federal budget shows the magnitude of government involvement in research and development. Since 1958, this federal investment has experienced a sharp rise, amounting in fiscal year 1964 to an estimated 15 billion dollars in expenditures. It has been stated that the research and development portion of these expenditures has risen to about one-third of our annual allocatable expenditures, exclusive of fixed charges in the budget for interest, veterans' benefits, subsidies, and prior-year commitments for capital expenditures.

These statistics must be examined carefully and in considerable detail to understand both the character and consequences of our current level of research and development (R&D) expenditures. All too often these activities have been collectively called "science" when in fact they represent a diversity of functions and interests as wide as the federal government itself. In fiscal year 1963, research obligations were 4.2 billion dollars, of which 1.4 billion was for basic research. The commitment for development was 13 billion. So when we talk about research and development, we must be aware of the distinction between the two processes, the amount of resources committed to each and the variety of activities that fall in both categories.

Development is largely related to particular and practical goals, often leading to the procurement of hardware by the government, to a preponderant degree in the defense area. Such practical goals also include improvement in power generation, mineral extraction from low-grade ore, water conservation, pollution control, fire protection, air and highway safety, and health, and reflect a response to familiar needs that is in no way unexpected or unjustifiable where our activities are increasingly involved and dependent upon technology. Because development and, to a major extent, applied research are pointed toward well-developed objectives, the total level of support and the balance between the alternatives can be decided by the American people through their legislative and executive representatives on a basis of some assessment of what each project can contribute to national goals. Here it should be possible to set priorities. Development planning is comparatively straightforward and quantifiable and the conduct of programs is subject to normal management principles and control over cost and quality. Choices in research are often far more complex.

Research is a relatively small though vital portion of our total effort in scientific and technological areas; only a limited proportion—around four per cent—of a federal budget of almost 100 billion dollars was for all research and less than two per cent was for basic research. In relation to our gross national product (over 500 billion dollars) the proportion of federally sponsored research is quite small, and the potential productive payoff immense. Federal expenditures for basic research, more than sixty per cent of the national total, constitute far less than ½ of one per cent of our annual gross national product, notwithstanding the fact that our present and future capabilities to meet technical objectives have become heavily dependent on progress in scientific research.

The systematic pursuit of new knowledge has become a key to meeting major national needs, yet no description of the process can accurately classify its ingredients. We know by hindsight that the development of the tools of our social purposes—like weapons or communications or vaccines—requires imaginativeness and ingenuity based on extensive and subtle understanding. We know too that energetic exploration often totally unrelated to any likely application of knowledge can lead to profound revolutions in our thinking, and that the fundamental nature of inquiry into the unknown is that the results are never likely to be more than hunches at the outset. Such imaginative inquiry has unlocked the secrets of the atom within this century, yielding practical results that have altered our world in ways that even now may not yet be fully apparent.

PART ONE Defense and the Economy

The General Problem of Nuclear War

ROBERT MC NAMARA

Robert McNamara was Secretary of Defense from 1961 to 1968, when he became head of the World Bank. Prior to 1961 he was president of Ford Motor Company. The following article is taken from his 1967 testimony before the House Armed Services Committee.

THE GENERAL NUCLEAR WAR PROBLEM

DURING the past several years, in my annual appearances before this Committee, I have attempted to explore with you some of the more fundamental characteristics of the general nuclear war problem and the kinds of strategic forces which it involves. I noted that our general nuclear war forces should have two basic capabilities: (1) to deter deliberate nuclear attack upon the United States and its allies by maintaining, continuously, a highly reliable ability to inflict an unacceptable degree of damage upon any single aggressor, or combination of aggressors, at any time during the course of a strategic nuclear exchange, even after absorbing a surprise first strike (2) in the event such a war nevertheless occurred, to limit damage to our population and industrial capacity.

The first capability we call "Assured Destruction" and in the second "Damage Limitation." The strategic *offensive* forces—the ICBMs, the submarine-launched ballistic missiles (SLBMs), and the manned bombers—which we usually associate with the first capability, can also contribute to the second. They can do so by attacking enemy delivery vehicles on their bases or launch sites, provided they can reach those vehicles before they are launched at our cities. Conversely, the strategic *defensive* forces—manned interceptors, anti-bomber surface-to-air missiles, anti-ballistic missile missiles—which we usually associate with the second capability can also contribute to the first. They can do so by successfully intercepting and destroying the enemy's offensive weapons before they reach our strategic offensive forces on their bases and launch sites.

As long as deterrence of a deliberate Soviet (or Red Chinese) nuclear attack upon the United States or its allies is the overriding objective of our strategic forces, the capability for Assured Destruction must receive the first call on all of our resources and must be provided regardless of the costs and the difficulties involved. Damage Limiting programs, no matter how much we spend on them, can never substitute for an Assured Destruction capability in the deterrent role. It is our ability to destroy an attacker as a viable twentieth century nation that provides the deterrent, not our ability to partially limit damage to ourselves.

What kind and amount of destruction we would have to be able to inflict on an attacker to provide this deterrent cannot be answered precisely. However, it seems reasonable to assume that in the case of the Soviet Union, the destruction of, say, one-fifth to one-fourth of its population and one-half to two-thirds of its industrial capacity would mean its elimination as a major power for many years. Such a level of destruction would certainly represent intolerable punishment to any industrialized nation and thus should serve as an effective deterrent to the deliberate initiation of a nuclear attack on the United States or its allies.

Assured Destruction with regard to Red China presents a somewhat different problem. China is far from being an industrialized nation. However, what industry it has is heavily concentrated in a comparatively few cities. We estimate, for example, that a relatively small number of warheads detonated over 50 Chinese urban centers would destroy half of the urban population (more than 50 million people) and more then one-half of the industrial capacity. Moreover, such an attack would also destroy most of the key governmental, technical, and managerial personnel and a large proportion of the skilled workers. Since Red China's capacity to attack the United States with nuclear weapons will be very limited, even during the 1970's, the ability of even a very small portion of our strategic offensive forces to inflict such heavy damage upon them should serve as an effective deterrent to the deliberate initiation of such an attack on their part.

Once sufficient forces have been procured to give us high confidence of achieving our Assured Destruction objective, we can then consider the kinds and amounts of forces which might be added to reduce damage to our population and industry in the event deterrence fails. But here we must note another important point, namely, the possible interaction of our strategic forces programs with those of the Soviet Union. If the general nuclear war policy of the Soviet Union also has as its objective the deterrence of a United States first strike (which I believe to be the case), then we must assume that any attempt on our part to reduce damage to ourselves (to what they would estimate we might consider an "acceptable level") would put pressure on them to strive for an offsetting improvement in their deterrent forces. Conversely, an increase in their Damage Limiting capability would require us to make greater investments in Assured Destruction, which, as I will describe later, is precisely what we now propose to do.

It is this interaction between our strategic forces programs and those of the Soviet Union which leads us to believe that there is a mutuality of interests in limiting the deployment of anti-ballistic missile defense systems. If our assumption that the Soviets are also striving to achieve an Assured Destruction capability is correct, and I am convinced that it is, then in all probability all we would accomplish by deploying ABM systems against one another would be to increase greatly our respective defense expenditures, without any gain in real security for either side. It was for this reason that President Johnson decided to initiate negotiations with the Soviet Union, designed, through formal or informal agreement, to limit the deployment of anti-ballistic missile systems, while including at the same time about $375 million in his FY 1968 budget to provide for such actions—e.g., protection of our offensive weapon systems—as may be required if these discussions prove unsuccessful.[1]

1. [In late 1967, the decision was made to deploy a "light" antiballistic missile defense system costing about $5 billion.—*Editor.*]

In this connection, it might be useful to reiterate another fundamental point, namely, that the concept of Assured Destruction implies a "second strike" capability, i.e., a strategic force of such size and character that it can survive a large scale nuclear surprise attack in sufficient strength to destroy the attacker. Thus, if Assured Destruction is also a Soviet objective, they must always view our strategic' offensive forces in their planning as a potential first strike threat (just as we view their forces) and provide for a "second strike" capability.

THE SIZE AND CHARACTER OF THE THREAT

In order to assess the capabilities of our general nuclear war forces over the next several years, we must take into account the size and character of the strategic forces which the Soviet Union and Red China are likely to have during the same period. Again, let me caution, that while we have reasonably high confidence in our estimates for the close-in period, our estimates for the early part of the next decade are subject to much uncertainty. As I pointed out in past appearances before this Committee, such longer range projections are, at best, only informed estimates, particularly since they deal in many cases with a period beyond the production and deployment lead times of the weapon systems involved.

The Soviet Strategic Offensive-Defensive Forces · Two significant changes have occurred during the last year in our projections of Soviet strategic forces. The first is a faster-than-expected rate of construction of hard ICBM silos; the second is more positive evidence of a deployment of an anti-ballistic missile defense system around Moscow. (Both of these developments fall considerably short of what we assumed in the "higher-than-expected" threat, against which we have been hedging for several years.) Our current estimates for other elements of the Soviet strategic forces are generally in line with those I discussed here last year.

Summarized in the table below are the Soviet's strategic offensive forces estimated for October 1, 1966. Shown for comparison are the U.S. forces.

United States vs. Soviet Intercontinental Strategic
Nuclear Forces, 1 Oct. 1966

	U.S.[a]	U.S.S.R.
ICBMs[b]	934	340
SLBMs (U.E. Launchers)[c]	512	130
Total Intercontinental Ballistic Missiles[d]	1446	470
Intercontinental Bombers[e]	680	155

[a] These are mid-1966 figures.

[b] Excludes test range launchers and Soviet MR/IRBMs capable of striking Eurasian targets.

[c] In addition to the SLBMs, the Soviets possess submarine-launched cruise missiles whose primary targets are naval and merchant vessels.

[d] In 1965, intelligence reports estimated Soviet intercontinental missiles as of mid-1966 to number between 430 and 500.

[e] In addition to the intercontinental bombers shown in the table, the Soviets possess medium bombers capable of striking Eurasian targets.

Intercontinental Ballistic Missiles · As of now, we have more than three times the number of intercontinental ballistic missiles (i.e., ICBMs and SLBMs) the Soviets have. Even by the early 1970's, we still expect to have a significant lead over the Soviet Union in terms of numbers and a very substantial superiority in terms of overall combat effectiveness. In this connection, we should bear in mind that it is not the number of missiles which is important, but rather the character of the payloads they carry; the missile is simply the delivery vehicle. Our superiority in intercontinental bombers, both in numbers and combat effectiveness, is even greater and is expected to remain so for as far ahead as we can see. There is still no evidence that the Soviets intend to deploy a new heavy bomber in the late 1960's.

Anti-Ballistic Missile Defense · We have been aware for many years that the Soviets have been working on an anti-ballistic missile defense system, just as we have been. After a series of abortive starts, it now appears that the Soviets are deploying such a system (using the "GALOSH" missile, publicly displayed in 1964) around Moscow. They are also deploying another type of defensive system elsewhere in the Soviet Union, but the weight of the evidence at this time suggests that this system is not intended primarily for anti-ballistic missile defense. However, knowing what we do about past Soviet predilections for defense systems,[2] we must, for the time being, plan our forces on the assumption that they will have deployed some sort of an ABM system around their major cities by the early 1970's. Whether made up of GALOSH only, or a combination of GALOSH and other types of missiles, a full scale deployment would cost the Soviet Union at least $20 billion to $25 billion.

The Red Chinese Nuclear Threat · There has been no basic change in our estimates of the Red Chinese nuclear threat. Their firing of a nuclear armed missile over a distance of a few hundred miles last October falls within the limits of that estimate. They will require many more tests before they achieve a truly operational capability with a medium or intermediate range missile, and this will take time.

With regard to an ICBM, we believe that the Red Chinese nuclear weapons and ballistic missile development programs are being pursued with high priority. On the basis of recent evidence, it appears possible that they may conduct either a space or a long-range ballistic missile launching before the end of 1967. However, it appears unlikely that the Chinese could deploy a significant number of operational ICBMs before the mid-1970's, or that those ICBMs would have great reliability, speed of response, or substantial protection against attack.

Red China also has some bombers which could carry nuclear weapons, but most of them have an operational radius of only a few hundred miles. It is highly unlikely, on the basis of cost alone, that they would undertake the development, production, and deployment of a new, long range bomber force. If they chose to do so, it would take them a decade or more before they could deploy it. Accordingly, we have no reason on this account to change our estimate that a significant Red Chinese nuclear threat to the continental United States will not develop before the mid-1970's.

---

[2] The Soviets for more than a decade have spent substantially more on air defense against strategic bombers than has the United States. But if our Strategic Air Command is correct in its judgment that a very high proportion of the United States incoming bombers could penetrate the Soviet defenses and reach their targets, and I have no reason to dispute it, then we must conclude that the bulk of these Soviet expenditures has been wasted.

Defense Expenditures and
the Domestic Economy

MURRAY WEIDENBAUM

Murray Weidenbaum is Professor of Economics at Washington University, St. Louis. This article first appeared in Defense Management, *published in 1967.*

NATIONAL-SECURITY EXPENDITURES—primarily the outlays of the Department of Defense (DoD) and the National Aeronautics and Space Administration (NASA)—exercise a limited but often catalytic role in the American economy. Using aggregate types of comparisons as a first approximation, defense and space spending appears to be of marginal importance in the economy: It accounts for less than one-tenth of the Gross National Product (GNP) and for a slightly smaller portion of the labor force. From a geographic viewpoint, most states and metropolitan areas are slightly affected by the economic impacts of these national-security programs; only a handful depend on them for as much as a third of their employment.

A similar situation prevails in the industrial economy. Most large industries—food, clothing, textiles, lumber, furniture, automobiles, mining, construction, machinery, retail and wholesale trade, and service establishment—find the military market to be a relatively small one for them. Even among the biggest defense contractors (the companies receiving the largest amounts of contract awards from DoD and NASA) the majority look to civilian markets for the bulk of their sales.

Nevertheless, because of the unusual nature of the resources devoted to defense and space programs, the American economy is affected in several important ways. The following is a sampling of these impacts:

1. Defense/space programs utilize a major share of the scientific and engineering talent in the United States; this tremendous demand may have created more than a little of its own supply,

and that for the rest of the economy as well.

2. Defense/space programs receive the bulk of all the goods and services purchased by the federal government; in creating this vast market for private industry, these programs have also served as the instrument for expanding the direct role of the federal government in the American economy as a purchaser and consumer of goods and services.

3. Because of the specialized nature of defense/space purchases—primarily high-technology weapon and space systems—a relatively few durable-goods industries provide most of these needs. In turn, these industries have become the leading growth industries in the nation and the regions in which they cluster among the fastest growing areas.

4. The expansion of defense/space programs also signifies that an increasing share of the national economy is independent of the level, or of changes in the level, of private consumption and investment; these government programs are independent of forces producing fluctuations in the private sector of the economy because they respond to a different set of demands.

Some statistical perspectives may be helpful in understanding the nature of the role played by defense and space programs in the national economy.

SOME AGGREGATE COMPARISONS

Until comparatively recently, expenditures for national security were a very minor factor in total economic activity. In the half century prior to 1930, such outlays normally equaled less than 1 per cent of the Gross National Product, except for the World War I period. From 1931 to 1939 military outlays averaged 1.3 per cent of GNP. World War II, of course, raised security programs to what appears to be a relatively permanent high level. Presently, purchases by DoD and NASA are $57 billion or 9.7 per cent of the total output of the nation. The proportion was even higher during World War II (peak of 48 per cent) and the Korean War (peak of 12 per cent).

An alternate measure of the economic impact of defense/space activity is the portion of the work force devoted to this activity.

Figures for 1963 reveal that 6.7 million workers were in defense-related employment, representing 9.4 per cent of total United States employment. A little over half were employed directly by the federal government, either in the Armed Forces or in defense-related work in federal agencies. The remainder were in defense-related employment in private industry, working for prime defense contractors, subcontractors, or firms providing materials and services to contractors.

The current level of military demand reflects an extended period of cold war, interspersed by incidents leading to limited conflicts, such as Korea and Vietnam, and temporary thaws and defense cutbacks, such as in 1957–58 and in 1963–64. An abrupt change in the nature of the external environment, and in the country's reaction to it, would cause another major shift from the present proportion of a little less than one-tenth of the nation's resources being devoted to armaments and related security programs. (See Table 1.) Clearly, the level and composition of

TABLE 1. *Measures of the Economic Impact of Defense/Space Programs Data for 1963*

GNP Comparisons (dollar amounts in billions)

Gross national product	$585.1
Purchases of good and services for national defense	$56.7
National defense as per cent of GNP	9.7%

Employment Comparisons (in millions)

Total U. S. employment	71.5
Estimated defense-related employment	6.7
Defense employment as per cent of total	9.4%

SOURCE: U.S. Departments of Commerce and Labor.

national-security demands are relatively independent of influences in the private economy. Defense and space spending does not regularly act as a stabilizer to counter swings in private consumption or investment, but neither does it necessarily move in parallel with the private economy to accentuate such destabilizing swings.

The impact of defense and space spending on the economy depends on many factors other than the level and rate of change of such spending. Heavy reliance on deficit financing during

World War II, in contrast to the tax financing of the Korean War, produced different results on consumer income and spending and, thus, different economic stabilization problems. Variations in tax structures to finance any given level of expenditures are likely to influence the impact of defense and space outlays. Also, consumer and business expectations may differ from one period to another. Finally, the availability of resources also affects the timing and extent of the impact on prices, production, and economic growth.[1]

BUDGETARY IMPLICATIONS

Military and space spending dominates the federal budget. From the viewpoint of economic activity, these programs account for over 85 per cent of all federal purchases of goods and services. In real terms (when the dollar figures are adjusted to eliminate changes resulting from inflation) virtually all the increase in the absolute amount of federal purchases during the past two decades has been accounted for by defense and space programs. In the aggregate, purchases of all other federal government agencies are at about the same level as in 1940. The large increases in federal civilian spending have been transfer payments and grants, which do not show up directly in GNP. Thus, the rise in the federal share of GNP from 6.2 per cent in 1940 to 10.3 per cent in 1964 has been accounted for entirely by defense/space expenditures. On this basis, it can be seen that these security-related expenditures have served, intentionally or otherwise, as the means for expanding the position of the federal government as a purchaser and consumer of goods and services.

The rather unique composition of military and space requirements affords useful insights into the nature of the resources required to meet these needs and of the resultant geographical and industrial distribution of these resources. As seen in Table 2, capital outlays—which roughly correspond to plant and equipment

1. Arthur E. Burns, "Military Expenditures, Economic Growth, and Stability," in U. S. Congress, Joint Economic Committee, *Federal Expenditure Policy for Economic Growth and Stability* (Washington: GPO, 1957), p. 509; M. L. Weidenbaum, "The Timing of the Economic Impact of Government Spending," *National Tax Journal* (March, 1959), pp. 79–85.

TABLE 2. *Composition of Defense/Space Expenditures, Fiscal Year 1964*

Capital Outlays:	Billions of Dollars	Per cent
Procurement of Weapon Systems:		
Department of Defense	15.4	26.4
Research and Development:		
Department of Defense	7.0	
NASA	3.3	
Subtotal	10.3	17.7
Construction:		
Department of Defense	1.3	
NASA	.4	
Subtotal	1.7	2.9
Total Capital Outlays	27.4	(47.0)
Operating Expenses:		
Department of Defense	30.5	
NASA	.5	
Total Operating Expenses	31.0	53.0
Grand Total	58.4	100.0

SOURCE: The Budget in Brief, Fiscal Year 1966.

expenditures in the private economy—receive 47 per cent of the funds. This is in striking contrast to other sectors of the economy, such as consumer purchases of goods and services. Consumer spending on durables (including residential housing) accounts for only 21 per cent of total personal-consumption expenditures plus housing. The volume of such hard goods or capital items produced for DoD and NASA is currently almost half as large as the total production of new plant and equipment for the private sector of the economy.

Within the capital-outlays segment, the concentration on research and development (R&D)—38 per cent of capital outlays —is noteworthy. These R&D disbursements of DoD and NASA, in turn, finance about three-fifths of all the R&D performed in the United States. They also represent the major element in the rising trend of R&D in the United States in recent years, far surpassing in dollar significance the increase in R&D funds supplied by all other sources, including private industry, colleges and universities, and other nonprofit institutions.

Reflecting the tremendous input of science and technology, the composition of the capital goods acquired by defense and space programs has changed substantially and frequently in the period since World War II. As shown in Figure 1, aircraft has gone through a cycle of decline and now expansion as well as through

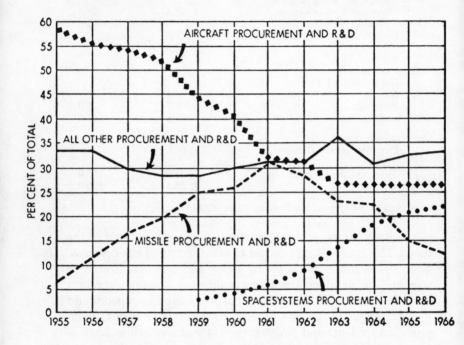

FIGURE 1. *Changing Composition of Defense/Space Procurement and R&D, Fiscal Years 1955–66*

SOURCE: Department of Defense and NASA.

a shift in emphasis from strategic bombers to tactical fighters and transports. With the advent of the Intercontinental Ballistic Missile (ICBM), missile procurement rose sharply. With the completion of much of the second generation of this type of weapon, such as Minuteman and Polaris, a decline has set in. Space systems—although still in the research stage—have expanded greatly, the bulk being accounted for by Project Apollo and other NASA programs. It should be recognized that the civilian space-exploration program, although it uses much of the same types of resources, results from a different set of national requirements. An expansion in defense outlays resulting from a limited war might have a neutral or even adverse effect on NASA funding; a cutback in military outlays resulting from arms control or disarmament agreements might lead to expanding NASA activities.

THE INDUSTRIAL BASE

The composition of the firms and industries supplying goods and services to DoD and NASA is determined in large measure by the changing nature of the requirements of these agencies. For example, during the period July 1950–June 1953, the time of peak procurement of Army ordnance equipment for the Korean conflict, General Motors, a major producer of tanks and trucks, was the number-one military contractor based on size of orders received. It had fallen to nineteenth position by fiscal year 1964. Aerospace companies, such as Lockheed, Boeing, and North American, provide the bulk of the aircraft, missile, and space sysems that now dominate DoD and NASA requirements.

The Industries Involved · Table 3 shows the current industrial distribution of the firms holding the largest value of military and space prime contracts. It is apparent that only a relatively few hard-goods producing industries account for the bulk of these contracts: aircraft, electronics, motor vehicles, petroleum refining, chemicals, rubber, and construction, in that order. A far greater variety of companies and industries, of course, participates at the subcontractor and supplier level. The funds for materials and parts reach many other industries in the form of subcontracts. This subcontracting does much to modify the concentration. Major Department of Defense prime contractors subcontract approximately half of all the contracts they receive, about 40 per cent of this amount going to small business firms. Data on NASA's subcontracts for 1964 show that of the 1,923 different subcontractors, 76 per cent were small business firms; they received 24 per cent of the subcontract dollars.

TABLE 3. *Defense/Space Contract Awards, by Industry, 1964 (percentages)*

Industry*	Standard Industrial Classification (SIC Code)	Dept. of Defense	NASA	Total
Aircraft	372	42.1	9.9	52.0
Electronics	481, 482 361, 365 366	22.8	2.3	25.1
Motor vehicles	371	3.6	0.7	4.3
Petroleum refining	291	3.6	—	3.6
Rubber	301	2.3	0.5	2.8
Construction	15, 16	1.8	0.4	2.2
Chemicals	281, 289	2.1	0.1	2.2
Education and nonprofit organizations	822, 892	1.4	0.6	2.0
Ship- and boatbuilding	373	1.9	—	1.9
Instruments	381, 383	0.8	0.5	1.3
Air transportation	451, 458	0.8	—	0.8
Primary metals	331, 333	0.4	0.1	0.5
Engine turbines	351	0.3	—	0.3
Industrial machinery	355, 356	0.2	0.1	0.3
Business services	739	0.26	**	0.3
Toy amusement and sporting goods	394	0.2	.66	0.2
Railroad equipment	374	0.1	—	0.2
Total		84.5%	15.5%	100.0%

* Companies are classified according to their primary area of business. This may not coincide with the categories in which they do the bulk of their defense/space work.
** Less than 1/10 of 1 per cent.

SOURCES: Listings of SIC codes were taken from S.E.C., *Directory of Listed Companies, 1963*, Dun and Bradstreet, *Million Dollar Directory*, and Aerospace Industry Association reports. Data on defense contracts were obtained from Department of Defense, *100 Companies and Their Subsidiary Corporations Listed According to Net Value of Military Prime Contract Awards*, for NASA contractors from NASA Annual Procurement Report, Fiscal Year 1964.

The extent of dependence on defense and space work varies widely among industries. It is estimated that 98 per cent of ordnance production is consumed by defense, 90 per cent of aerospace, 60 per cent of shipbuilding, and 35 per cent of electrical equipment. In contrast, the proportion is less than 5 per cent for many important industries, including food, apparel, leather, lumber and wood, wholesale and retail trade, services, finance, and construction.

A relatively few large corporations receive the bulk of the defense-contract awards. In fiscal year 1964, the one hundred companies receiving the largest dollar volume of military prime contracts accounted for 73 per cent of the Department of Defense's total. The top one hundred companies accounted for 91 per cent of NASA's prime contracts.

Concentration of economic activity is a long-standing and pervasive attribute of the American economy. By way of perspective, the 139 largest manufacturing corporations accounted for 46.5 per cent of the assets of all manufacturing corporations in 1931. Likewise, the eight largest firms in 1954 accounted for a third or more of the total shipments in 108 of 164 manufacturing industries for which data were available.

Defense contracts have been concentrated in a relatively few companies for some time. In World War II the one hundred largest contractors ranked by dollar volume of contract awards accounted for 67 per cent of the value of all military contracts, and among these the top twenty-five companies had 46 per cent. In their study of the weapons-acquisition process, Merton J. Peck and Frederic M. Scherer concluded that ". . . the weapons business is apparently less concentrated than the most highly concentrated of American industries such as automobiles and aluminum. It is still, however, competition among the few."[2]

The extent of dependence on defense work varies widely among major contractors. Of the thirty-five largest such contractors in 1964, defense-space sales represented over 75 per cent of the total company sales in the case of nine of these firms, from 50 to 74 per cent in seven firms, and less than half in the case of nineteen of the thirty-five.

Specialized Resources · Another aspect of the industrial impact of defense and space programs is the specialized nature of the resources used by the supplying companies. In contrast with the situation during World War II, and even with that during the

2. Merton J. Peck and Frederic M. Scherer, *The Weapons Acquisition Process* (Boston: Graduate School of Business Administration, Harvard University, 1962), p. 118. [See also the selection from this study included below, pp. 132–144.—*Editor.*]

Korean conflict, a far greater share of the work is currently being performed in highly specialized facilities that have been specifically built for the purpose, often at the initiative of DoD or NASA, which still may retain title to the factories and the equipment therein. In 1941, less than one-half of the total material needs of warfare consisted of special-purpose equipment. Most of this was material that could be produced by converting ordinary peacetime facilities. Currently, the great bulk of the material needs of defense and space programs consists of specialized equipment that is produced in special facilities built for the purpose.

Moreover, many of the companies involved in the aerospace and electronics industries were set up for, and so much of their experience is limited to, the design and production of military weapon systems and related aerospace vehicles. As a consequence of the technical requirements of defense and space work, these companies have tremendous numbers of scientists and engineers, compared with the more commercially-oriented industries. The typical company or division of a company specializing in defense and space work hires four or five times more scientists and engineers than the most technically-oriented commercial company to support the same volume of sales. For a typical company producing aerospace systems, engineers and related technical personnel no longer constitute merely a single important but limited department. They may exceed in actual numbers the total of factory or "blue collar" employment. In large measure, these companies have become primarily aggregations of R&D resources.

Aircraft and missile companies alone employ more scientists and engineers on research and development work than does the combined total of the chemical, drug, petroleum, motor-vehicle, rubber, and machinery industries. It has been estimated that about 52 per cent of all the scientists and engineers doing R&D work in American industry are engaged on projects funded either by DoD or NASA.

The defense and space programs, however, act as more than sources of demand for scientists, engineers, and other technical employees. Both directly and indirectly, they serve to increase the supply of such personnel. The direct means include university fellowships, aid to research funding, and training programs. The more indirect influence on the supply of scientists and engineers is the creation of a favorable labor market for them, by means of increasing pay rates and employment opportunities.

In addition, there has been a significant movement from defense employment to the private economy. Numerous veterans of the Armed Forces are now using skills, such as those in the field of electronics, that were acquired in the military service (over 16 per cent of enlisted-personnel separations from the Armed Services during the period 1957–63 were trained in electronic skills). An example of the movement of defense-industry personnel to civilian work occurred as the result of the Dyna-Soar cancellation: Two-thirds of the laid-off employees found jobs in nondefense fields.[3]

REGIONAL IMPACTS

The concentration of military and space production in certain industries and companies has been accompanied by a high degree of geographic concentration. Firms in the East North Central states supplied over 73 per cent of the tanks and related automotive equipment ordered by DoD in 1964; the Pacific Coast states supplied 51 per cent of missile and space systems; and the Middle Atlantic states furnished 35 per cent of electronics and communication equipment.

Thus certain states and communities, because of their relatively high degree of dependence upon specific categories of defense work, are especially affected by shifts in size and types of DoD and NASA programs. In fiscal year 1964, the ten states receiving the largest dollar volume of DoD and NASA contracts accounted for 68 per cent of the total.

Subcontracting affects a significant geographic redistribution of the contract dollars. Although records of DoD's subcontract distribution are not available, a look at NASA's subcontracts gives an indication of the effects. A sample of first-tier NASA subcontracts shows that 68 per cent were awarded to companies in states other than those in which the prime contractors were located; many of these states do not participate in NASA activities

3. Robert Brandwein, "The Dyna-Soar Contract Cancellation—A Statistical Summary," *University of Washington Business Review* (October, 1965).

at the prime-contract level at all. The lack of comprehensive data on subcontracting is a major handicap in analyzing the industrial and geographic impacts of DoD and NASA spending (efforts to fill this gap are now underway, however).

Dollar procurement by state fluctuates from year to year. An illustration is the case of Missouri, whose military prime-contract dollars increased 53 per cent from fiscal year 1963 to 1964, moving the state from the tenth highest state to the third. At the same time Ohio fell to eighth from third, with a 28 per cent decrease in dollar volume.

Three key factors underlie the geographic shift and concentration or dispersion of defense procurement: the product mix or the kind of product being purchased, the upward or downward trend of a few large individual projects, and the kind of industries located within each state and their ability to compete for military business.

In some states large amounts of defense/space work represent comparatively small portions of total employment and payrolls because of the broad industrial base. This factor cushions the impact of defense/space programs. Certain states and communities, because of their relatively high degree of dependence on defense and space work, are especially affected by shifts in these programs. One indication of the magnitude of this dependence is the portion of the state's personal income derived from military payrolls and from wages and salaries of defense workers in private industry. Six states depend directly on defense and space work for at least 10 per cent of personal income—Virginia, Utah, Washington, California, Alaska, and Hawaii. For all other states, the proportion is less than 10 per cent.

Within various states, the concentration is far greater; important examples are such metropolitan areas as Washington, D.C., Boston, Wichita, Cape Kennedy, Los Angeles, Seattle, and Huntsville, Alabama.

Much of the income generated directly by defense expenditure in a given region is spent locally on retail goods, services, housing, and other consumer items. This creates additional income, business investment, and, thus, employment. This induced employment should be added to direct employment, swelling the local effect of defense expenditure. A study of Los Angeles estimated the combined effect at 43.5 per cent of total employment. Estimates for the Seattle-Tacoma, Washington, area show a similar relationship—42 per cent of total employment could be related to defense and space expenditures.[4]

The tendency of defense and space programs to cluster in a relatively few areas, and in a pattern different from that of American industry generally, is of fairly recent origin. In World War II, the distribution of defense contracts more or less followed the then prevailing pattern of manufacturing activity. The major industrial states—Michigan, New York, Pennsylvania, Ohio, and Indiana—ranked high in prime-contract awards.

As long as automotive and conventional-ordnance products were a substantial part of defense procurement, the capabilities of established manufacturing firms were drawn upon. Korea marked the beginning of the change. With the increasing role of aircraft, missiles, electronics, and space systems, newer firms became of greater importance, and they tended to locate in the newer industrial states of California, Texas, Washington, or in rejuvenated New England states. The dominance of California is even more striking at the present time, and Washington State, another center of aerospace activity, also appears high on the list of defense/space industrial activity.

TECHNICAL FALLOUT AND OTHER LONG-TERM EFFECTS

The impacts of defense and space expenditures on the economy manifest themselves in various ways. The incomes of government and private-industry employees working on these programs show up directly in personal income and are also reflected in the Gross National Product. The investment outlays by government contractors also are reported in GNP. In addition, as the recipients of defense-related income respend the proceeds for various types of consumer and investment items, further effects are felt of an induced nature (so-called multiplier and accelerator effects). The multiplier effect of government purchases from private industry

4. Charles Tiebout, "The Regional Impact of Defense Expenditures: Its Measurement and Problems of Adjustment," in U.S. Congress, Senate Committee on Labor and Public Welfare, *Nation's Manpower Revolution*, Part 7 (Washington: GPO, 1963), pp. 2516–2523.

has been estimated in the neighborhood of 1.3. Of some interest also is the further estimate that a billion dollars of such public outlay would generate additional federal tax revenues of about 488 million dollars, state and local revenues of 30 million dollars, and would reduce unemployment-insurance costs by 160 million dollars.[5] Thus the net budgetary costs of defense and space programs would appear to be rather less than the gross or clearly visible expenditures.

There is yet another aspect of the economic impact of defense/space programs that may be more illusive and controversial, but possibly of greater significance in the long run. This feature is the "spillover," "fallout," or transfer of defense and space technology to other areas of the economy. There is no simple method of measuring the dollar impacts on the economy of national-security spending for research and development.

From the point of view of investment in the private sector, four main effects have been identified;[6]

1. The emergence of the new technologies, such as electronics, is stimulating investment in new industries.

2. These technologies are enabling existing industries to develop a new range of equipment, instruments, and materials that are replacing, improving, or extending old types of production. Computing machines, control devices, and synthetic chemicals are examples of private investment's being so induced to create new facilities or modify old factories and production equipment.

3. The tools and materials created by the new technologies make possible economies of production in other industries, calling forth new investment to finance cost-saving innovations and increased output. Examples include computers and record-keeping equipment in the office and automatic controls for factories and railroads.

4. Induced investment results from changes in the location of

5. Daniel Suits, "Econometric Analysis of Disarmament Impacts," in *Disarmament and the Economy*, ed. Emile Benoit and Kenneth Boulding (New York: Harper & Row, Publishers, 1963), p. 104.

6. George H. Hildebrand and Norman V. Breckner, "The Impacts of National Security Expenditure Upon the Stability and Growth of the American Economy," in U. S. Congress, Joint Economic Committee, *Federal Expenditure Policy for Economic Growth and Stability* (Washington: GPO, 1957), p. 536.

industry made possible by the new technologies.

Attempts to quantify these effects of defense/space technology have yielded extremely limited results. One detailed survey resulted in an impressive catalogue of the various types of technology which have had effects on the civilian economy. But no comprehensive quantification was available.[7]

A more limited survey of large aerospace companies reported that, other than the few firms selling equipment to the airlines, the large defense suppliers obtain only 1 or 2 per cent of their sales from products based on their defense/space work that are sold in commercial markets. The list of abandoned commercial ventures is long, ranging from stainless-steel caskets to powered wheelbarrows to garbage-reduction machinery.[8]

Reasons offered for the inability of the large, specialized defense/space companies to utilize their resources in commercial endeavors include their lack of marketing capability and their inability to produce large numbers of items at low unit prices. These weaknesses are not necessarily handicaps in defense and space work. For example, the lack of commercial marketing capability of these firms results from their preoccupation with meeting the rigorous technical requirements of the government customers. Their inability to produce large volumes at low cost also reflects their unique capability to design small numbers of large-scale systems of great technical complexity.

Nevertheless, additional undertakings continue, particularly attempts to transfer advanced technology to government and industrial areas rather than to consumer markets that require so many of the capabilities found in such short supply by defense/space contracts. More recent attempts include an automatic parcel-sorting system for a railway terminal, the conversion of jet airplane engines to pumping gas and generating electricity for public utilities, and computerized systems to maintain inventory records for retail firms.

NASA, through its technology-utilization program, has been

7. John G. Welles *et al., The Commercial Application of Missile/Space Technology* (Denver: University of Denver, Denver Research Institute, September, 1963).

8. Murray L. Weidenbaum, "Adjusting to a Defense Cutback: Public Policy Toward Business," *Quarterly Review of Economics and Business* (Spring, 1964), pp. 7–14.

attempting to accelerate the flow of space technology to business firms that can apply it to commercial goods and services. Universities and research institutes are cooperating in order to serve as a transmission belt between government and industrial defense laboratories and commercial industry.[9]

ECONOMIC CONSTRAINTS ON DEFENSE/SPACE SPENDING

The question has been raised as to how much national-security spending the economy can afford; the companion concern is that short-run considerations may impair the long-term capability of the economy to support a large and sometimes expanding array of national-security programs.

There is no simple or generally agreed-on method to measure the "burden" of defense and space programs on the economy, much less, the economic ceiling, if any, that exists on such programs.

Using the GNP comparison, the portion of our national resources devoted to armaments has tended to diminish rather than increase in recent years, from 10.5 per cent in 1957 to 8.4 per cent in 1964. During much of that period, considerable unutilized or underutilized capacity existed in the economy, far more than was generally desired. Inflation has not been particularly troublesome in recent years; the wholesale price index has fluctuated within the narrow range of 99.0 to 100.7 from 1957 to 1964 (base of 1957–59 = 100).[10]

As to the concern over budgetary deficits, the major increases in federal spending in recent years have occurred in the domestic civilian area, particularly in education, welfare, and health programs. The balance-of-payments problem continues; however, the impact of national-security programs here is not in terms of its total but of the allocation between domestic and overseas outlays. In this connection, NASA programs have little impact on the balance of payments, and DoD has taken numerous steps to re-

9. National Aeronautics and Space Administration, Technology Utilization Program; Charles Kimball, "The Relationship Between Economic Growth and the Transfer of Technology," in 1963 Proceedings of the National Association of Business Economists (1963), pp. 80–90.

10. [Note that this was written before the intensification of the Vietnam conflict.—Editor.]

duce its adverse influence on U.S. international accounts.

The real cost to society of allocating productive resources to defense and space programs may be that these resources are unavailable for other purposes. Yet, such resources may not be entirely diverted from other uses in practice. Some or all of the resources so used might have remained unemployed but for the expansion of defense or space activities. On the other hand, if there is any such sacrifice in a given time period, and if the loss is in investment, additional sacrifices will accrue in subsequent time periods as society foregoes the returns on the foregone investment.

Even where resources utilized by defense and space programs are diverted from other sectors, the value of the resultant output does not necessarily measure the value of the output diverted from the civilian sectors. For example, when resources shift from comparatively low-valued products such as agriculture to high-valued products such as space-exploration systems, the portion of GNP utilized by the defense program exceeds in value the output yielded by the private sector; thus a net increase may occur in the level of economic output. Such structural shifts are a characteristic of the development of the American economy and a manifestation of its relatively rapid growth pattern.[11]

There still may be an important opportunity cost involved in some of the highly specialized resources required by DoD and NASA. The most striking case may be that of R&D, where over half of all the work performed in private industry is financed by these two agencies. Those who decry private affluence amid public poverty may reflect on the allocation of one of our most vital resources, science and technology.

Overall, available analyses of the "burden" of defense/space expenditures have generally concluded that, if necessary for military or political reasons, the American economy could handle, with a minimum of dislocation or hardship, a far higher level of such spending than has been experienced in recent years. Studies or statements of this type have been made by such diverse groups as the Committee for Economic Development, the National Planning Association, a panel of the United States Arms Control and

11. Burns, *op. cit.*, pp. 512–513.

Disarmament Agency, and a group of outstanding university and research economists appearing before the Joint Economic Committee of the Congress. But many such analyses also concluded that the long-term growth and prosperity of the United States do not require even the current level of national-security spending.[12]

Thus, economic constraints do not appear to be an important limitation on the level of defense or space spending—directly. Indirectly, and essentially through the federal budgetary process, financial constraints have restricted (and are likely to continue to restrict) the portion of the nation's resources devoted to these purposes. This reflects the fact that government appropriations for these items are not made in isolation but result from the interplay of many conflicting requirements and demands, including those of numerous other federal programs and of taxpayers who wish to reduce the portion of their incomes taken by the federal government.

The nation's experience testifies to the ability of the economy to adjust successfully to major reductions in national-security spending. Demobilization after World War II was extremely rapid, and no sizable unemployment problem developed. Between June, 1945, and June, 1946, over 9 million men were released from the armed forces, about three times the present total of military personnel. Between 1945 and 1946, national defense purchases of goods and services were reduced by 75 per cent. This reduction was equivalent to more than 25 per cent of the GNP in 1945, about three times the present proportion of GNP that is represented by defense/space spending. The accumulation of savings due to wartime scarcity and the large pent-up demand for durable goods contributed to the ease of the postwar transition.

The end of the Korean conflict involved a much smaller reduction in defense spending, which in turn started from a much lower peak than that at the end of World War II. Tax reductions helped to maintain aggregate consumer income and spending.

---

12. Murray L. Weidenbaum, "Costs of Alternative Military Strategies," in *National Security, Political, Military and Economic Strategies in the Decade Ahead,* ed. David Abshire and Richard Allen (New York: Frederick A. Praeger, Inc., 1963), p. 792. [Again note that this was written before the extension of our role in Vietnam—*Editor.*]

The level-off in the total of defense and space spending in 1963-64 was accompanied by a decline in the national unemployment rate, clearly indicating the capability of the American economy to adjust rapidly at least to moderate changes in defense or space expenditures.

Numerous studies of the economic impact of arms control and disarmament have concluded that the United States is capable of making the necessary economic adjustment to fundamental reductions in the level of national-security expenditures; the limitations are considered to be mainly in the political sphere—the willingness of the nation to take measures of sufficient magnitude and promptness to utilize the resources that would be released in such an eventuality.[13]

IMPACT OF ECONOMIC ENVIRONMENT ON MILITARY DECISION MAKING

Over the years numerous local pressures have arisen to require the Department of Defense to take account of the impact on the economy of its decisions on such military matters as choice of weapon systems contractors, location and retention of bases, and so forth. The official position has been that these substantive decisions will be made on the basis of meeting military requirements in the most efficient manner, without limitation regarding the effects on individual employees, companies, and communities.

In accord with this philosophy, a number of limited actions have been taken to assist in the economic adjustments to change in the level or pattern of defense spending. For example, in major curtailments, such as those involving the closing of ninety-five installations announced in October, 1964, the Department of Defense guarantees another job opportunity to every permanent employee whose job has been abolished. Where possible, it offers alternative choices of location to those whose jobs have been transferred.

13. See Emile Benoit and Kenneth Boulding, eds., *Disarmament and the Economy* (New York, Harper & Row, Publishers, 1963); U. S. Arms Control and Disarmament Agency, *Economic Impacts of Disarmament* (1962); United Nations, Department of Economic Social Affairs, Economic and Social Consequences of Disarmament, 1963, *Report of the Committee on the Economic Impact of Defense and Disarmament* (July, 1965).

There is much less that the military establishment can do to assist employees of its contractors. Under cost-type contracts, separation or retirement expenses can be allowable costs as can, in some instances, the costs of training and job-related education.

The Department of Defense maintains a special office whose task it is to help communities adversely affected by base closings or contract terminations. This Office of Economic Adjustment visits these communities and provides ideas and advice. It often serves as a focal point for community efforts to launch industrial-development programs.

Government officials on numerous occasions have stated that there is no public obligation to maintain any given defense contractor. Consistent with this, however, the federal government does a number of things that are deemed appropriate for a large, responsible customer. One such action is to give the specialized military suppliers the maximum feasible advance information concerning the future defense markets. The newest such program of the Department of Defense was a series of industry "briefing sessions" held early in 1965. The President's Committee on the Economic Impact of Defense and Disarmament recently recommended that maximum advance notice of cancellations and cutbacks of defense contracts be given to the contractors and localities involved, so that they can properly plan to cope with the situation.

Both the Department of Defense and NASA revised their procurement regulations in 1964 to state clearly that companies may charge to their defense or space contracts an allocable share of the costs of generalized long-range management planning, including planning for the possibility of economic dislocation or fundamental alterations in the company's present markets.

All these and related government programs are designed to alleviate the side effects of military-program actions rather than to influence them. To the extent that they are successful, these ameliorative-type programs should reduce local political pressure on defense decision making.

On the Economic Burden of Defense

James Tobin is Sterling Professor of Economics at Yale University. This paper was originally published in Reports and Speeches *of the Eighth Yale Conference on the Teaching of the Social Studies, April 1963.*

THE OCEANS NO LONGER guarantee the North American continent immunity from military attack, and nothing seems likely to take their place. Absolute security is a thing of the past; and the imperfect and uncertain defenses now available to us are, unlike the natural barriers that once protected us, very, very expensive. I propose here to discuss some of the economic implications of this revolution. I shall consider first the effects of the domestic economy, and second the profound change in the international economic position of the United States.

The security of the nation costs roughly one tenth of our Gross National Product every year. I count this as a burden, but I know that some critics of American capitalism argue that it is not. There are two versions of the argument that defense production is really free—one that the resources devoted to defense would simply be unemployed otherwise, the other that they would be wasted in frivolities and luxuries our society could well do without. I shall take up these two versions in turn.

According to the first view, it is only the stimulus of defense demand that has kept the U.S. economy from relapsing into the mass unemployment and stagnation of the 'thirties. In the absence of this stimulus, not only would the labor now employed to make and man armaments be unemployed, but many other workers, through indirect effects, would be out of their jobs also. The industrial capacity now committed to armament either would lie idle or would never have come into being.

History has not performed this experiment for us. But the evidence is against so pessimistic an assessment of the vitality of

33

our economic and political system. Although defense expenditures have been high by historical standards ever since the Second World War, we have taken in stride two cutbacks in military spending—one spectacular reduction immediately after the war, amounting to $65 billion, over one quarter of GNP, and a second, amounting to $10 billion, nearly 3 per cent of GNP, in the first Eisenhower Administration following the Korean settlement. During the first postwar decade our primary economic problem was much more typically excess demand and inflation than inadequate demand and unemployment. If the defense program was really a mammoth WPA, we were surely overdoing it.

The American people have taxed themselves heavily to pay for defense, suppressing private consumption in order to make room in the economy for defense production. In 1929 consumption took 75 per cent of GNP; now it takes 65 per cent. The number of federal personal income taxpayers has increased twentyfold, and the rates they pay, which ranged from ⅞ of 1 per cent to 24 per cent in 1929, now start at 20 per cent and rise to 91 per cent. Without the defense burden our taxes would be much lower, our private consumption spending higher, and our civilian public expenditures higher too.

The germ of truth in the view I am discussing lies in the politics and ideology, rather than the economics, of government budgets. The sheer size of defense expenditures even when they are matched dollar for dollar by taxes, is an expansionary economic influence. The reason is that taxes are paid at the expense of saving as well as spending. To put the point another way, if government expenditures were lowered by, say, $25 billion (about half the present defense budget) it would be necessary to cut tax receipts by more than 25 billion—perhaps $30 billion—in order to induce taxpayers to replace the $25 billion of government spending with $25 billion of their own spending. This means that if government expenditures were substantially lower, we would probably need *more* frequent and *larger* budget deficits to maintain prosperity and high employment.

There is nothing frightening about this conclusion except that it is so poorly understood in this country. If we must assume that the balanced-budget fetish would have ruled fiscal policy regardless of the consequences for the economy, then economists do have cause to be thankful for high defense expenditures. These outlays have made the fetish less damaging than it would have been with small government budgets. Indeed, through much of the postwar period the urge to balance the federal budget has helped to contain inflationary pressures. The renewed popularity of the balanced-budget principle since the war is probably in some degree an adaptation to this situation.

From an economic standpoint, it is perfectly feasible, through proper fiscal and monetary policy, to sustain prosperity and high employment with much smaller government expenditures. I am optimistic enough about American democracy to believe that the political and ideological obstacles to the use of such policies would melt away if circumstances were obviously and persistently different from those of 1947-57—less danger of inflation, more threat of unemployment and excess capacity. After all, the experience of the 'thirties led the American people to resolve solemnly, in the Employment Act of 1946 that their government would never again sit idly by and permit large-scale unemployment and depression.

I have been discussing the view that defense has not been an economic burden, because the manpower and the other productive resources devoted to it—and perhaps many more—would have been unemployed otherwise. There is a second line of reasoning that might lead to a similar conclusion, namely that if these resources were not actually idle, at any rate they would be wasted. They would be producing socially useless goods and services. Affluent America, in this view, is already saturated with consumption goods. The nation can keep its vastly efficient, increasingly automated, productive machine occupied only by continuously creating artificial wants—wants for things that the same process soon renders obsolete. Keeping up with the Russians in missiles is just a substitute for keeping up with the Joneses in advertised gadgets.

Without doubt trivia and status symbols are a large component of U.S. private consumption. But economic progress has always been a race between productivity, on the one hand, and rising standards and aspirations, on the other. There is no reason to believe we have won that race today, any more than we had won it in the New Era of the 'twenties. As social scientists, we are inclined to believe we can never really win it.

Certainly a look at the incomes and consumption patterns of a large part of the American population today should disabuse any observer of the illusion that consumption levels cannot be usefully increased. Americans do not exhibit by their behavior any signs of saturation. Married women, teenagers, retired people seek jobs when they can. Breadwinners cherish the opportunity to work overtime and even to engage in "moonlighting." Americans spend, as they consistently have done, about 93 per cent of their earnings after taxes. They seek to improve their houses, to see the country and the world, to camp and to boat, to buy paperbacks and high-fidelity records, to improve their health and medical care, to fix and straighten their children's teeth, and to send the children in droves to colleges. To the extent that defense has been purchased at the expense of private consumption, it has not been free but has been a real burden on the nation.

It is easy to see why civilian government has suffered from the defense program. Defense is a government activity, and the economies it entails fall naturally on other government activities. Since defense makes government budgets frighteningly large and taxes unpleasantly high, political instincts and pressures work to restrain the growth of other government activities and of revenues to finance them. The nation can well afford expansion of these activities, many of which deserve higher priority than the private activities with which they compete for resources. But we are accustomed to looking narrowly at what government can afford, instead of broadly at what the nation can afford. Thus President Kennedy found it necessary to give the economy its much-needed boost by cutting taxes to encourage private spending rather than by increasing non-defense spending. No other course is politically feasible, and the President must couple his plea for tax reduction with a pledge to keep civilian government expenditures in check. I think it is fair to conclude that in the absence of the defense program there would be more funds, at all levels of government, for schools, colleges, hospitals, roads, parks, urban rehabilitation, urban transport, and social welfare.

There is another sense in which the defense effort may have been an economic cost to the American people, but it is difficult to assess. Has the concentration of research and development efforts on defense slowed down the rate of technical progress in civilian production? Research and development have become bywords in American industry since the war, and we have increased dramatically our expenditures for these purposes, until they now amount to about 3 per cent of GNP. But most of this is oriented to defense. Half of it is federally financed, and a large share of the privately financed effort occurs in defense and space industries. Most of the scientific and technological talent of the country is devoting itself to building better weapons rather than better mousetraps. Although there is undoubtedly some spillover —new techniques and products designed for defense purposes turn out to have civilian uses too—it is not easy to find examples. Clearly the same mobilization of talent and resources to improve civilian productivity would have set us much farther ahead.

On the other hand it is equally clear that this is not a real alternative—we just do not set up Manhattan Projects to solve problems like suburban commutation and urban congestion. If the defense effort has monopolized physicists and engineers, it has also induced a faster increase in their supply. Sputnik appears to have set off a slow revolution in the quality of American education, which eventually may turn out to contribute greatly to our national well-being as well as to our national strength.

The postwar rate of growth in productivity in the economy as a whole has been within the range of normal historical experience. I find it difficult to assign the defense effort either a plus or a minus on this score.

I have discussed some of the major domestic economic consequences of the passing of the age of free security. I turn now to some of the consequences for the external economic position of the United States. There the revolution in military technology has had dramatic effects, particularly on our economic relations with Western Europe.

Before the Second World War Europe was militarily and politically vulnerable. The United States was not. The United States was the safe haven for property, and our vaults filled with the world's gold as money was invested here for safekeeping. This consideration overrode normal economic calculations of profitability. Now Western Europe is as safe as America; the differential risk that led to concentration of capital in dollar assets has vanished. Europe has reclaimed its natural economic share of the investments of its own citizens, and of Americans and others as well. As a result, much of the gold that fled to this country in the 'thirties and 'forties has departed.

The process has been painful to us in many ways. We became accustomed to thinking of the dollar as unique among national currencies, and of all other currencies as funny money. Now we find that other currencies—Deutschemarks or francs or guilders or Swiss francs—can be strong too, and since currency strength is purely relative, their strength makes the dollar look weak. More important, the reversal of capital movements in favor of Europe has hampered our domestic economic policy. Accustomed to pursuing fiscal and monetary policies for domestic objectives alone, we now find that we must worry about the effects of our policies on our balance of payments and our gold reserves. This has long been an everyday preoccupation of our European friends, but it is new to us and somewhat mysterious. We are not, in fact, as free as we were before to adopt expansionary measures to stimulate the domestic economy. And we overreact in fear of the unknown—warnings about "gold losses," "loss of confidence in the dollar," and the balance-of-payment deficit are potent new weapons in the hands of financial conservatives who always oppose expansionary policies anyway.

The same revolution in military technology has reversed the world roles of the United States and Europe. Formerly, we were sheltered by the British navy, and in a sense by the French army; today our nuclear deterrent and our armed presence shelter Western Europe. We cannot guarantee their security any more than our own, but the security we do provide comes at little cost to Europe itself. At the same time, the United States has of necessity assumed many of the former responsibilities of Europe toward the rest of the world, all the more difficult and expensive because of the Cold War, the breakup of colonialism, and the aspirations of the new nations for rapid economic development.

These reversals of role have signaled a decline in Europe's power and political influence in the world, but they have been accompanied by the most remarkable economic progress within Europe since before 1913. Relatively unburdened by defense and released from overseas commitments (France must be excepted on both counts), most European economies have grown much faster than our own since 1950. European exporters have strengthened their competitive positions in world markets. The move toward continental European unity, of which the Common Market is the principal achievement, may be seen as a compensation for the decline in European political power in the world. We have supported it for political reasons, but it is making life more difficult for our exporters, especially our farmers, and it is another factor encouraging the flow of investment capital to Europe. Meanwhile our defense and foreign aid activities have poured billions of dollars overseas. Many of these dollars have come into the possession of European central bankers who can and sometimes do exchange them at the U.S. Treasury for gold. Here is another way in which the new military situation has weakened the international monetary position of the United States.

This is not a calamity, and I do not mean to exaggerate its importance. Monetary arrangements are means, not ends; and the external position of the dollar or any currency is not of such overriding importance as bankers and central bankers are disposed and obliged to believe. We are certainly wealthy and productive enough to afford troops in Germany, bases in Italy, and aid to India—even if they do require us to buy, directly or indirectly, European currencies with dollars. We still sell more goods abroad than we buy. Our balance-of-payment deficit, troublesome as it is, amounts to less than ½ of 1 per cent of our Gross National Product and essentially reflects the exchange of gold and short-term debt for less liquid but more remunerative and productive assets abroad. The chronic glut of dollars is likely to be no more permanent than the dollar shortage that preceded it.

Meanwhile, however, we face the difficult task of adapting to a new and more symmetrical world monetary situation. The dollar has been serving as an international currency, and the United States has been the world's banker. These functions will be shared more and more with Europe, and more and more internationalized. In this, as in other respects, the military revolution has brought the United States down to earth, subject to the same burdens, frustrations, and problems as the ordinary run of mortal nations.

The Industrial-Military Complex: I

DWIGHT D. EISENHOWER

This selection is from former President Dwight D. Eisenhower's speech to the nation on January 17, 1961.

A VITAL ELEMENT in keeping the peace is our military establishment. Our arms must be mighty, ready for instant action, so that no potential aggressor may be tempted to risk his own destruction.

Our military organization today bears little relation to that known by any of my predecessors in peacetime, or indeed by the fighting men of World War II or Korea.

Until the latest of our world conflicts, the United States had no armaments industry. American makers of plowshares could, with time and as required, make swords as well. But now we can no longer risk emergency improvisation of national defense; we have been compelled to create a permanent armaments industry of vast proportions. Added to this, 3.5 million men and women are directly engaged in the defense establishment. We annually spend on military security more than the net income of all United States corporations.

This conjunction of an immense military establishment and a large arms industry is new in the American experience. The total influence—economic, political, even spiritual—is felt in every city, every statehouse, every office of the federal government. We recognize the imperative need for this development. Yet we must not fail to comprehend its grave implications. Our toil, resources, and livelihood are all involved; so is the very structure of our society.

In the councils of government we must guard against the acquisition of unwarranted influence, whether sought or unsought, by the military-industrial complex. The potential for the disastrous rise of misplaced power exists and will persist.

We must never let the weight of this combination endanger

our liberties or democratic processes. We should take nothing for granted. Only an alert and knowledgeable citizenry can compel the proper meshing of the huge industrial and military machinery of defense with our peaceful methods and goals, so that security and liberty may prosper together.

Akin to and largely responsible for the sweeping changes in our industrial-military posture has been the technological revolution during recent decades. In this revolution, research has become central; it also becomes more formalized, complex, and costly. A steadily increasing share is conducted for, by, or at the direction of the federal government.

Today the solitary inventor, tinkering in his shop, has been overshadowed by task forces of scientists in laboratories and testing fields. In the same fashion, the free university—historically the fountainhead of free ideas and scientific discovery—has experienced a revolution in the conduct of research. Partly because of the huge costs involved, a government contract becomes virtually a substitute for intellectual curiosity. For every old blackboard there are now hundreds of new electronic computers.

The prospect of domination of the nation's scholars by federal employment, project allocations, and the power of money is everpresent and is gravely to be regarded.

Yet, in holding scientific research and discovery in respect, as we should, we must also be alert to the equal and opposite danger that public policy could itself become the captive of a scientific-technological elite.

It is the task of statesmanship to mold, to balance, and to integrate these and other forces, new and old, within the principles of our democratic system—ever-aiming toward the supreme goals of our free society.

The Industrial-Military Complex: II

ADAM YARMOLINSKY

This article by Adam Yarmolinsky, Professor of Law at Harvard University, comes from the Atlantic Monthly, *March 1967.*

THERE ARE AT LEAST three kinds of decisions that face the policy maker as he goes through the piles of papers on his desk. The first are the either-or, yes-or-no decisions, where the choices are mutually exclusive. Then there are the now-or-later issues. And last there are the how-much or how-far decisions, where the question is one of degree.

All these decisions, if they are important enough to reach the men who sit in the status three-window offices on the E Ring, involve a balancing of values and risks. These are values and risks not only for the country, and often for the world, but also for interest groups within the Pentagon, across the Potomac, and down Pennsylvania Avenue to the Capitol. The pressures for some accommodation of these competing forces are enormous, and, in part because of the complexity of the issues, the opportunities for compromise are not inconsiderable. Even in the first kind of decision, there is room for accommodation. A yes on one issue may be balanced by a no on a related one. On the other hand, an unbroken series of "no" answers to any bureaucracy tends to inhibit communication altogether, rather like the labor relations concept of failure to bargain in good faith. No Secretary of Defense can regularly reject proposals from his military advisers, particularly where both their professional competence and the lives of American boys are at issue; and no analytical arguments will modify the effect of a blanket rejection on the continuing workable relationship between the Secretary and the generals. Indeed, the remarkable thing is not how many compromise decisions are made in the Pentagon, in the face of all the pressures for compromise, but how few.

It is here, if anywhere, that the so-called military-industrial complex comes into play. When President Eisenhower, as he left office, warned of the growing power of the military-industrial complex, he may only have been giving vent to his frustrations at his inability to hold down the Defense budget. At the end of his term, he still thought a President ought to be able to give orders like a general, and when he found the orders were not directly obeyed, he chose to blame it on a conspiracy.

Surely the military-industrial-congressional complex is not a conspiracy. But there are coincidences of interest among the military project officer who is looking for a star, the civilian who sees an opening for a new branch chief, the defense contractor who is running out of work, the union business agents who can see layoffs coming, and the congressman who is concerned about campaign contributions from business and labor as well as about the prosperity of his district. Each of these constellations of interests wants to expand the Defense Establishment in its own direction. In the early sixties, the Pentagon was an expanding universe, one of the few fortuitous advantages McNamara enjoyed at the beginning of his tenure. Resources that were cut out of unnecessary activities could often find employment in areas that needed to be strengthened. A similar situation prevails today. Until very recently, Army training camps simply were not available for the training of less essential reserves mandated by a congressional lobby, because the training camps were fully utilized readying active forces for Vietnam. But when the war in Vietnam is brought to an end, the pressures of the military-industrial-congressional complex will necessarily be increased.

The pressures can still be resisted, and there is every evidence that they will be. But it is unreasonable to expect any Secretary of Defense to resist them alone, or supported only by the few people within the Department who are entirely his own men. Over the past six years, the Pentagon has developed the kind of organizational and analytical instruments that permit effective communication between the bureaucracy and the responsible political leadership, and among the elements of the bureaucracy with conflicting institutional interests. That communication has been taking place about fundamental changes that have been and are necessary to make the military establishment a better servant of United States foreign policy.

PART TWO   Decision Making in the
Department of Defense

Program Budgeting

*David Novick is Head of the Cost Analysis Department of the
RAND Corporation. This paper comes from his book,* Program
Budgeting, *published in 1965.*

UNTIL THE END OF WORLD WAR II we managed our military affairs
through two executive departments—War and Navy. The decision
to re-examine our defense posture and our defense organization
came about as a result of our experience with joint operations
during the war, dissatisfaction with the handling of materiel
and manpower problems, and the insistence of the Army Air
Corps that it become a separate establishmet.

At that time there were two schools of thought on how to or-
ganize the departments. Mr. Stimson and Secretary of War Pat-
terson argued for a single unified department. But Secretary of
the Navy Forrestal and Mr. Ferdinand Eberstadt [1] were in favor
of creating a new top layer that would be a coordinating layer.
In the conflict between Army and Navy views, Congress adopted
the Navy position.

1. Mr. Eberstadt, a New York investment banker, was a close friend
and former business associate of Secretary Forrestal and had been chosen
to represent the Secretary of the Navy on the drafting committee appointed
to propose changes in the defense organizations. See *Unification of the
War and Navy Departments and Postwar Organization for National Security,
Report to Hon. James Forrestal, Secretary of the Navy,* Committee on Naval
Affairs, Senate, 79th Cong., 1st Sess. (Washington, D.C.: U.S. Government
Printing Office, 1945); referred to as the Eberstadt Report.

In the National Security Act of 1947, Congress set up a National Military Establishment headed by a Secretary of Defense with general authority over three executive departments—Army, Navy, and Air Force. Congress also recognized the World War II Joint Chiefs of Staff and gave them statutory authority as principal military advisers to the President, Secretary of Defense, and National Security Council.

Mr. Forrestal became the first Secretary of Defense and worked under this system for two years, by which time he was convinced that the view he had espoused just would not work. He recommended the establishment of a single executive department to President Truman, which the President proposed to Congress.

A major objective of the President's proposal was that "we should have integrated strategic plans and a unified military program and budget." The legislation, as enacted, fell far short of these goals. It authorized the Secretary to establish broad policies and programs but in no way moved to integrate the separate military departments. In 1949 amendment to the National Security Act asserted the role of the Secretary of Defense, and the Army, Navy, and Air Force lost their status as executive departments. In addition, a Title IV was added to the act creating a Comptroller at the Department of Defense level and in the offices of each of the service secretaries. The objective was to provide similar administrative integration at the resource or budget level to that sought for military activities.

By 1958 President Eisenhower recognized the need for expediting and strengthening the unification process. In his Defense Reorganization Message of 1958 he declared that "all doubts as to the authority of the Secretary of Defense" had to be settled once and for all. The further reorganization he initiated at that time created unified and specified commands, which were a formal recognition of the fact that the operations of each of the services were important, not so much as individual Army, Navy, or Air Force actions, but more properly as part of a combined effort responsible, through the Joint Chiefs, to the Secretary of Defense and the President. At that point the stage was set for full integration of our military activities, but fuller realization of these potentials was to await the appointment of Robert Mc-

Namara as Secretary of Defense in January 1961.

Mr. McNamara's forceful personality combined with the recognition of a legal basis for action was to result in a major movement toward integrated action in defense planning. The reorganization of 1958 and the introduction of the new Secretary need not in themselves have provided the major change that we have now seen. In addition, a change was needed at the administrative level which, although recognized formally in the 1949 amendments creating the Office of Assistant Secretary of Defense (Comptroller), had not yet moved toward the kind of integration at the resource level that was now necessitated by the other moves.

Prior to 1961 despite many innovations and reforms in the financial management of the Department of Defense and the separate military departments, the Secretary of Defense did not integrate his military planning with his resource requirements or budget.[2] Although the Secretary presented an overall DOD budget to the Executive and Congress, it was a combination of the three separate departmental budgets rather than a completely integrated one. In addition, the requirements for resources (appropriation money) were organized in terms of activities or functions (such as "Construction") rather than that of major military or strategic objectives, as may be seen in Table 1. Consequently, the further detailed breakdowns were in terms of these same budget appropriation categories, and there was no device for transposing the conventional budget codes into a meaningful identification of resources required for major national security objectives. The budget, when stated in terms of procurement, construction, military personnel, operation and maintenance, etc., did not provide either the Secretary of Defense, the Executive, or Congress with any way of sorting out these major categories of resources and relating them to such major military objectives as defense of the continental United States or strategic offensive capability. The weaknesses of this method of financial planning have been summarized by Alain C. Enthoven as follows:

It (the pre-1961 system) had several important defects, perhaps the most important of which was the almost complete separation between planning and decision-making on weapon systems and forces, on the one hand, and budgeting on the other . . . In other words, the long-range plans for weapon systems, forces, and all of their supporting elements were made by the Services on the basis of their estimates of the forces required to assure our national security. Generally speaking, costs were not introduced systematically, either to test the feasibility of the whole program or for purposes of evaluating the efficiency of the allocation.

Budgeting, on the other hand, had as its point of departure the guideline dollar totals laid down by the Administration and based on estimates of the burden the economy could or should bear. The result was a gap. The "required forces" always cost much more than the Administration and the Congress were willing to pay. The process by which the conflicting interests were resolved was unsystematic and wasteful because it led to unbalanced programs.

Furthermore, the Secretary of Defense did not receive adequate cost data. The budgetary system identified cost by object classes—Procurement, Military Personnel, Installations, etc.—the *inputs* to the Defense Department, rather than by weapon systems and forces, such as B-52 wings and Army divisions, which are the tangible *outputs* of the Department . . . Moreover, cost data were presented and financial management was conducted at the Defense Department level on a year-at-a-time basis. The full time-phased costs of the proposed forces were not presented to the Secretary of Defense. Because the costs of most programs are small in their first years, this led to the starting of many programs that could not be completed at anything like existing levels. Although a certain amount of this is a desirable hedge against uncertainty, it is clear that there were a great many wasteful stretch-outs and cancellations of programs that would not have been started if the costs of all of the approved programs had been anticipated.[3]

Lacking management techniques for identifying resources to objectives, the Secretary of Defense did the budget and planning job by first bringing the overall defense budget into line with the fiscal policy of the administration. He then divided the total

2. A proposal for a new budget concept that would integrate the planning, programming, budgeting, and accounting activities of the Department of Defense was made by the writer in 1954 in *Efficiency and Economy in Government Through New Budgeting and Accounting Procedures*, R-254 (Santa Monica, Calif.: The RAND Corporation, February 1, 1954), and again in 1956 in *A New Approach to the Military Budget*, RM-1759 (Santa Monica, Calif.: The RAND Corporation, June 12, 1956).

3. Address before the American Economic Association, Pittsburgh, Pa., December 29, 1962.

TABLE 1. *Summary of Budget Authorizations and Expenditures (in millions of dollars)*

Title of appropriation groups	New obligational authority			Expenditures		
	1959 enacted	1960 estimate	1961 estimate	1959 actual	1960 estimate	1961 estimate
Military personnel: Total[a]	11,463	11,658	11,837	11,801	11,959	12,146
Active forces[a]	10,174	10,262	10,426	10,544	10,592	10,741
Reserve forces	649	681	612	616	667	611
Retired pay	640	715	799	641	700	794
Operation and maintenance	10,195	10,317	10,527	10,384	10,137	10,321
Procurement: Total	14,293	13,090	13,085	14,410	13,943	13,602
Aircraft	6,134	6,143	4,753	7,658	6,670	6,027
Missiles	4,107	3,244	3,825	3,339	3,500	3,479
Ships	1,947	1,139	2,035	1,493	1,651	1,644
Other	2,105	2,563	2,471	1,921	2,121	2,451
Research, development, test, and evaluation	3,775	4,189	3,910	2,859	3,680	3,917
Construction: Total	1,384	1,364	1,188	1,948	1,670	1,359
Active forces	1,358	1,291	1,153	1,862	1,608	1,302
Reserve forces	26	73	35	86	62	57
Revolving and management funds	57	30	30	—169	—444	—350
Total, military functions	41,168	40,647	40,577	41,233	40,945	40,995
Military assistance	1,515	1,300	2,000	2,340	1,800	1,750
Grand total, Department of Defense: Military	42,683	41,947	42,577	43,573	42,745	42,745

a Additional obligational authority available by transfer: $535 million in 1959, $430 million in 1960, $350 million in 1961.

budget among the three military departments. The departments were then, for the most part, left alone to allocate their funds as they saw fit. As a result, each department tended to favor its area and special interests, often without concern for the total problem. Understandably they sought to guarantee larger shares in future budgets by concentrating on dramatic new weapons. The Navy concentrated on its newly developed nuclear capability, emphasizing attack and missile-carrying submarines and aircraft carriers. The Air Force centered its interest on strategic equipment—bombers and missiles. The Army focused on new defenses against aircraft and missiles. And probably more important, all these new developments were undertaken without much interest in, or information about, their resource requirements. There was some effort to determine development and procurement costs, but little attention was paid to the other resources (real estate, personnel, associated equipment, etc.) necessary for a weapon to become a usable weapon system.

The budget was projected for only one year into the future, and the Secretary of Defense and the Secretaries of the three departments put all their emphasis on "next year's budget"—a budget that could not translate resources into objectives, could not project the future resource implications of proposed actions, and that did not distinguish between one-time investment outlays and recurring, or annual operating, expenses.

By January 1961 there had been quiet but long-standing recognition of this deficiency in relating military budgeting to planning. The RAND Corporation in 1954 had issued a report[4] suggesting a method for considering resource requirements in military planning, a method called "Program Budgeting." It proposed the identification of four major mission areas for the Air Force—strategic, defense, tactical, and transportation. It also proposed identifying to each of these mission areas not just equipments but the complete weapon system packages and support system packages necessary for their implementation. Finally, it proposed and demonstrated a new method for developing resource requirements in terms of weapon and support system packages so that they could in turn be related to the appropriate major mission area and this into a total Air Force posture. Perhaps more im-

4. Novick, *Efficiency and Economy in Government.*

portant, the RAND resource proposal was a part of a series of RAND developments in the field of weapon system analysis in which a major feature was the concept of evaluating alternatives and tradeoffs with a view to illuminating possible preferred solutions. Other requests for a "functional" or mission-oriented budget that had appeared by 1961 may have been motivated by a desire to use the information in seeking out preferred ways for applying resources to objectives, but no method for preparing such budgets was indicated.

There was then in 1961 a well-established legal basis for change and a recognition, at least in some quarters, of the need for major change. It was in this context that the new administration in 1961 embarked upon the planning for its military activities. One of the major features it introduced was the recognition of the need for a method for integrating resource programming and budgeting into military planning.

PROPOSAL FOR A PROGRAM BUDGET

The use of the term "program" in Washington had originated during World War II when it was used to describe a combination of activities to meet an end objective.[5] With the war's end, "program" was taken over by the Bureau of the Budget, but here it dealt with components such as personnel or the training of personnel rather than major end objectives. In the same way, "program" was used to lump together related administrative activities, such as procurement of equipment items. In none of these cases was the term "program" used to mean the output or ultimate goal of many interdependent activities (e.g., the combination of equipment, people, real estate, and related activities necessary for a military mission such as strategic bombardment or continental defense).

It was in this atmosphere that, in 1954, the new concept of program budgeting was projected for the Defense Department and the military services. Here "program" was to mean an inte-

5. David Novick, *Which Program Do We Mean in "Program Budgeting"?* P-530 (Santa Monica, Calif.: The RAND Corporation, May 12, 1954). See also Don S. Burrows, "A Program Approach to Federal Budgeting," *Harvard Business Review,* May 1949, p. 272.

grated planning-programming-budgeting process that would bring together all of the resources to be applied to specific missions. The significant feature of this process is its effect on decision-making and control in the vital area of defense expenditures. This innovation is having a notable impact on financial management, but as now administered, is leaving the traditional fiscal process relatively unchanged.

The new program-budget procedure has two primary aims: first, to permit analysis of total force structures for all of the services in terms of common missions or national objectives; second, to project the resource impact (or financial requirements) of the proposed force structures over an extended period of years. To achieve the first objective we identify, for example, the Navy's Polaris weapon system as an element of the strategic retaliatory forces and have it compete for resources against other elements of the strategic forces such as Titan and Minuteman. This may be contrasted with the previous rationale, which put the Polaris in competition with other Navy programs having varying objectives, such as aircraft-carrier construction, anti-submarine warfare, etc. To accomplish the second objective, we project all of the development and procurement activities required to buy a new equipment; then add all the real estate, stocks, training, and other resources that are needed to put a new weapon system into the military inventory. To these investment outlays we add the recurring expenses that must be met each year we operate the equipment, and carry this process forward for a period of years that is either the expected life of the system or is administratively specified.

THE ROLE OF LONG-RANGE FINANCIAL PLANNING

Several major factors have in recent years created a new emphasis on unified longer range financial and nonfinancial planning for the entire military establishment. Such planning is in terms of missions, forces, and weapon systems, which are the actual products of defense expenditures, rather than in terms of the standard appropriation categories.

The strongest factor has been the diminishing relevance of the traditional military service boundaries in the implementation of the major missions or programs, such as continental defense or limited warfare. Today, responsibility for a major program is no longer within the exclusive province of an individual military service, but rather, in varying degrees, is shared by all of the services. Therefore, a budget organized in terms of the traditional services and the standard appropriation categories of procurement, construction, personnel, etc., is not readily adaptable for effective implementation of such interservice programs.

Beginning in the early 1950's weapon systems, because of their extreme technical complexity and increasing sophistication, have become enormously costly. This has made it more desirable, consequently, to be able to estimate in advance probable weapon system performance and cost and thus assist in the eventual choice between alternative weapons. Cost-effectiveness analysis [6] of alternative forces and weapon systems has therefore grown in importance. This technique stems basically from operations research in World War II.

The distinction between cost-effectiveness analysis and its predecessor, operations research, is very important. The emphasis of operations research, as the name implies, is on operations, while the emphasis in cost-effectiveness analysis is on forward planning. Freedom to allocate one's resources is usually severely limited in typical problems of operations research, whereas the purpose of cost-effectiveness analysis is to examine the effects of such alternative resource allocations.

Perhaps some mention should be made of how military planning has become the most important function in the military establishment. The swift nature of nuclear warfare with its requirement for response time measured in minutes, airborne alert, and so forth, resulting from the enormous speed of modern missiles carrying nuclear warheads, has shifted the emphasis in modern warfare from operations to planning. In the past, the relatively slow pace of military operations made it possible to deploy forces and weapons as the need arose, with a minimum of long-range advance planning. Today military planning has been cast in the central role not only because of the accelerated pace of nuclear war but also because of the long lead times necessary

6. This term is the one usually employed in the Department of Defense.

for weapons procurement, the enormous cost of weapons, and the wide choice of weapons through advanced technology.

The interest of Secretary of Defense McNamara is planning and management sciences has led him to seek out those who could help in this task. His interest has provided the needed impetus to effect a major change in the immense and complex Department of Defense. Equally important, the extraordinary capacity of the Secretary to master the complexities of vast programs has given vitality and stature to the new planning tools.

When Assistant Secretary of Defense (Comptroller) Charles J. Hitch first took office in 1961, he envisioned the introduction of the program-budgeting process over a period of several years. This span, however, was compressed by Mr. McNamara, who set as an initial objective the formulation of the FY 1963 defense budget in terms of major programs and weapon systems.

The new planning-programming-budgeting structure consists of five major elements:

1. A program structure in terms of missions, forces, and weapon and support systems.

2. The analytical comparisons of alternatives.

3. A continually updated five-year force structure and financial program.

4. Related year-round decisionmaking on new programs and changes.

5. Progress reporting to test the validity and administration of the plan.

The establishment of this system has considerably reduced the incidence of what Secretary McNamara has called "hectic and hurried" [7] decisions on major programs in the course of budget review. The annual budget now is essentially an increment of a longer range plan, although a substantial process is still involved in converting the program budget into the one used in the appropriation process.

The longer range plan, it should be made clear, is a unified Department of Defense plan rather than an aggregation of sepa-

7. "Annual Report of the Secretary of Defense, July 1, 1960, to June 30, 1961," Department of Defense, *Annual Report for Fiscal Year 1961* (Washington, D.C.: U.S. Government Printing Office, 1962), p. 27.

rate service plans. However, each service is still encouraged to assess competitive means for accomplishing a mission in which it has an interest. In this way service rivalries are maintained on a more productive basis. Service primacy has now become a less important issue than the relative importance of the missions and the potential contribution of each service to them. This may prove to be a primary advantage in the further implementation of a planning and programming framework in terms of missions, forces, and weapon systems.

With regard to possible implications of the new process for the organization of the services within the Defense Department, Secretary McNamara has disclaimed any intention to shift organizational responsibility from one service to another. He has, in fact, pointed out that the new process may serve as a substitute for such change. The actual execution of each mission is, after all, the responsibility of the interservice and functional commands. Thus, the continued organization of the services on a nonmission basis is no disclaimer of the importance of planning by mission.

The change of emphasis from annual budgeting in terms of appropriations to longer range planning in terms of missions, forces, and weapon systems has naturally had an impact on financial improvement programs. The emphasis on cost fostered by Public Law 863 [8] is seen now as only part of the answer to the objective of achieving "cost-based" budgeting. Assistant Secretary Hitch in a speech to an accounting group explained the relationship of the new to the old: [9]

Cost-based budgeting and accrual accounting deal primarily with costs over shorter time periods and with the performance of all of the many tasks which go to make up an effective fighting machine. The program system is concerned with costs over a longer period of time and with performance in terms of acquiring and deploying the forces and equipment in accordance with program goals and plans. Both objectives are important, but we believe first attention must be given to the

8. "An Act To Improve Governmental Budgeting and Accounting Methods and Procedures," August 1, 1956, United States Statutes at Large . . . 1956 and Proclamations, Vol. 70, 84th Cong., 2d Sess. (Washington, D.C.: U.S. Government Printing Office, 1957), pp. 782–783.

9. Presented before the Federal Government Accountants Association of Washington, D.C., April 12, 1962.

accounting needs of our programming system.

Much work remains to be done to derive the full benefits of the new process. The discussion to follow will highlight the more important remaining tasks.

PLANNING AND PROGRAMMING

Planning and programming, which are words that have been used often in this discussion, are really aspects of the same process; they differ only in emphasis. *Planning* is the production of the range of meaningful potentials for selection of courses of action through a systematic consideration of alternatives. *Programming* is the more specific determination of the manpower, materiel, and facilities necessary for accomplishing a program. In addition, except in the very short term where dollars are in effect "given," programming entails interest in the dollar requirements for meeting the manpower, materiel, and facility needs.

The new process results in improved planning through the designation of major "programs," and of "program elements" within them, as the units for planning and programming of forces, dollar costs, and manpower. Major programs represent the primary missions to be performed. The nine major programs currently identified in the Department of Defense program-budget structure are listed and described briefly below. Program elements are the forces, weapon (or support) systems, and similar types of integrated activities by means of which the missions are accomplished. As an example, the program elements that make up Program I: Strategic Retaliatory Forces, are also listed below.

Major Programs in the Department of Defense Program-Budget Structure [a]

PROGRAM I

Strategic Retaliatory Forces: the forces that are designed to carry out the long-range strategic mission and to carry the main burden of battle

[a] Excerpted from statement of Secretary of Defense Robert S. McNamara before the Committee on Armed Services on the Fiscal Year 1965–1969 Defense Program and 1965 Defense Budget, January 27, 1964, *Hearings on Military Posture and H.R. 9637*, House of Representatives, 88th Cong., 2d Sess. (Washington, D.C.: U.S. Government Printing Office, 1964).

in general. They include the long-range bombers, the air-to-ground and decoy missiles, and the refueling tankers; the land-based and submarine-based strategic missiles; and the systems for their command and control.

PROGRAM II

Continental Air and Missile Defense Forces: those weapon systems, warning and communications networks and ancillary equipment required to detect, identify, track, and destroy unfriendly forces approaching the North American continent.

PROGRAM III

General Purpose Forces: the forces relied upon to perform the entire range of combat operations short of general nuclear war. These include most of the Army's combat and combat support units, virtually all Navy units, all Marine Corps units, and the tactical units of the Air Force.

PROGRAM IV

Airlift and Sealift Forces: those airlift and sealift forces required to move troops and cargo promptly to wherever they might be needed. Included in the airlift forces are both the MATS transports and the Air Force Tactical Air Command troop carrier aircraft. The sealift forces include the troop ships, cargo ships, and tankers operated by MSTS and the "Forward Floating Bases."

PROGRAM V

Reserve and National Guard Forces: equipment, training, and administration of the Reserve and National Guard personnel of the several services.

PROGRAM VI

Research and Development: all research and development effort not directly identified with elements of other programs (i.e., where there has been no decision to produce for inventory).

PROGRAM VII

General Support: support activities of the several services and the agencies that serve the entire Department of Defense. It constitutes an "all-other" or residual category of activities or programs and includes all costs not capable of being directly or meaningfully allocated to the other major programs.

PROGRAM VIII

Military Assistance: equipment, training, and related services provided for armed forces of allied and friendly nations.

PROGRAM IX

Civil Defense: federal assistance for fallout shelters, warning and radiological monitoring systems, training and education for emergency preparedness, etc.

Program Elements Contained in Program I:
Strategic Retaliatory Forces

Aircraft Forces	*Missile Forces, Sea Based*
B/EB–47	Polaris System
RB–47	Regulus System
B–52	*Command Control, Communications*
AGM–28A/B	*and Support*
GAM–87	SAC Control System (465L)
B–58	PACCS (KC–135/B–47)
KC–97	UHF Emergency Rocket Communi-
KC–135	cations System
RC–135	Base Operating Support
Missile Forces, Land Based	Advanced Flying and Missile Train-
Atlas	ing
Titan	Headquarters and Command Support
Minuteman	

The subdivision of the entire defense program into over 800 program elements could not have been accomplished in the limited time available without deferring many possible questions regarding the scope of each program element. Because the scope of many program elements was not necessarily matched to existing appropriation activities or organizations, it was initially somewhat indefinite. Further study in this area is still required.

Particularly troublesome has been the question of the proper distribution of the costs of supporting activities. Although such activities are not in themselves output-oriented in the same sense as a B-52 squadron, their costs must be allocated on some appropriate basis to the proper program elements. An installation or base, for example, may support two or more force units, and in some cases it is necessary to divide the support costs correctly between the units. More explicit rules must be developed to assure reliability in cost distribution methods. Without this reliability, comparison between one cost analysis and the next cannot be meaningful.

Within the program budget structure, planning decisions are made after comparing projected costs and effectiveness of feasible program choices. In such comparisons a methodical examination of alternatives is made in terms of quantitative estimates of cost (including manpower, equipment, facilities, etc.) and of the expected military benefits ("effectiveness") to be derived from the systems. A typical comparison might involve the merits of buying more Minutemen squadrons versus more Polaris submarines. Illustrative formats for presenting cost-effectiveness data to the Secretary, which were put into the *Congressional Record* by Assistant Secretary Hitch,[10] are shown in tables 2, 3, 4, & 5.

The programming aspect of the process consists of an eight-year force structure and a five-year financial program in terms of major forces, dollar costs, and manpower—all by program element within each of the major programs. This relates financial to nonfinancial planning in a way that is not possible with the standard appropriation structure. The Basic National Security Policy, the Joint Strategic Objective Plan, and the service plans can now be meshed with the Secretary's five-year plan.

TABLE 2. *Alternative Force Structures*

This part of the summary would normally include:
(a) The currently approved program.
(b) The alternative (if any) proposed by the relevant service.
(c) The JCS recommended force structure.
(d) Other significant alternative possibilities.
The format for describing each alternative normally includes a projection of the relevant part of the force structure. For example:

Alternative I. Numbers of Aircraft, End of Fiscal Year
(figures and models are hypothetical)

Aircraft	1961	1962	1963	1964	1965	1966	1967
F–18	800	767	658	493	325	275	150
F–21	412	510	620	620	610	585	570
F–28	—	—	—	200	315	385	510

And similarly for each alternative.

SOURCE: Statement of Assistant Secretary of Defense (Comptroller) C. J. Hitch, *Systems Development and Management (Part 2), Hearings before a Subcommittee of the Committee on Government Operations,* House of Representatives, 87th Cong., 2d Sess. (Washington, D.C.: U.S. Government Printing Office, 1962), App. IV (b), pp. 643–644.

10. Statement of Assistant Secretary of Defense (Comptroller) C. J. Hitch before the Military Operations Subcommittee, July 25, 1962, *Systems Development and Management (Part 2), Hearings before a Subcommittee of the Committee on Government Operations,* House of Representatives, 87th Cong., 2d Sess. (Washington, D.C.: U.S. Government Printing Office, 1962), pp. 513-547.

TABLE 3. *System Costs*

For each alternative force structure, a summary of complete system costs is shown. For example:

Alternative I. Total Obligational Authority, End of Fiscal Year
(in millions of dollars)

System	1961	1962	1963	1964	1965	1966	1967
F–18							
R&D							
Initial investment							
Annual operating							
Subtotal							
F–21							
R&D							
Initial investment							
Annual operating							
Subtotal							
F–28							
R&D							
Initial investment							
Annual operating							
Subtotal							
Grand total							

SOURCE: See Table 2.

Funding considerations no longer need be the overriding factor to which plans are adjusted. Former Deputy Secretary Roswell L. Gilpatric contrasted this earlier type of planning process with the present one in the following words: [11]

In the past, the Defense Department has often developed its force structure by starting with a budget and sending it off in search of a program. Our new system of program packaging has reversed this procedure, by first determining our over-all strategy, then fitting the hardware and the manpower to those objectives.

This does not mean that the overall defense cost level is of no concern. It certainly is, but arbitrary ceilings are no longer used.

Financial planning for a period longer than a year must always carry the qualification that the actual provision of adequate resources cannot be guaranteed. If resource levels are changed, however, a financial plan that is more directly translatable to program output simplifies the revision of nonfinancial goals.

11. "Defense—How Much Will It Cost?" *California Management Review,* vol. V, no. 2, Winter 1962, p. 53.

TABLE 4. *Evaluation of Effectiveness*

This section will, of course, vary with the weapon systems and forces in question, with the objectives, mission, etc. Moreover, various areas are more or less amenable to quantitative analysis. The following two examples are illustrative of evaluations of alternative strategic retaliatory forces and tactical attack air forces.

Strategic Retaliatory Forces

	Alternative Forces, FY 1967			
	I	II	III	IV
Population and floor space destroyed:				
United States				
Population				
Floor space				
Allied				
Population				
Floor space				
Sino-Soviet				
Population				
Floor space				
Expected number of targets destroyed:				
Category I				
Category II				
Category III				
Category IV				
Category V				
Category VI				
Others				

Tactical Air Forces (attack mission)

	Alternative Forces, FY 1966			
	I	II	III	IV
Per day:				
Tons of ordnance delivered				
Aircraft hours on station				
Sorties				
Expected number of targets destroyed:				
Category I				
Category II				
Category III				
Category IV				
Others				

SOURCE: See Table 2.

TABLE 5. *Summary of Comments or Recommendations*

    (a)   By Services.
    (b)   By Joint Chiefs of Staff.
    (c)   By Director of Defense Research and Engineering, Comptroller, and others.

SOURCE: See Table 2.

Financial planning in terms of major programs and program elements, and budgeting in terms of appropriations, are linked by use of the same measure of cost—total obligation authority. They are also linked by the use of planning and programming cost categories that can be related by appropriations. The principal cost categories are research and development, investment, and operations. These highlight the key decision points in the life of a weapon system. Each of the cost categories is related to several of the appropriation categories, and in time it may be possible to achieve an even closer coordination between the two classifications.

Translation of financial planning in terms of major programs and program elements to budget activities can be made somewhat easier by further analysis and revision of the program element structure. Effective work of this kind has already been accomplished for the Research and Development and General Support programs. The frequent costings now required on a program element basis have brought increasing attention to programming-budgeting consistency and understanding of relationships.

Slow-Down in the Pentagon

HANSON W. BALDWIN

Hanson W. Baldwin is Military Editor for The New York Times.
This article comes from Foreign Affairs, *January 1965.*

In 1947, THE "Bible" of the nation's military contractors—Armed
Forces Procurement Regulations—was a slim volume about 100
to 125 pages long. Today, the A.F.P.R., which governs in minute
detail all those who do business with the Pentagon, has expanded to four huge volumes totaling something like 1,200 pages
with new ones added daily.

Five to seven years ago, according to a careful statistical average compiled by one major defense contractor, it required four
to five months to execute a contract from the time an acceptable
price quotation was received in the Pentagon to the time the
contractor received the final document. Today, the same contractor estimates that an average of nine to twelve months is
needed for the same process; a very few may be completed in 30
days; some may require 23 months.

Parkinson's law of bureaucracy—the less there is to do the
more people it takes to do it, and the simpler the problem the
longer the time required for the solution—appears to be operating
in Washington, particularly in defense contracting. There are
many reasons for this state of affairs.

Secretary of Defense Robert S. McNamara the apostle of
"cost-effectiveness" these past four years, must share the blame
for many of them as well as the credit for some improved management procedures. But the lengthening delays in the development and production of new weapons started long before he
took office, and no one man, no one cause, is responsible.

A rough rule of thumb used to hold that it required about
seven years (in the United States) from the gleam in the eye of
the designer to the finished operational product. This time span
which has been compared unfavorably with the lead time re-

quired for the development and production of new weapons in Russia, has been steadily lengthening, and there is no sign at the moment that the process is being checked.

Even more important, there appears to have been in the first half of the 1960s a definite reduction, as compared to the 1950–1960 period, in the evolution and production of new weapons. The Republicans protest too much when they allege that the Pentagon, under Mr. McNamara, has not produced a single new weapon system. But it is at least true that virtually all the major —and most of the minor—weapons systems in operation or in development today (Polaris, Minutemen, B-70, T.F.X. or F-111, AR-15 rifle, etc.) were already in production, development, or in preliminary design and specification form back in the 1950s. The Pentagon in recent years has certainly instituted some much needed management reforms, effected some economies, and added considerably to our ready strategic strength and our conventional war and general support forces. But it has probably canceled more development contracts (the nuclear-powered aircraft Dynasoar, the mobile medium-range ballistic missile Skybolt, etc.) than it has initiated new ones.

Two principal and telling criticisms have been leveled at the Pentagon's present policies, trends and procedures by scientists who can be in no way accused of political parochialism.

Dr. James R. Killian, Jr., Chairman of the Corporation of the Massachusetts Institute of Technology, cautioned recently against an attitude that is too prevalent in and outside of the Pentagon—a belief that the technological revolution is over. No one in the Pentagon has ever explicitly stated such a belief, but the attitude of skeptical "show-me-ism" widely held there acts as a very definite brake upon the excited enthusiasm which should energize new research projects. Mr. McNamara's "whiz kids," complete with slide rules and computers, brushed aside the factor of professional judgment or scientific hunch when they took office, and their emphasis upon "perfection on paper" and the cost part of the cost-effectiveness formula has definitely slowed the pace of military development.

Behind this attitude in the Pentagon is an even broader trend. Part of it is a belief expressed by many scientists—notably by Dr. Jerome B. Wiesner and Dr. Herbert F. York in a recent issue of *Scientific American*—that disarmament, or arms limitation, is the only way to political salvation, and that therefore continued technological military development worsens the situation. This somewhat simplistic viewpoint has had an increasing public and political appeal and indeed has its adherents in the Defense Department. And even so hardheaded a man as Representative Melvin Price, chairman of the research and development sub-committees of the House Armed Services Committee and the Joint Congressional Atomic Energy Committee, recently warned that "we are entering a leveling-off period, a plateau, in the total dimensions" of the Government's research program. This feeling of disillusionment on the part of scientists, and of fear of economic limitations on future "breakthroughs" in weapons research, comes at a time when the military technological revolution is far from finished.

Despite our present great strength, Dr. Killian has said, we cannot "rest on our oars," thinking the race is won. "We may be only at the beginning of unexampled scientific and engineering achievement," he notes, and the "high confidence" and sheer size of the present research and development effort may "obscure weaknesses still present in our program and lead us once again into complacency."

The second major criticism leveled at present weapons development policies comes from James T. Ramey, Commissioner of the Atomic Energy Commission, and Dr. Edward C. Welsh, acting chairman of the National Aeronautics Space Council. Mr. Ramey in a recent speech urged the Government to rid itself of what he called the "requirements merry-go-round." He pointed out that every new project had to be justified on the basis of "military requirements," and that many promising developments —particularly in space—could never be pushed, or even demonstrated, if development had to wait for the establishment of requirements. Invention has never followed this path; the machine gun and the tank would still remain blueprint dreams if their development had awaited the specifications of clear-cut military requirements. One cannot state a requirement for an inventor's hopes. As Dr. Welsh has pointed out, "If we had required a clear-cut prior mission, we would probably have developed no airplanes, no spacecraft, or, in fact, no wheel."

Other causes for the delays in development and production of new weapons have their roots in the past, well prior to the present Administration, and the responsibility extends far beyond the Pentagon. A $50 billion annual defense budget attracts the eager interests of many government agencies.

The sprawling bureaucracy of Big Government; the control of major military or para-military projects by agencies over which the Defense Department has no direct authority, including the Atomic Energy Commission, the National Aeronautics and Space Administration, the Central Intelligence Agency, the Bureau of the Budget; Congressional legislation and executive regulation —social, political and economic; the tremendous size and complexity of the armed forces; over-centralization and over-regulation in the Pentagon; too much service rivalry and not enough service competition—all these and other factors have become built-in roadblocks in defense development and contracting.

Big Government itself is undeniably one of the roadblocks to speedy performance. Everybody must get in on the act, particularly if a new development project involves sizable sums of money or promises numerous jobs, or involves systems or components which must be provided by foreign governments or by other agencies of government.

The "advice"—and the actual control—exercised on military projects by executive agencies outside the Pentagon is sweeping but almost completely negative. They delay and they criticize and they inhibit; they do not expedite.

Congressional legislation and executive regulation complicate, restrict, and delay research and procurement contracts. The contractor must comply with hundreds of laws or executive orders. Accounting procedures, minimum wages, civil rights, veterans' preferences, subcontracting, profit limitations and so on and so forth, all are roadblocks to speed. The Armed Forces Procurement Regulations reflects in its bulk size, and complexity how social, political, and economic considerations, as well as those that are military and technical, influence the awards of contracts.[1]

1. A.F.P.R. regulations require the proposals of the contractor to be reviewed before submission by engineering, pricing, auditing, data, legal, civil rights, subcontracting, and many other experts, and in turn various Pentagon and government agencies must review the proposals for compli-

Economic considerations—the need, for instance, to funnel defense contracts into depressed areas—and political pressure— the need to win an election or placate a pressure group—play their part in consideration and delay in contracts. Normally, as the T.F.X. investigation brought out, no major defense contract is awarded without Presidential approval, and the Democratic (or as the case may be, the Republican) National Committee representatives always have their opportunity to urge contractual rewards to the party faithful. The F-111 (T.F.X.) contract went to the General Dynamics Fort Worth plant, although the services in three separate evaluations preferred the Boeing proposal. Many in Washington believe this was the result of political pressure.

All of these practices—all of this red tape—"jest growed" as part of Big Government and a big defense budget.

II

But the major causes of recent delays are to be found in the Pentagon itself, and they stem from the over-centralized organization established by Mr. McNamara and the attempts made to achieve "perfection on paper" before any steel is bent.

Centralization—"unification," the public calls it—has been steadily increasing, particularly since the passage of the 1958 modifications to the National Security Act. But Mr. McNamara has used the power every Secretary of Defense has always had to a far greater extent than any predecessor. There is no doubt that he has run the show. Any major contract must be approved by him; even relatively minor modifications must pass the gauntlet of his numerous assistants.

The checkreins Secretary McNamara has used were, without doubt, needed to halt the proliferation of unneeded weapons systems and the expenditure of billions on projects that turned out to be "duds" or duplications of others.

---

ance. Even so, A.F.P.R. regulations are sometimes vaguely worded. A Congressional investigating subcommittee recently requested the Department of Defense to alter those regulations dealing with employee health and recreation expenses. The wording of some of the regulations permitted the charge-off of losses for operating factory cafeterias, and contractors could also charge cocktail parties to the taxpayer if they were billed as "employee welfare."

It is an axiom of sound military research practices that in the early stages two or more parallel lines of development should be followed leading to the same end—a weapons system of given characteristics. In case an unexpected engineering problem of insuperable difficulty is encountered in one developmental effort, the second may offer an alternative. But to avoid unnecessary duplication and expense once the teething troubles are over, one of the two lines should be abandoned and full efforts concentrated on the more hopeful one. In the pre-McNamara era this decision was often left until too late. This was the case, for instance, when the Air Force developed the Thor Intermediate-Range Ballistic Missile and the Army developed Jupiter. Because of service rivalries and pressures, both missiles were developed to final "hardware" stages and both were produced in small but expensive quantities, although one virtually duplicated the other and either could have done the job of both. Mr. McNamara, therefore, had some justification for his "show-me" attitude and for the elaborate system he has established of evaluating and analyzing all new projects. But he or "the system" has over-compensated. The "cost" part of the "cost-effectiveness" formula has been emphasized and underscored at the expense of speedy development and new ideas. Never in the history of competition have so many been able to say no, so few yes.[2]

In the past, technological development and research and procurement contracting were largely decentralized; the individual services were responsible to a major degree for their own weapons development. Service competition, in the happiest sense, produced the air-cooled aircraft engine (sponsored by the Navy) and the liquid-cooled engine (sponsored by the then Army Air Corps) with which the United States fought and won World War II in the air. One without the other would have been incomplete; a service competition produced both.

2. Management experts and contractors have pointed out that the exercise of centralized control by the Department of Defense over the services requires information and reports from the services. The self-generating and self-defeating nature of the work load imposed becomes apparent. The tighter and more centralized the control, the more reports that are required. The more authority taken away from the working level, the more paper work that is required from those at the working level to back up their diminished authority.

When a new aircraft was required, the service needing it determined the characteristics wanted to perform the specialized missions contemplated. Competitive contracts were then let for a small number of planes, and actual flight competitions between competing companies were held, with the big payoff production contract going to the contractor who built the best plane, as actually determined in the air.

The services formerly had, within overall policy and budget limitations, a considerable degree of autonomy, and weapons development and procurement were largely decentralized. What can be done when red tape is cut, authority and responsibility are coupled, and organization is decentralized to the working levels is shown by the production of the Polaris missile and the A-11 aircraft. The highly successful and extremely complex Polaris was pushed to completion as an operational weapon in about three and a half years, well ahead of schedule. One man, Vice Admiral W. F. Raborn, was given authority and responsibility to cut across organizational lines, and he was fully backed by the Navy and the Department of Defense. There was then no such centralization in the Pentagon as exists now. The A-11, successor to the famed U-2 high-flying reconnaissance plane, was a secret project, amply funded by the C.I.A. and by the Air Force. With ample funds, full authority and responsibility and a high degree of autonomy, Lockheed Aircraft was twice able to produce—in the U-2 and its successor—world-beating aircraft in the abbreviated timespan. Similarly, Vice Admiral Hyman G. Rickover, who wore two hats—one Navy, one A.E.C.—and whose authority therefore spanned the bifurcated organizational structure, was able to produce what was essentially a new weapons system with minimum delay. The key to these and other successful development and production efforts is the coupling of authority and responsibility at working levels.

Today the entire picture has changed violently. Under the law, separate service departments must be maintained and the services cannot be directly merged; Mr. McNamara has merged them "indirectly," as John C. Ries points out in his new book.[3] A fourth service—the Office of the Secretary of Defense—has been

3. *The Management of Defense* (Baltimore: The Johns Hopkins University Press, 1964).

built up as an all-powerful apex. It is far more than a policy-making and coordinating agency, as it was originally intended to be under the National Security Act of 1947; it administers , operates, contracts, develops, procures, and commands. Super-agencies, superimposed over the service departments, are answerable only to the Secretary of Defense and the Joint Chiefs of Staff.

Former service functions have been assumed by the Defense Supply Agency, which procures items common to the services; by the Defense Intelligence Agency, the National Security Agency. (communications, intelligence and security; codes and ciphers, etc.), the Defense Communications Agency (common and longlines communications) and the Defense Atomic Support Agency. These have added new super-echelons to the Pentagon bureaucracy.

Mr. McNamara came into office intending—he let it be known —to streamline top echelon Defense Department management. There were some 15 Presidential appointees of the rank of Assistant Secretary of Defense or higher in January 1961 when he took office; there are 16 today. There were 11 Deputy Assistant Secretaries of Defense two years ago; there are about 30 today.

The Joint Staff of the Joint Chiefs of Staff was originally limited by law by Congress to 100 officers, then increased to 400, a specific limit intended to prevent the development of a super-General Staff; it now numbers the full 400, plus another 1,170 military and civilian personnel. The additional personnel are labeled members of the Organization of the Joint Chiefs of Staff, a euphemism which permits evasion of the legal restriction (with both Executive departments and Congress winking at the extra-legality). This staff, rich with rank, now has three lieutenant-generals or vice admirals assigned to head its more important sections or divisions, and its director—a three-star general— may be given four stars if current suggestions are carried out.

As one would expect with gigantic staff which tends to generate its own paper work, the work load of the Joint Chiefs of Staff steadily increases—from 887 persons or reports requiring some action by the J.C.S. in 1958 to about double that number today. Something like a de facto hierarchical general staff now exists, with the Chairman of the Joint Chiefs as a kind of overall Chief of Staff; and it busies itself with the ridiculous and the petty as well as the crucial and important. (The Joint Chiefs, for instance, determine the details of the administration and curriculum of the National War College and other joint service schools and have even solemnly considered such important matters as the advisability of establishing an all-service soccer team which might compete with European all-stars, and the numbers of cooks, and which services should furnish them, for a U. S. headquarters in Europe.) Representative Charles S. Gubser of California has estimated that there are now a total of some 34,000 employees responsible to the Office of the Secretary of Defense (exclusive of separate service departments in Washington). Statistics like these indicate the revolutionary changes that have occurred within the Pentagon in the past fifteen—particularly in the past four—years. As Mr. Ries puts it, the "dogma of centralization" has triumphed.

Many besides Mr. Ries worry about the capability of the present defense organization to withstand the strain of real war or protracted crises. There have been some disturbing signs of faltering and confusion during the Berlin crisis, the Cuban missile crisis, and one of the Gulf of Tonkin incidents.

The present Secretary of Defense has a computer mind, capable of absorbing and recording immense quantities of detailed data. He also has ferocious energy. The combination of these two qualities has enabled him, so far, to deal with what Mr. Ries calls the "minutiae that floods upward in a centralized organization." But even Mr. McNamara has several times given evidence of strain, and after Mr. McNamara—who? To decentralize the department so that the Secretary could have time, opportunity, and assistance to cope with major decisions would require a decrease rather than an increase in the staff of the Secretary—something that no democratic bureaucracy seems capable of accomplishing.

The centralized organization of the Pentagon and the accompanying growth of a bureaucracy—particularly in the upper echelons—explain in part the delays in development and procurement of new weapons systems. In effect, responsibility and authority have been separated in the Pentagon. Vice Admiral Rickover gave several instances of delays caused by bureaucracy in testimony to a Senate Committee in 1958. Purchase of nuclear cores was delayed for six months "just because one staff person with no responsibility but with authority had on his own decided" against the purchase. In March 1964, he testified before a House Appropriations subcommittee on the question of nuclear power for a new aircraft carrier. The carrier itself was already approved by both Congress and the Defense Department. The Navy and most Congressmen felt that such a major new investment should be as modern as possible, and that it should be powered with nuclear reactors rather than with oil, even though the initial cost would be considerably greater. But the subject was studied to death. Admiral Rickover testified: "The Department of Defense itself caused much of the delay. They considered the Navy's request to change it to a nuclear carrier for a year. The Department of Defense kept on asking for more information, more studies, more analyses. New studies and analyses are under way now on nuclear propulsion for the next carrier and other surface warships. These studies never end, and we don't build ships."

The services still have the legal responsibility for development and procurement but not the authority to implement their responsibility. Similarly the responsibility for planning and execution has been separated. The Joint Chiefs no longer legally command anything; in the procurement field the services must often execute or carry out procurement plans they have not formulated (i.e., the T.F.X.).

In an admirable attempt to promote some much-needed long-range planning in the armed forces and to control costs, Mr. McNamara instituted what is called the Five Year Force Structure and Financial Management Program, often dubbed "The Book." "The Book" tries to chart and elaborate all major details of service force structures (including sizes, types) and weapons systems required, being procured or developed, for the next five years. Any significant change in "The Book," including research expenditures, requires consideration by hundreds of people, including the Joint Chiefs of Staff and the Secretary himself, and an elaborate process of justification, review, and approval all along the line from lowest to highest echelons. Contracting, budgeting, progress on weapons systems—and even lawn cutting —are programmed and controlled in detail from various echelons of the Secretary's office, with streams of reports required. The services have complained that there is an inherent, built-in inflexibility and rigidity in this system.

In addition to the Secretary of Defense and his deputy and the Chairman of the Joint Chiefs and the 1,570 supporting staff, all of the Assistant Secretaries of Defense have become, not de jure, but de facto, line *operators* as well as *staff* assistants. By virtue of authority delegated by the Secretary, they can and do cut across service lines and intervene at the lowest echelons. Two offices, in particular, have a major influence in weapons development and procurement; unfortunately they are too often delaying factors rather than expediters.

The Office of the Assistant Secretary of Defense (Controller) has completely changed its character under the McNamara regime. Charles J. Hitch, the incumbent, has, with the Secretary's approval, applied the methods he developed as an economic theorist at the RAND Corporation to military strategic programming. The cost-effectiveness of various weapons systems is analyzed on paper by his office, and he and his associates have a powerful voice in determining what kind of weapon will go to what service. Dr. Brown, the director of Defense, Research and Engineering, does another analytical job, supposedly from the technical and engineering feasibility point of view. His analyses are particularly important in the research and development stages.

Any projected weapons system has to run the gauntlet between the Charybdis of Mr. Hitch and the Scylla of Dr. Brown; but many other high and low echelon perils confront it also. The McNamara administration has established "for all large endeavors" (and for some that are not so large) what it calls a "Project Definition Phase" (P.D.P. in Pentagon jargon). In Secretary McNamara's words, "before full-scale development is initiated, the specific operational requirements and the cost effectiveness of the system must be confirmed, and goals, milestones and time schedules must be established. . . . All the aspects of a development are tied together into a single plan which defines, for Government and industry alike, what is wanted, how it is to be designed and built, how it will be used, what it will cost, and what systems and techniques will be used to manage the program. . . ."

The P.D.P. represents the Pentagon's search for "perfection on paper" before any operation begins. There is no doubt that it is an attractive theoretical management tool, but there is also not much doubt that it has delayed development and procurement of new weapons systems, and whether or not the end result in the form of "finished hardware" is actually any better or less expensive, it is still too soon to tell.[4] The T.F.X. (F-111) aircraft for the Air Force and Navy has been programmed and evaluated, analyzed and costed in detail on paper in the "P.D.P."; it is still in the development stage and may not be operational for years to come.[5] This plane, which can vary the sweep of its wings (their angle to the fuselage) in flight, was forced into a preconceived and theoretical mold in the P.D. phrase. Mr. McNamara insisted, against service objections, that Navy needs and Air Force needs could be satisfied by a single all-purpose plane, which could be flown from land fields and carrier decks on several entirely different types of missions. The attempt to achieve this—in theory and in blueprint form—required many months before

4. Stanley Bernstein, of the Raytheon Company, in a paper, "The Impact of Project Definition on Aerospace System Management," delivered at the first annual meeting of the American Institute of Aeronautics and Astronautics (June 29–July 2, 1964), used the Mobile Medium-Range Ballistic Missile as a case history. He pointed out that contractors were expected to meet some 20 different requirements in a final P.D.P. report. ". . . one may consider the several contractors who participated in the M.M.R.B.M. effort," he said. "Even prior to Department of Defense program authorization in January 1962, companies like Hughes, Thiokol, Martin, and many others had been engaged in significant engineering efforts. When Program Definition was authorized, originally as a four-month effort, nine prime companies and many subcontractors and suppliers geared for maximum effort. The four months stretched to almost one year. Motivation has to be maintained. The present status of M.M.R.B.M. is clouded [Since this paper, M.M.R.B.M. has been virtually killed] Yet the participants must retain a level of interest in order to be ready to proceed if the program should become active. The maintenance of this motivation is a major management challenge. The requirement for stated performance incentive goals will, inevitably, lead to more conservative design and engineering during the Program Definition Phase. . . . P.D. contracts should not be used as a means of postponing difficult government decisions or to decide what kind of military capability is required."

5. The practice of "super-study" is extending beyond the Pentagon. The S.S.T., or Supersonic Commercial Transport, is now called the "Super-studied Transport." Najeeb E. Halaby, head of the Federal Aviation Agency, recently said, "Whether or not it ever flies, it will easily be the most analyzed project in the Government's history." If so, this is quite a record.

designs acceptable to both services were evolved. The development contract was finally awarded to Convair and the first of the developmental T.F.X. planes is nearing completion. The Navy fears the finished version may be too heavy for carrier decks.

The finest fighter in the world today, the Navy's McDonnell F-4-B Phantom II, which the Air Force is now buying in quantity in a slightly modified version, was the product of flight competition back in the 50's when the P.D.P. in its present rigid form was unheard of, and centralization in the Pentagon had not reached today's extreme. The McDonnell and Chance-Vought aircraft companies, in response to a Navy need for a supersonic fighter of certain given specifications, were each awarded developmental contracts for a small number of planes. The results were then actually flight-tested in competition. McDonnell won, but the Chance-Vought product was also good and was procured in more limited quantities for specialized reconnaissance and other missions for the fleet.

Many believe that this type of flight and inter-service competition produces the best dividends. One service evolves the plane or engine and (after actual competition between several bidders) contracts for and procures the one best suited to its own specialized needs. That one may well be adapted—after it is operational—to the needs of another service.[6] Each gets the type it wants, and a better plane or weapon than if it had been forced, on paper, into a common mold. For there frequently are incompatible requirements among service weapons systems, and the attempt to provide "commonality" in the interest of reducing costs may well increase cost and reduce combat effectiveness.

It is true, of course, that major weapons development projects have become far more complex and costly than they were ten to twenty years ago. In theory, the attempt of the Department of Defense to "define" a project and to refine it on paper before the steel is bent has a great deal of attractiveness. Many authorities who are loud in condemning the delays of the P.D.P. system do not believe it is economically feasible—at least in all

6. There are countless instances of this kind of adaptation. In addition to the liquid and air-cooled engines and the F-4-B, the Air Force, for instance, uses the Navy-developed Sidewinder and Bullpup missiles.

cases—to return to the old era of actual competitive service tests. Others, however, think that competitive testing of several different models, while more expensive initially, may actually save money eventually, chiefly because it may result in a better product. Eugene E. Wilson, retired naval officer and retired vice chairman of United Aircraft Corporation, wrote in the September –October 1964 issue of *Shipmate*, the magazine of the U.S. Naval Academy Alumni Association, that "the current practice of awarding production (and development) contracts to a single supplier, on the basis of contract guarantees unsubstantiated by competitive prototype performance . . . will not protect a hapless purchaser (the government) willing to risk his all on computation." The fundamental difficulty with P.D.P. is that it has been invoked as an answer to *all* development and production problems, that it is interpreted too rigidly, and that there has been far too much dependence in the Department of Defense on what is essentially a management tool at the expense of judgment and engineering and scientific intuition.

It is only fair to add that recently the complaints of the services and of industry have resulted in a recognition in the Defense Department of some of these faults. A new and standardized procedure for rating, evaluating, and selecting the winning contractors in a screening competition has been under preparation for two years and is now being presented—possibly for final approval—to the Office of the Secretary of Defense. For any large projects (exceeding $100,000,000 in production costs) authority will still remain at the highest levels; for smaller projects authority may be delegated to lower echelons. The procedure may—but probably will not—lessen the time lag; certainly it will not change the recent emphasis on "perfection on paper."

In the Program Definition Phase of weapons development three high hurdles, in addition to countless evaluation procedures, cause many projects to stumble and fail.

One is the eruption of inter-service rivalry instead of—in the best sense—inter-service competition. A proposal for a new weapon or aircraft by one service is now picked to pieces and studied on paper by all services before even a minor development contract is approved. Now that their former degree of autonomy is restricted and actual development competition discouraged, the services know that the P.D. phase offers a now-or-never chance. Each service may produce a different concept or a different set of desired performance figures; a long "hassle" ensues to try to put them all into one weapons system. This occurred, notably, in the case of the T.F.X.; it is happening now with the new COIN (counter-insurgency) aircraft which the Marines want to develop. The result is delay, sometimes a compromise as to performance.

A second factor causing delay and difficulties is the attempt by the Secretary's numerous assistants to eliminate what they call "gold-plating," or unnecessarily high performance figures or standards. The attempt is laudable, but it is sometimes carried to extremes, and it has been difficult, as Admiral George W. Anderson, former Chief of Naval Operations, pointed out, for men in uniform to adjust to the idea that a ten-mile-an-hour speed differential between our own aircraft and enemy planes may not—in the eyes of the Department of Defense—be important. To a pilot, that ten miles an hour, even though costly in terms of dollars, may be the difference between life and death.

It is in the P.D. phase, too that the old bogey of "no operational or military requirement" becomes a major obstacle to weapons development. It is invoked at both high and low levels. Mr. McNamara has been rigid—though with some signs of a slight relaxation recently—about the statement of specific needs before development can start. The "operational requirement," as an experienced naval officer puts it, "is another of the paper obstacles which are intended to insure proper planning but which, when operated by people who have no real knowledge of the problems involved, frustrate progress."

In the military exploitation of a new medium, like space, it is completely impossible to define, in the terms required by the P.D.P. evaluations, the need for, or the performance characteristics of, a new vehicle. How can even a prescient scientist predict what usefulness a Manned Orbiting Laboratory will have? Yet the invocation of "no specific operational requirement" has delayed Air Force development of this highly important new project for at least two to three years.

Representative Chet Holifield's Military Operations Subcommittee of the House recently gave its view of what's wrong with the Pentagon. After a thorough study of Mr. McNamara's protracted efforts to merge military and commercial satellite systems, the subcommittee reported that two years had been wasted. It said: "We still detect uncertainty and overeconomizing in the Defense Department approach . . . there has been overmanagement and underperformance . . . too many layers of supervision, the lack of clear-cut responsibilty . . . and sluggish channels of . . . communication."

Senator John Stennis, in common with many others, has decried the tendency to be negative, to object, to try to refine requirements in too much detail, to evaluate and study too much. Some weapons systems, he has said, "have literally been studied to death." He cites the B-70 (which dates back in inception to 1954) as a prime example of what happens to a weapon system development "when it is subjected to repeated stops and starts and when there is not a strong, orderly and continuous program to bring it to completion." This bomber, designed for long-range, high-altitude flights at three times the speed of sound, has encountered many technical difficulties and is well behind even a revised schedule. This was made certain by off-again-on-again programs in the Pentagon and by the multi-layered, centralized organization there.

Before a final contract for a project is signed and actual development starts, an average of at least 50 signatures or approvals is required—sometimes as many as 100 to 200. Some individuals, required by legal or administrative reasons to sign twice, have had to be briefed twice; by the time the second signature was needed they had forgotten what the contract was about.

It is true that centralization in the development and procurement field, epitomized by the Five Year Force Structure and the Program Definition Phase, was in part the outgrowth of inadequate management by the services of some research and development contracts. It was also the result of the failure of past Secretaries of Defense to exercise the power they have always had by eliminating—not service competition—but duplicatory and unnecessary service rivalry. But the cure has proved worse than the disease.

Healthy service competition can be encouraged and unhealthy service rivalry can be discouraged by:

1. Abandonment of attempts—keyed primarily to costs, not effectiveness—to force service weapons systems into "all-purpose" molds. "Commonality" develops naturally from actual technological accomplishments, not from P.D.P.'s or paper plans.

2. Return, insofar as possible, to competition in hardware rather than competition on paper. The end product is almost certain to be better, and ultimately may cost less.

3. Sponsorship, within a service, or by two or more services, of competitive research and development projects, all having a common goal, but each following different technological paths to that goal.

4. Definite selection by the Defense Department at the earliest possible stage of the best project; cancellation of the others.

The key lessons for tomorrow are two. Responsibility and authority must be coupled at *working levels* in the management of research and development and production contracts. And there must be a much higher degree of job stability and continuity in management than the rotational policies of the services have made possible in the past.[7]

7. As Representative Melvin Price notes, one reason, for example, that the Army (nuclear) reactor program (a program for developing a small portable nuclear reactor which could provide power in remote areas) has fallen flat on its face is that the Army kept transferring out the managers of the program. There were six different managers in five years.

The Case for Cost-Effectiveness Analysis

CHARLES HITCH

Charles Hitch was Assistant Secretary of Defense (Comptroller) from 1961 to 1965. He is now President of the University of California. This article comes from his book, Decision-Making for Defense, *published in 1966.*

THE EXTENSIVE AND COMPREHENSIVE use of "cost-effectiveness" studies or systems analyses was . . . [a] major innovation introduced into the decision-making process of the Defense Department [during the early sixties]. Although the introduction of the programming function was generally well received, considerable controversy arose over this extensive use of cost-effectiveness studies in the decision-making process, and some of this controversy continues. Why this is so is something of a mystery to me. We have made repeated efforts to explain the essential nature of these studies and the contribution that they make to the achievement of greater military effectiveness as well as economy in the defense establishment. But the suspicion still persists in some influential quarters that, somehow or other, cost-effectiveness studies put "dollars before national security," or will result in our going to war with "cut-rate, cut-quality, cheapest-to-buy weapons." Virtually every attempt we have made to explain the inexorable logic of relating cost to military effectiveness seems to shatter itself on the argument—"Nothing but the best will do for our boys." And the "best" usually refers to some particular characteristic of physical performance, such as speed, altitude, or firepower, or even unit cost!

Implicit in this challenge is the deeply rooted feeling that national defense is far too important a matter to be inhibited by cost. If one weapon system performs better than another, then we should buy the higher performance system, regardless of cost; the country can afford it. Indeed, the people who hold

79

this view feel that it is somehow sinful, or at least unpatriotic, to try to relate performance or military effectiveness to costs; that considerations of military effectiveness and cost are antithetical.

To anyone trained in economics, this is a most puzzling attitude. We know that the very act of making a choice—and that is all we are doing when we choose weapons—involves weighing the utility or benefit to be gained against the cost which must be incurred. Why is that so? It is so because benefits *cost* resources and we live in a world in which resources are limited. If we use more for one purpose, less remains for other purposes —even in as rich a nation as the United States.

Certainly, most of us are continuously being forced to make such choices in our personal lives. Although explicit calculations may be rare in these personal choices, they are common, if not quite universal, in business affairs. Indeed, the weighing of benefits against costs is one of the imperatives of any good business decision. The fact that one machine can produce twice as much or twice as fast as another must obviously be weighed against its additional cost in order to determine which is the more profitable. The principle is exactly the same in defense, except that in private business the manager is guided by the profit goal and the market prices of what he buys and sells; whereas in government the decision-maker, since he is not selling in a market, must determine the worth of his "product," e.g., of added performance, by careful analysis and the application of experienced judgment. In this respect, cost-effectiveness analysis is more difficult in defense than in a private firm operating in a market economy, and even more important.

Contrary to the suspicion in some quarters, the scarcity of resources and the consequent necessity for economic choice is not the invention of economists or defense comptrollers, or even of the Democratic administration. The Hoover Commission in its report of June 1955 pointed out that:

The question of "quantity" cannot be considered except in conjunction with that of "cost." Just as in a business, one cannot make a decision to buy material or equipment without simultaneous consideration of price, so the Government cannot intelligently consider the wisdom of embarking on any program without a similar consideration of its cost. A decision to increase or decrease the number of air wings is intimately connected with consideration of the cost at which an air wing can be equipped and operated.

The role of the cost-effectiveness study is to assist management in making just such decisions by bringing into clearer focus the impact on overall military effectiveness of an increase or decrease in the number of air wings and the specific cost implications of such changes.

I was somewhat startled about a year ago to read a statement by a leading member of the Congress:

There is no hard evidence that the Soviet Union is applying cost-effectiveness criteria in its planning for future weapons systems. In fact, many knowledgeable students of Soviet thinking believe that the opposite is quite probably the case.

It reminded me of a statement made some years earlier by Hanson Baldwin to the effect that:

In the Western World—though not in Russia—costs are a more decisive factor in shaping defense than is military logic.

The idea that the Soviets pay little attention to cost is a very common misconception in this country. At the risk of opening up a new controversy on the "cost-effectiveness gap," let me assure you that the Soviet leaders are most sensitive to the need for applying cost-effectiveness principles in all of their economic planning, and there is no reason to doubt that they follow the same approach in the military area. For example, here is a statement from the program adopted by the 22nd Congress of the Communist Party of the Soviet Union in 1961:

Chief attention in all links of planning and economic management must be focused on the most rational and effective use of material, labor, financial and natural resources, and on the elimination of excessive expenditures and losses. It is an immutable law of economic construction to achieve, in the interests of society, the greatest results at the lowest cost.

The formulation is not elegant, or even accurate, but the sense of it shines through.

That military expenditures were not excluded from this consideration was made evident by Mr. Khrushchev's explanation of the cutback in the Soviet military forces announced in January 1960. At that time he said:

The elimination of nonproductive expenditures and the search for additional possibilities for economic development are tasks that constantly confront not only us but any state. I repeat that this matter is always urgent and will always attract unflagging attention. . . . The proposal to reduce the Soviet Armed Forces . . . will yield an annual saving of approximately 16,000,000,000 to 17,000,000,000 rubles [old rubles]. This will be a very tangible saving for our people and our country. It represents a powerful reinforcement for fulfilling and over-fulfilling our economic plans.

Thus it seems plain that the Soviets, too, realize that they are not immune to the laws of economics, that they are not exempt from having to choose among the various alternative claims on the limited resources available to them. Nor do they appear reluctant to make use of the most modern methods and techniques to assist their managers in making these choices. Clearly, the Soviets have also realized that the modern world is far too complex to rely solely on intuitive judgment and that their decision-makers must be supported by quantitative analysis.

But opposition to cost-effectiveness studies stems not only from a suspicion of quantitative analysis but also from the conviction—completely unsubstantiated but nevertheless firmly held —that these studies inevitably lead to decisions favoring the cheapest weapon. Nothing could be further from the truth. Cost-effectiveness analysis is completely neutral with respect to the unit cost of a weapon. What it is concerned with is: Which strategy (or force, or weapon system) offers the greatest amount of military effectiveness for a given outlay? Or looking at the problem from another direction: How can a given level of military effectiveness be achieved at least cost?

In some cases the most "economical" weapon may be the one with the highest unit cost; in other cases, it may be the one with the lowest unit cost—it will depend on the relative military worth of quality and quantity in the particular circumstances. Unit cost, by itself, is simply an index—an inverse index—of quantity. There have been many cases in history where the cheaper and technically less efficient weapon proved to be the "best," simply because its lower cost permitted it to be acquired in much greater numbers.

It should always be our policy to spend whatever is necessary for defense, but to spend whatever is spent in such a way as to achieve the greatest possible military capability—not to buy quality when the same amount spent on quantity will purchase greater effectiveness, and vice versa. Sometimes a weapon system with less than the maximum unit cost and effectiveness does win out as in the case of the new Navy attack aircraft, the A-7, which is far slower than many other aircraft now in the forces —and also much cheaper. The A-7 promises to be not only satisfactory for the missions it is intended to perform, but superior in those missions to alternatives which cost more per aircraft. As a Marine Colonel pointed out in an article last year—"Speed is not necessarily progress. . . . If . . . targets cannot be found and accurately hit, the effort is wasted."

But sometimes it is just the other way around—cost-effectiveness studies lead us in the direction of higher quality, higher performance, higher unit cost. For example, during the past three years we have vastly increased the procurement of such relatively complex air-to-ground weapons as the radio-controlled BULLPUP close support missile, the SHRIKE antiradar missile, and other quality modern ordnance. They are far more expensive per unit than the older "free fall" bombs they displaced, but also far more effective. Our cost-effectiveness studies have shown that we get a more economical defense from these weapons than from bombs—even if the bombs are inherited and therefore almost cost free.

Cost-effectiveness studies or systems analyses are needed in the defense decision-making process for yet another purpose. This purpose might be labeled "how much is enough?" . . . Military requirements in the Department of Defense tend to be stated in absolute terms. The traditional military requirements study was typically a calculation of the forces required to achieve a single hypothesized objective.

To give an oversimplified example, suppose the objective were to achieve an expectation of destroying 97 per cent of 100 targets, using missiles having a 50 per cent single-shot "kill" capability. The traditional requirements study would conclude that 500 missiles were needed because 100 missiles would achieve an expectancy of 50 kills, 200 missiles—75 kills, 300 missiles—87 kills, 40 missiles—94 kills, and 50 missiles—97 kills. This, of course, merely reflects the operation of the familiar law of diminishing returns. But the significant point is that the last 100 missiles would increase the "kill" expectation by only three extra targets, from 94 to 97. Thus, we should not only ask the question, "Do we need a capability to destroy 97 per cent of the 100 targets?"; we should also ask the question, "Is the capability to raise expected target destruction from 94 to 97 per cent worth the cost of 100 extra missiles?" In other words, we must not only examine total costs and total products but also marginal costs and marginal products.

Of course, when dealing with defense problems, data on marginal costs and marginal products do not, in themselves, imply mathematically what the number should be, i.e., the number we should buy. Since we do not operate in the market place, we cannot usually calculate the point where, in the business world, marginal cost equals marginal revenue. The defense decision-maker must exercise his own judgment as to whether the last 3 per cent of kill capability is worth the cost of another 100 missiles. But data of this kind can contribute a great deal to making that judgment an informed one.

The example I used is a relatively simple problem. At a much higher level of difficulty are such questions as whether an air defense system capable of destroying say 95 per cent of all the bombers an enemy could possibly launch against us is a desirable military objective. This depends not only on the cost of the air defense system itself but also on the relative cost and effectiveness of *other ways* of limiting damage to the United States, such as producing and deploying an antiballistic missile defense system, increasing our civil defense program, or adding to our strategic offensive forces. Thus, what are military objectives when viewed from one level, are simply means to a still higher objective when viewed from another level; and any given objective is likely to be only one of a number of alternative ways of achieving a still broader objective—in this case, limiting damage to the United States. The tradeoffs or substitution possibilities among them depend upon questions of cost and effectiveness, which in turn depend upon technology.

Although our national security objectives, in the highest sense of the word, reflect essentially the composite value judgments of the American people, the choice of a particular military strategy or military objective cannot be divorced from the cost of achieving it. Systems analysis at the national level, therefore, involves a continuous cycle of defining military objectives, designing alternative systems to achieve these objectives, evaluating these alternatives in terms of their effectiveness and cost, questioning the objectives and other assumptions underlying the analysis, opening new alternatives and establishing new military objectives, and so on indefinitely.

Thus, the problem of allocating resources within the Department of Defense itself involves the choosing of doctrines, weapons, equipment, and so forth, so as to get the most defense out of any given level of available resources or, what is logically equivalent, to achieve a given level of defense at the least cost. Approaching the problem from the first point of view—getting the most defense from a given level of resources—we work in terms of marginal rates of transformation and substitution. Approaching the problem from the second point of view—achieving a given level of defense at the least cost, which is the way Secretary McNamara prefers to look at the problem—we work in terms of marginal products and marginal costs in order to help the top decision-maker choose the appropriate level of resources.

Regardless of which approach we use in allocating resources within the defense establishment, we must recognize that, at the highest level of government, there remains the problem of optimizing the allocation of resources across the entire spectrum of our national needs, and this means exercising choice among many desirable objectives. This in itself imposes certain constraints on the size of the defense budget at any particular time and under any particular set of circumstances. Certainly, if the international situation were to worsen, the value of an additional increment to the defense budget would be relatively greater than before, compared with other needs and concerns of the U.S. Government. Conversely, if the international situation were to improve markedly, then the value of the last increment of the defense budget would be relatively smaller than before, compared with our other needs. This problem of national choices is not unique to the United States. It is one with which the government of every nation has to cope, even, as we have seen, the Soviet Union.

But let me hasten to say that systems analysis or cost-effectiveness studies are by no means a panacea for all the problems of defense. Costs in general can be measured quantitatively, although not always with the degree of precision we would like. Measuring effectiveness or military worth poses a much more difficult problem. Reliable quantitative data are often not available. And even when such data are available, there is usually no common standard of measurement. This is particularly true with regard to systems analyses involving complex new technologies. Here, even reliable cost data are seldom available. Accordingly, the preferred alternative can rarely, if ever, be determined simply by applying a formula.

It has long been my contention:

that economic choice is *a way of looking at problems* and does not necessarily depend upon the use of any analytic aids or computational devices. Some analytic aids (mathematical models) and computing machinery are quite likely to be useful in analyzing complex military problems, but there are many military problems in which they have not proved particularly useful where, nevertheless, it is rewarding to array the alternatives and think through their implications in terms of objectives and costs. Where mathematical models and computations are useful, they are in no sense alternatives to or rivals of good intuitive judgment; they supplement and complement it. Judgment is always of critical importance in designing the analysis, choosing the alternatives to be compared, and selecting the criterion. Except where there is a completely satisfactory one-dimensional measurable objective (a rare circumstance), judgment must supplement the quantitative analysis before a choice can be recommended.

I am the last to believe that an "optimal strategy" can be calculated on slide rules or even high-speed computers. Nothing could be further from the truth. Systems analysis is simply a method to get before the decision-maker the relevant data, organized in a way most useful to him. It is no substitute for sound and experienced military judgment, and it is but one of the many kinds of information needed by the decision-maker.

It is my experience that the hardest problems for the systems analyst are not those of analytic techniques. In fact, the techniques we use in the Office of the Secretary of Defense are usually rather simple and old-fashioned. What distinguishes the useful and productive analyst is his ability to formulate (or design) the problem; to choose appropriate objectives; to define the relevant, important environments or situations in which to test the alternatives; to judge the reliability of his cost and other data; and finally, and not least, his ingenuity in inventing new systems or alternatives to evaluate. My friend and former colleague, Albert Wohlstetter, used to insist that the systems analyst could contribute much more by inventing new systems than by comparing proposed systems; his own inventions are eloquent testimony to the validity of this view.

The analysis of rapid deployment of forces to trouble spots around the world illustrates many of these points. Early analyses concentrated on the question: what is the most economical type of aircraft to procure for the purpose? Sealift was regarded as much too slow to be a competitor. From an early date, extensive prepositioning of men and equipment, or of equipment only, was recognized as an alternative, or a partial alternative, and included in the analysis.

Then a systems analyst made an invention. A great problem with prepositioning is the difficulty of acquiring real estate for the purpose in foreign countries and the likelihood that the real estate, if acquired, and the prepositioned stocks will turn out to be in the wrong country (or even the wrong continent) when hostilities actually threaten or break out. So this analyst thought: why not preposition on ships? A pregnant thought. We now have many "forward floating depots"—Victory ships stocked with Army equipment—in the Western Pacific, ready to steam to any threatened area and substantially augmenting our airlift rapid deployment capability.

At about the same time a more straightforward design development or "invention" produced the Roll-on/Roll-off, or "Ro-Ro," ship which can rapidly load and unload Army vehicular equipment at even primitive ports.

Then a third invention was made by an ingenious systems analyst who simply combined the characteristics of the forward floating depot and the Ro-Ro ship and developed an appropriate operational concept for the combination. This definitely made sealift competitive with airlift for rapid deployment in many situations, and we have asked Congress in the 1966 budget for four specially designed Ro-Ro's to be used as forward floating depots.

Meanwhile some design inventions stimulated by airlift analyses promise us much more efficient airlift aircraft. The most important enables us to combine the marked economies of a very large aircraft with a landing gear and power plant which permit operations from short, primitive forward air bases. This combination promises to reduce or even eliminate the ground line of communication in the combat theater, with substantial savings in time, troops, and equipment. We are starting full-scale development of such an aircraft—the C-5A—this year.

Our analytic problem now is to determine the best mix of this better sealift and this better airlift. In many situations (e.g., close to the shore in Southeast Asia and Korea), the ships can win handily on cost-effectiveness criteria. In other hypothetical situations (e.g., farther inland), the C-5A wins handily. Each system has capabilities the other has not. And problems the other has not. And different and difficult-to-analyze vulnerabilities to enemy action. No computer will automatically provide the answer to this problem of optimum mix, although a carefully formulated computer program can, under specified conditions, give valuable insights about break-even points and regions of sensitivity.

Typically in major systems comparisons this is the situation. There are multiple objectives or payoffs—not just one which is well defined and clear-cut. There are multiple circumstances in which the system may be called upon to function. And there are usually great uncertainties about costs, enemy intentions and capabilities, and other factors. This kind of systems analysis makes great demands on the analyst's ingenuity, his experience, and above all his judgment and common sense. When Ellis Johnson called it "quantified common sense," he was not far off the mark.

Finally, we must recognize that if the objectives or the costs or the measurements of military effectiveness are wrong, the answers will also be wrong. The SKYBOLT air-to-ground missile is a case in point. A gross underestimate of costs in 1961 led to a decision to carry that project into the production stage. When the full dimensions of the ultimate cost later became apparent, the decision was made to drop the project since it was not worth the increased cost in the light of the other alternatives available, namely, expanding the MINUTEMAN force and retaining more of the HOUND DOG air-to-ground missiles which were already in the inventory. You may recall that this decision led to some very painful moments with our British colleagues as the United Kingdom had also planned to use the SKYBOLT missile with its bombers. Our decision to drop the project created some very difficult problems for the British Government at the time and led to a meeting at Nassau between President Kennedy and Prime Minister Macmillan. Yet, no responsible military or civilian official in our Defense Department or, I believe, in the British Defense Ministry, would argue in favor of the SKYBOLT today.

But notwithstanding all of these dangers I have mentioned, the need for systematic quantitative analysis in defense is much more important than in the private sector of the economy. Almost never do we find one person who has an intuitive grasp of all the fields of knowledge that are relevant to a major defense problem. We may be able to assemble a group of experts, each of whom has a good intuitive grasp of the factors relevant for answering one of the many subquestions and after discussion emerge with a fairly unequivocal answer. But in general, and especially when the choice is not between two but among many alternatives, systematic analysis is essential.

Moreover, in contrast to the private sector where competition provides an incentive for efficiency, efficiency in government depends on the conscious and deliberate selection of techniques and policies. And wherever the relevant factors are diverse and complex, as they usually are in defense problems, unaided intuition is incapable of weighing them and reaching a sound decision.

The need for systems analysis exists not only in the Office of the Secretary of Defense, that of the Joint Chiefs of Staff, and the headquarters of the military departments, but also at the other levels of the management structure in the defense establishment. After all, the purpose of this function is to help reduce the uncertainties involved in making choices among alternatives, and such choices have to be made at many different echelons. The areas of interest, the problems, and the subject matter will be different at these different levels, but the general approach—the way of looking at a problem—and the techniques will be basically the same.

Our objective, therefore, has been to build an integrated and mutually supporting structure of systems analysis throughout the defense establishment, with the broadest kind of exchange of information and techniques at and between various levels. This arrangement provides the checks and balances so essential to minimizing parochial viewpoints and organizational bias. The systems analyst, like any other scientist, must always be prepared to submit his work to critical scrutiny, and not just by other systems analysts. This is one of the great merits of the scientific method—it is an open, explicit, verifiable, and self-correcting process.

Because all major defense programs are now projected at least five years ahead, some early critics of the new system feared that it would tend to stifle change and place the defense effort in a straitjacket. I can assure you that their fears are unfounded. The Five-Year Program has proved to be quite amenable to change. Each year we consider three or four hundred program change proposals which, if they were all to be approved, would cause gross shifts in individual program amounts of $25 to $30 billion over the five-year planning period. Actually, the total gross value of changes, both plus and minus, which are approved each year, amount to somewhat less than half of this sum. I think we can safely conclude that constant change is likely to remain a characteristic of the Five-Year Force Structure and Financial Program.

However, the high volume and value of changes to the forward program do not lessen its worth to us as a management device. Indeed, one of the important purposes of any future plan is to indicate the areas where change may be desirable while there is still time to study, consider, and make such changes. In this respect, I think it is important to appreciate the role of the present leadership in instigating change. In developing the program, Secretary McNamara has chosen not simply to make decisions, but also deliberately to create opportunities to make decisions. He is constantly asking questions, requesting studies, goading the services and his staff to propose new alternatives, better alternatives to programs currently incorporated in the Five-Year Program. The criticism that the Secretary's management techniques stifle initiative and the development of ideas at the middle and lower levels of the Department seems to me to be the exact reverse of the truth.

Another criticism of both the programming system and the increased reliance on systematic quantitative analysis is that they have acted to "downgrade" the role of military judgment. I do not think they have. There is nothing inherent in the programming system or in systems analysis that calls for downgrading military judgment or for relying on computers for anything other than computation. In fact, I would say that the uniformed military planners have in recent years been given a greater opportunity to influence the Department's programs than they ever had previously. When planning and budgeting were separate, the planners, both in the JCS organization and the services, proceeded on their own, with little or no civilian control. But the plans they produced, because they were divorced from budget realities, were largely ignored in the actual decision-making process which determined the defense program. Prior to very recent years the Joint Strategic Objectives Plan [JSOP] was duly noted and filed, and the effective "real-world" decisions were made by the Secretary of Defense in the budget process, with no systematic participation by the military planners.

This has completely changed. The Joint Chiefs of Staff, through the JSOP, now initiate the major proposals for changes in the approved Five-Year Force Structure. Moreover, their advice is solicited on every other program change proposal. In every way, the entire JCS organization is enmeshed in the planning-programming-budgeting system to a far greater extent than ever before. And with respect to the differences of opinion which inevitably arise, the truth is that on practically every serious issue affecting the defense program there are military and civilian partisans on both sides.

Criticism of the programming system is sometimes coupled with criticism of an alleged overcentralization of defense management generally. It is true, of course, that the institution of unified Defense Department-wide programming has provided the conceptual framework, the administrative mechanism, and much of the data needed to facilitate top-level decision-making. But these top-level decisions have always been made—if not explicitly, then implicitly by the imposition of ceilings. As I noted earlier, priorities among major program objectives can be rationally determined only in the context of the total program, and balance among all elements of the defense effort can be achieved only at the Department of Defense level. The proper size of the MINUTEMAN force cannot be determined simply in terms of our ICBM requirements, or even in the context of the entire Air Force program. Being simply one element of the Strategic Retaliatory Forces, the MINUTEMAN program must be considered together with all of the other elements including the Navy's POLARIS force and, indeed, with all aspects of the general nuclear war problem. Similarly, the requirement for air-lift aircraft operated by the Air Force could hardly be established independently of the requirement for sealift, and neither, independently of the requirement for lifting Army ground forces. This kind of centralized planning and decision-making is essential if soundly balanced military programs are to be pursued, and I think that few in the Department would now disagree.

However, there still exists, within the Pentagon, some scepticism as to the permanence of this particular management innovation, predicated on the proposition that "it takes a McNamara to make it work." Often, of course, this is intended not as a serious indictment of programming, but simply as a kind of backhanded compliment to the talents of the Secretary. Yet some—remembering the relatively passive decision-making roles played by some other Defense Secretaries—are convinced that, under a significantly different style of leadership, the programming system and the data it generates would tend to go unused, and that the system itself would eventually atrophy and be discarded.

I will readily admit that to push through the development of the programming system in so short a time and make it work required a Secretary as strong and decisive as Robert S. McNamara. But I believe that the programming system can be adapted without too much difficulty to almost any style of leadership we are likely to have in the future. Every Secretary will have his own style—his own manner of approaching and making decisions —and management techniques must be adapted to the Secretary. I can easily imagine that some future Secretary, for example, will not want to get involved in as much program detail as Mr. McNamara. I see no particular problem in modifying the programming system to accommodate such a preference—without doing violence to any of the principal objectives of the system. We have "thresholds" in the system now, below which program changes can be made by the Secretaries of the military departments or at lower echelons. There is nothing sacrosanct about the level at which such thresholds are established. But I cannot imagine a Defense Secretary who would willingly forego the assurance, provided by the new planning-programming-budgeting system, that his military plans are in proper balance and that the budgets he proposes are both fiscally responsible and actually provide the capabilities that his military planners are counting on. As President Truman pointed out at the end of World War II in his Message to the Congress proposing a single Department of Defense: ". . . strategy, program and budget are all aspects of the same basic decisions." To this I would like to add, if I may be permitted to quote myself, that "the job of economizing, which some would delegate to budgeteers and comptrollers, cannot be distinguished from the whole task of making military decisions."

But if programming, at least in its basic essentials, is here to stay, can the same be said for its partner in arms, systems analysis? I have pointed out that the programming system facilitates the use of systematic quantitative analyses comparing the costs and effectiveness of alternative programs. But programming is possible, indeed has been used, without systems analysis, and can achieve some of its important objectives—order, consistency, and rough intuitive balance among programs—without it.

I noted some of the objections raised against the use of systems analysis or cost-effectiveness studies in the solution of defense problems. Just the other day, I came across a new one in a study on "Science and Defense" prepared by Klaus Knoor and Oskar Morgenstern for the Center of International Studies of the Woodrow Wilson School of Public and International Affairs at Princeton. The authors raised the question ". . . whether the recent emphasis on cost-effectiveness may not be too much of a good thing." They went on to say:

Admittedly, sophisticated cost-effectiveness studies played too small a role until Mr. McNamara became Secretary of Defense. But there are fairly widespread feelings that its present role may be excessive and constitute an overreaction to the previous lack.

The authors agree that cost-effectiveness studies are valuable in comparing similar weapon systems, but they question their utility in choosing between dissimilar weapon systems since they may "act as too sharp a brake on the innovating process that is concerned with radically new ideas."

Their main concern is with our ability to measure "effectiveness" in terms of numbers. This is a difficulty we have long recognized. Indeed, in our book on *The Economics of Defense in the Nuclear Age,* we devoted a separate chapter to incommensurables and uncertainty.

But most surprisingly, the authors raised the question ". . . whether the POLARIS system would have been developed if cost-effectiveness notions had been applied then as they are today." They express ". . . grave doubts that the POLARIS system would have been developed or, if introduced, have been pushed as hard as has been the case. . . ." The fact of the matter is that almost no one was as enthusiastic about POLARIS as the systems analysts who were using *survivable* power as their measure of effectiveness. In 1961 almost the first thing Secretary McNamara did was to recommend to the President a doubling of the fiscal years 1961 and 1962 POLARIS programs from the then existing rate of five boats per year to ten per year. In addition, the entire program was accelerated so as to complete the tenth to the twenty-ninth POLARIS submarines in twenty months, viz., one per month, instead of the previous five per year schedule. At the same time we accelerated the development of the longer range POLARIS A-3 missile. I recall that at the time this action was taken, we estimated that the average systems cost per POLARIS missile on or near station was probably two to three times that of a MINUTEMAN. An old-fashioned budgeteer using a simple *cost* criterion would indeed have looked askance at POLARIS. But its high survivability made it extremely attractive on a *cost-effectiveness* criterion. Thus, in this case, the application of the cost-effectiveness principle led to the program expansion of a relatively costly system.

With regard to the broader question concerning the proper role of cost-effectiveness studies or systems analysis in planning the research and development program, let me recall that it was only in the third stage, "advanced development," that we "begin to explore the costs of the more likely applications in order to determine whether the potential operational benefit would be worth the cost of development, production, and deployment"—and even then the requirements test is a weak one. Projects proposed for the first two stages, "research" and "exploratory development," are not required to meet that test at all. And it is from these first two stages that the radically new ideas come.

It is worth noting that annual expenditures for research, exploratory development, and advanced development, which together constitute the area of new technology formation, have increased by 25 per cent since fiscal year 1962, to over $2.3 billion.

But although research and exploratory development, and even advanced development, do not necessarily have to be directly related to specific military requirements, full-scale engineering development or an operational system development—i.e., a decision to spend on the order of $1 billion or more—can be justified only in terms of its potential contribution to our strategy, considering both its costs and military effectiveness, as well as the relative cost-effectiveness of other alternatives. All too often in the past, systems development work was started before consideration had been given to how the proposed weapon system would be used, what it would cost, and whether its contribution to our military capability would be worth its cost.

PART THREE Military Research and Development

Policy Issues Involved in the Conduct of Military Development Programs

BURTON H. KLEIN

Burton H. Klein, formerly head of the economics department at the RAND Corporation, is Professor of Economics at California Institute of Technology. This paper first appeared in Economics of Research and Development, *published by Ohio State University in 1965.*

THE MAIN PURPOSE of this paper is to discuss some of the issues involved in the conduct of military research and development. But before turning to policy matters, it may be a good idea to spend some time asking ourselves, "What is the essential nature of this activity?" Unless those who are interested in policy matters can come to some agreement on the kinds of uncertainties that underlie R&D decisions and, therefore, on the environment in which these decisions have to be made, discussion of policy matters hardly can be very fruitful.

While we can agree that the nature of an activity ought to be taken into account in devising policies for its effective conduct, it unfortunately is not easy to characterize this activity—"military development"—in a meaningful way. To be sure, development can be defined in terms such as "the identification, modification, and combination of feasible components and devices to provide a distinctly new application practical in terms of performance, reliability, and cost." But such a definition does not provide much of a flavor as to what development is all about.

The one characteristic that is most common to military development projects, I have no doubt, is the sharp changes in the attitudes taken toward their outcome as they progress through various stages toward completion. The point was illustrated in a talk given by General Clifton Von Kann, Director of Army Aviation:

Let's examine the typical peaks of joy and valleys of depression in the life of an ordinary helicopter.

First, the highest peak. It is hot out of the design concept stage and into the cocktail brochure. It will never be as good again. It is the finest thing since Coca-Cola and is a panacea for any problem you care to mention.

Then comes the first valley. The engine that was to power this dream ship is found to be made of metal, weighs a few pounds, and burns fuel. The original concept did not take this into consideration. Obviously, performances will suffer.

Next peak—the mock-up. Now we can show something. You can just see by looking at it that here is a real machine. Potential customers seem to come from everywhere to take a look, make a few sage remarks, and leave the impression that they're ready to buy a few thousand.

Valley—slippage. If the target date for first flight were met, it would mean taking off without rotor blades or engine installed. Careful engineering department types are mad at sales-happy promotion types in front office for setting such an impossible goal. Front office types are mad at foot-dragging, super-meticulous engineers who want to turn this stage into a lifetime project.

Peak—first flight. There will always be a great number of people who do not understand why a helicopter flies. This includes many helicopter engineers. So naturally they are elated and fascinated when a new one actually gets airborne.

Then the lowest valley. Sometimes in the testing stage, just as real production is being geared up, there is bound to be full panic. It may stem from anything—paint peeling near the exhaust—seat covers not holding up—the horrible realization that the engine life is not eternal —anything can trigger it. But the conclusion is always the same. "Let's stop this thing now and not throw good money after bad!"

The next peak is perhaps not very high in the terms of absolute altitude, but looking back into the very low valley we have just left, it is very impressive and gratifying. A couple of our potential owners have actually bought a few articles and are trying them out. Preliminary reports indicate a few "bugs" but generally they are satisfied and pleased. There is every indication that they will order more and that the helicopters will join the ranks of the accepted standard family.

The only thing I find wrong with General Von Kann's story is that it ends a little bit too abruptly—he fails to mention the trough that often comes after the operational organization in question has bought a few of the articles and has tried them out. Sometimes this is the lowest valley in the entire scenario, and assuming that a very large development program ends as of the time a new capability is initially introduced into operational use can lead to some very mistaken ideas as to how long it actually took to complete a program and how much money was actually involved.

General Von Kann's illustration also brings out another much more significant characteristic of military development projects: not only were the attitudes taken toward his helicopter constantly changing, but so was the helicopter itself. Though the tendency depends somewhat on the ambitiousness of the advances being sought, all of the evidence I have examined strongly suggests that it is seldom indeed that the differences between the system as it was initially conceived and as it emerges from development are only of a minor sort. For example, the congressional hearings on the missile programs show that almost all the major subsystems now being used in the Atlas missiles are of a different kind from those initially planned. Moreover, the differences are considerably greater than such as exist between, say, Boeing's 707 and Douglas' DC-8. The Atlas is not, of course, a unique example among missile systems. Others also have displayed a strong tendency to end up with technological ingredients not initially intended for them. In fact, a reasonable operational definition of a missile system would be that it is a system mainly made up of components and subsystems initially developed for other missile systems.

That pronounced changes in characteristics occur even when the advances sought are not so ambitious as they have been in some of our missile programs is indicated by a study we did at RAND of six fighter plane development projects. All of these planes were designed for some particular mission—all-weather interception or ground support, for example. All of the aircraft manufacturers based their airframe design on some particular engine design furnished by one of the engine manufacturers. In almost all of these cases, there were also programs for developing specialized electronic as well as other kinds of equipment. To what extent did these plans materialize? Four out of the six planes ended up with different engines; three with different electronic systems. In order to make them satisfactory flying machines, five of the airframes had to be extensively modified; three of the fighters came out of development essentially different airplanes. Of the six airplanes, three ended up by having quite different operational roles from what was originally planned for them. Only one of the airplanes possessed the same technological ingredients and had the same kind of operational role that had originally been planned for it. This plane, however, will have a much less important role than it was intended to have, in part because another fighter, whose development was started for a very different kind of role, has already provided quite as good a capability.

Many more such examples could be cited to illustrate changes in the course of development. The question remains as to why such changes are experienced.

I

One of the main causes for change during development, we are often told, is the compulsion that engineers have for squeezing the last ounce of performance out of their systems. If anyone wants to study this tendency, a good place to look, I suggest, is the space business. Here, almost every space vehicle is specially tailored to take utmost advantage of its inherent payload lifting capability right through the development process, sometimes up to and including the day of launch. With regard to most of the military development projects I have looked into, however, I notice no substantial propensity to add refinements for performance after the system is in active development. In military programs the tendency to ask for everything usually gets so adequately expressed in the initial planning and design work that in development there is no longer a question as to whether further performance-oriented improvements ought to be added. One of the main problems in military development, then, and one of the main reasons for modifications, is simply that of getting a system into tolerable working order. To do that, often some performance has to be given up.

A frequently claimed cause of changes in configuration that occur after development starts is that the initial planning was poorly done—for if it wasn't, why, then, the many changes? If there is anything in this allegation, one might expect to find a high degree of correlation between those projects that received the most attention in the initial planning stage of development and those that turned out to be most successful. But all the evidence that I have examined indicates that the correlation, if anything, is negative. For example, in the field of radar development, those radars that were most meticulously designed were almost invariably those radars that took the longest time to get into tolerable working order and whose development cost the most; measured either in terms of time or dollars, the differences were of the order of 2 or 3 to 1.

To continue along this line of thought, consider a radar known as side-looking radar, and more specifically one that operates at a very short wave-length, say, .86 centimeters. The main virtue of this kind of radar over the conventional scanning radar is that it provides fantastically good resolution, almost approaching that of photographs. Scientists were aware that such a radar could provide much better resolution during World War II. It was known that exploitation of the shorter wave-length bands would result in improved resolution; it was also known resolution could be improved by using larger antennas. And, as a matter of fact, there were some experimental attempts during the war to develop a radar which utilized, instead of the conventional scanning antenna, long antennas mounted on the side of an airplane —hence the term "side-looking radar."

Why then didn't the staff at the Radiation Laboratory go ahead and build a practical device that would exploit the potentialities of side-looking, very-short-wave radar? Let's ask first why they didn't develop a side-looking radar with the short wave-length characteristic of present-day side-looking radars. The answer is this: While it was believed that such a radar would have very good resolution, it also was believed—on the basis of experimental evidence—that such a radar would have extremely limited range. An experimental 1.25 centimeter radar had been developed toward the end of the war which, though it gave quite remarkable resolution, had a range of only several miles. From this it was generally concluded that a radar with a wave length less than 2.0 centimeters would have no military utility.

Had it not been for some experiments conducted by British scientists this probably would have remained the general conclusion for some time. What their experiments proved was that the choice of 1.25 centimeters as a radar frequency was a very unfortunate choice indeed, for at frequencies slightly higher (1.8 centimeters) and slightly lower (.86 centimeters), atmospheric attenuation was far less serious than at 1.25 centimeters and other neighboring frequencies. In other words, these experiments proved that the function was not a monotonic one. Thus, although a good deal was known about radar at the time, and although a good deal more than routine engineering talent was devoted to the selection of the 1.25 centimeter frequency, a side-looking radar such as we have today wasn't built during the war simply because the necessary knowledge did not exist.

The same is true in trying to predict the performance of a particular configuration of a missile, a rocket engine, airplane, or almost any other development project. Contrary to all the allegations that have been made, I don't think that the lack of larger rocket engines has been entirely responsible for holding up our space program. What has been at least as responsible is all that has had to be discovered about making a variety of components and subsystems perform reliably.

In one sense, the radar example just quoted is not typical of the problems that come up in development; that is, whereas in the case of short wave-length radar, the "windows" came out in the form of "peaks," it is more usual for them to come out as "troughs." No matter how many factors are taken into account in the design study, there will invariably be some reactions not taken into account, and sometimes they may be very important. Because such reactions are not taken into account, radars can turn out to have very bad antenna patterns, airplanes can be prone to structural fatigue, and space vehicles to blowing up.

It is true, of course, that none of these kinds of problems is insurmountable—true, that, given enough time and effort, any system can be developed to have more or less the performance characteristics originally predicted for it. In other words, one can be fairly sure that at some finite cost, or in some finite period of time, something more or less like the specified article can be developed. The only hitch is that it might take eight years instead of the originally forecast three years, and development might well cost five or ten times as much to achieve rigidly prescribed performance and input characteristics in the final product. Even in those cases in which there is a wide measure of agreement among experts, their advice may not always turn out to be good advice or their experiences relevant.

The last sentence is illustrated by the case of a radar whose design was laid down during the last part of the war, and whose development became a very high priority matter right after the war. It was generally agreed that this radar would take no longer than two or three years to develop. The advances that it incorporated were regarded as being less ambitious than those incorporated in the wartime radars; and the same organization that had developed several radars during the war to the point of an airborne reliability of greater than 90 per cent in less than two years worked on this new radar. But a host of unanticipated problems came up, and it was much longer than the entire length of World War II before the new radar was made into a reasonably reliable instrument.

To turn to a different field: Some years ago it was believed that ramjet engines were simple devices; and even though no large ramjet engines had ever been developed, no more than a simple scaling job seemed to be involved. On this premise the Navaho missile project was started. Needless to say, the development of large ramjet engines is now considered anything but a simple, straightforward undertaking.

Or consider the case of titanium, which, contrary to all the prophesies, has not been extensively used in airplanes and missiles. The fortunate aspect of titanium is that although its weight-saving characteristics have not proved nearly as useful as was initially contemplated, its non-corrosive qualities will lead to a series of applications that hardly anyone foresaw—from marine vessels to ordinary kitchen utensils.

One final example of the experts' consensus being slightly off the mark. Immediately after World War II, it was widely believed that the turboprop engine would be far better for bomber aircraft and transport airplane applications than the ordinary jet engine, and that the development of such an engine would not be a much more difficult task than the development of an ordinary jet because, after all, the differences between the two engines were only some gears, a propeller, and a few other "simple" items. Because it was believed that the turboprop offered the only way of getting the required range, the B-52 was initially designed as a turboprop airplane. Actually, the development of the turboprop engine took years longer than it was generally supposed to take, in part because the propeller mechanism turned out to be a nasty bottleneck. On the other hand, progress in reducing the fuel consumption of the jets was much more rapid than many experts thought it would be. Fortunately before development work got actively underway, a jet had been substituted.

Note that each of these examples, in its way, illustrates (1) rather substantial changes in a system between its inception and the time it could be called a useful device, and (2) that substantial revisions in delivery time and costs are commonly required. In other words, development is a business in which errors of 30 or 40 per cent can hardly be regarded as errors.

It is true, of course, that if military planners had been willing to settle for the kinds of advances that have typified commercial projects, the outcome of military development projects would be far more predictable than it has been. All that I am pointing out is that highly predictable kinds of advances and highly rapid advances are not the same thing.

The next question is, When in the development process can reasonably accurate estimates of performance, total cost and delivery time be made?

At the beginning of a development project, there is a tendency to plan as though the future course of events were known with great certainty, although a large number of unexpected events occurred in every previous program with which the planners were connected. Arguments will go on almost endlessly about details of the design that have nothing whatsoever to do with the fundamental technological problems. In estimating the procurement cost, extreme care is taken to make sure that no item, however small, is left out of account—for example, the cost of the fence that is to enclose the missile site is estimated down to a gnat's eyelash. Kill probabilities are spoken of in terms such as 83 per cent, missile accuracies in numbers more precise than measurement techniques can provide. The development schedules are so meticulously worked out as to imply that development itself is no more than a routine process of confirming them. I often wonder how I *myself* can become so absorbed in a study involving some new kinds of missiles, say, that the computations become the reality, and all that's happened to past estimates becomes as unreal as something that might have happened two hundred years ago.

Sharp improvements in estimates begin to occur only after the missile, radar, or engine is in test. This is not to say that after an aircraft engine has been first put on the test stand, or after the first three shots of a new missile, estimates of cost, performance, and development can be accurate within a margin of error of 2 per cent. On the contrary, some terrible mistakes have been made by concluding on the basis of the first few tests that an end product was practically developed. On the other hand, it is often true that some impressive facts are learned as the result of the initial tests. For example, we at RAND tried to find out why the predictions that Pratt and Whitney made for its engines almost invariably turned out to be better than the predictions made by the other engine companies. One of the reasons, we discovered, is that unlike the other companies, Pratt and Whitney almost always had a preliminary model of the engine in test before they made the prediction. Earlier, I talked about side-looking radar. When an experimental .86 centimeter side-looking radar finally was put into development, it took just ninety days to get it ready to be tested, and the cost of finding out what resolution it actually would provide came to some three million dollars. As it turned out, this was actually a much smaller amount than the government had spent on past studies.

Some time ago, we looked into the accuracy of the estimates of production costs for a number of missiles and aircraft as a function of the phase of development the system had reached when the estimates were made. What we found was that when half of the development time has elapsed in a missile or aircraft development program, estimates could be made with twice the confidence as at the beginning of the program. What it cost to get this improvement in the estimates will ordinarily be a good deal less than half of the total development cost, since the amount spent in the first half of the development period is ordinarily a good deal less than half of the total development cost.

I might point out that the evidence that I have cited reflects, among other things, the kinds of development practices that were used in the programs we studied. I myself am convinced that if the major aim in the programs had been to find out as quickly and cheaply as possible what would be involved in getting a satisfactory capability, the improvement in the estimates would have been much more rapid. In a few of the programs, this was the major aim. But in the vast majority of others, it wasn't.

So far I have been talking about the conditions under which new weapon systems are supplied. One of the two main points I have been trying to make is that initial estimates of a system's performance, reliability, and cost are subject to very large errors —errors that can be substantially eliminated only by developing systems that incorporate more modest advances than have typified military development projects. The other is that there are ways of reducing the risks in relying on initial estimates. Short of making a major decision to develop an entire system, there are commonly many kinds of tests and experiments which, if conducted, will result in decided improvements in the estimates. In short, whether or not it is so regarded, development is essentially a process of learning.

Now let us turn to the demand uncertainties that underlie development decisions. These are quite as important as the supply uncertainties, although my discussion of them will be much briefer and much more in the way of generalizations.

One of the factors that is important in determining the demand for particular weapon systems is the rate of progress in related technologies. The extraordinary progress that has been made in reducing the weight of fission and fusion weapons, for example, has had a very considerable influence on determining the preferred kinds of missiles. Progress that was made some

years ago in overcoming the problems associated with large
solid-fuel motors also has had a good deal of influence. Development
of vertical take-off airplanes could have a good deal to do
with the kinds of naval forces we will have in the future. But
though developments in related fields may be very important
in determining the demand for particular kinds of systems, predicting
the course of these technologies is subject to the same
kinds of difficulties I already have discussed. If progress in related
fields had been better foreseen, some major decisions on the
development and production of weapons systems would have been
very different from what they were.

Another factor of obvious importance in making decisions
on weapon systems is a knowledge of the demands imposed by
our actual or potential enemies—of what Russia, for example, is
up to in her own military programs. Once having determined
who our enemies are now or might be (and a brief glance at
the alliances of World War II will reveal that this in itself is
not always easy), it would be nice if we could plan our own
military procurement programs so that the actions we took
were not sensitive to those taken by them. To a certain extent we
do this, but to carry this idea very far would require a much
higher level of military spending than we now have. Within
anything like the current budget level, the programs for our
strategic forces have to be premised on some kind of projection
of Russian capabilities. We cannot hope to build enough flexibility
into our own forces so that their effectiveness is not affected by
whatever course of action other nations may take.

However, it should not be necessary for me to belabor the point
that there is a very wide range of uncertainties indeed in projecting
opposing forces over a period of five, ten, or fifteen years.
Besides the ordinary kinds of problems involved in making intelligence
estimates and intelligence projections, there are, in the
case of Russia, some very special problems. Contrary to what is
often assumed, the Russians, in fact, do not give the impression
of a highly rational set of decision-makers carefully using the
country's resources to maximize some well thought out set of
objectives. The strategic notions in back of their planning are at
best often very difficult to understand, as are many of their
weapon systems choices.

All things considered, it is clear that the factors influencing the demand for new weapon systems are no easier to predict than those influencing the conditions on which they will be supplied.

II

There are two main implications of the foregoing for R&D policy decisions.

First, I think it is important that the government should be devoting a very significant proportion of its R&D expenditures to research and development activities falling outside the major weapon systems programs. I have in mind here expenditures, not only on basic research, but also in those activities directed to experimenting with new techniques and to obtaining measurements. I stress experimental activities because one of the most important prerequisites to rapid technological progress is a very considerable willingness to try out new ideas. Very seldom indeed have studies alone led to the decision to go ahead with the development of a major technological advance. In fact, in many cases the effect of conducting long, drawn out "scientific" investigations has been to dampen enthusiasm for trying out a really good idea.

Beginning in the late 1920's, for example, almost every study that was made of the jet engine came to dimmer conclusions on the feasibility and value of a jet engine than the study preceding it. Shortly before World War II, a study group composed of some very distinguished American scientists proved more conclusively than anyone had before that the idea didn't make any sense. Shortly thereafter, the British let us in on their wartime secrets, and one of the U.S. engine companies that had earlier debunked the idea became the leader in developing the jet engine in this country. An experimental engine had been developed in Britain only because a British investment company decided a jet-powered airplane would have an enormous advantage for carrying airmail. It is of interest to note that the amount the company risked in demonstrating the feasibility of the jet engine came to something like twenty or twenty-five thousand dollars. This, essentially, is the amount scientific committees spent nearly ten years arguing about.

I do not regard the only purpose of a large program in basic research and exploratory development to be the discovery of strange new techniques. As I tried to point out earlier, the strategic uncertainties facing this country are so large that it would be extremely costly indeed to insure ourselves against all reasonable contingencies in our weapon systems programs. A much less expensive method of buying flexibility—of buying a capability to adapt our weapons programs to the actual strategic situation quickly—is to develop a large menu of technology. In saying this I am not suggesting that we should attempt to carry the development of components so far that weapon systems could be assembled from previously developed components with no technical risks involved. It is true that experimental projects often have been carried too far—that too much money has been spent on them before deciding which, if any, systems will use them. But one of the often-suggested cures for that problem— making decisions on the basis of paper studies—is not a well-advised cure.

If one of the main purposes of these research and development activities is to insure against strategic uncertainties, a very significant part of the research effort should *not* be directed to work which is ordinarily regarded as extending the frontiers of technology. In fact, I personally believe that this country is not doing nearly enough R&D work on kinds of techniques that do not get into the headlines. Even though the less exotic techniques often promise to be of very considerable military value, it's hard to drum up enthusiasm for them.

A second major implication of the nature of military R&D, which experience strongly suggests—at least to me—concerns the kind of strategy that should be pursued in weapon systems programs. What it suggests is that the approach taken in systems development projects should be a frankly experimental approach. Initially the requirements for the system should be stated in very broad terms, and considerable emphasis should be placed on keeping the system very flexible until the major technological difficulties have been resolved. To expedite their resolution, equipment should be put to test as rapidly as possible. Decisions on the best set of compromises should not be made until there is some basis for making them; specifically, these decisions should not be made until a preliminary version of the system is in test.

I would also urge that parallel approaches be taken in attempting to overcome difficult technological problems. Part of the reason for this is implicit in what I have already said. Carrying, say, three component development projects into the initial stages of development is often likely to cost a good deal less in terms of both time and money than selecting the wrong approach initially and proceeding into a full-scale development program on the basis of that approach. Another part of the reason is that the return from putting more and more engineers on the same project or subproject is apt to be rapidly diminishing. Typically, the success of any particular subproject will depend almost entirely on a relatively few individuals. Give these individuals more and more people to supervise and all that you will have accomplished is to substitute complexity for ingenuity. Once you have three hundred instead of fifty engineers on a fighter plane project, for example, a devilishly complicated device is the price that you have to pay in order to allow all those people to express themselves.

Finally, I want to say something about the obstacles in getting R&D policies more oriented toward the directions I have indicated. The one that has been given most publicity is the extensive review process that projects must go through before they are approved. Committees often impose elaborate requirements on weapon systems long before such requirements should be imposed; and in the course of satisfying all the committee members, systems are often made more complex than they need to be. Committees also constitute an enormous obstacle when it comes to getting action on any really new ideas.

But we all know that all this reviewing is not going to be stopped, or even substantially curtailed. I think that a good deal could be accomplished, however, by making the reviewing process reflect the kind of decision being reviewed. The kind of review that is appropriate before a weapon system project is started is very different from the kind required when development has been carried far enough that detailed considerations are really worth arguing about. And the kind of review that is appropriate for experimental projects not likely to cost more than a few million dollars is certainly very different from that appropriate for major systems projects likely to cost hundreds of millions. But the way the decision-making machinery works at present low- and high-cost risks are often regarded in the same way.

A second major obstacle to getting policies that will make for more rapid progress in R&D is, I think, the widespread belief that in minimizing the total amount of time required to get a system ready for operational use, production problems are likely to prove a more serious constraint than research and development problems. The belief that production problems are likely to be the dominant problems leads to the initiation of large-scale production preparation early in a development program, even at the expense of minimizing the program's flexibility. Moreover, initiating programs in this way is so costly that the number of options that can be carried into development is substantially smaller than it could be if the programs were initiated on a different basis.

As I have said, this belief is very widely accepted; I myself, however, have seen very little evidence that production problems are a serious constraint on the time required to get a system into operational use. An examination that we made of some twenty development programs failed to disclose that those begun on the basis of very large production preparations furnished operational systems sooner than those that were not so begun. Moreover, I don't know of a single program in which the dominant problems turned out to be production, not technical problems.

But there is a more fundamental objection to making minimal procurement lead times a dominant objective in research and development policies. It is simply that given the uncertainties that exist both in the supply and in the demand conditions, such a policy will not lead to an efficient allocation of the research and development budget. If the military research and development programs had been entirely concentrated on those systems that were regarded as the favorite choices ten years ago, we would not be in a very good strategic position today.

There is, in addition, a more deep-rooted obstacle in the tendency present not only in the Defense Department but also, I suspect, in all large organizations to overestimate the costs of flexibility and to underestimate its benefits.

At least two kinds of flexibility are relevant here. First, there is the type of flexibility that is built into military forces so they can handle a wide range of contingencies—Type I flexibility if you will. There are many matters likely to remain just as uncertain after the forces are built—for example, how a war might get started—as they are today; and Type I flexibility buys insurance against the kinds of uncertainties that are likely to remain uncertainties. It is the type of flexibility that Stigler had in mind as he wrote his famous article on what kind of a plant to build when the demand for a product is very uncertain.

Type II flexibility, on the other hand, attempts to reduce the uncertainties confronting the decision-maker by buying information on competing development alternatives. It is premised on the assumption that some of our resources can be used to reduce these uncertainties before military forces are actually procured and put on the line, that the greater knowledge attained by comparing development alternatives will contribute directly to widening the range of alternatives available and to reducing the number of uncertainties confronting those responsible for using our Type I flexibility. Recently, increasing attention has been focused on measures that would result in more Type I flexibility, but I have the feeling that still far too little attention is being given to flexibility in the development process itself.

The reasons that far too little Type II flexibility is purchased —aside from a development philosophy which results in large technical as well as financial commitments very early in the game—are, as I have suggested, that its costs are typically overestimated (in time as well as in dollars), and that its benefits are typically underestimated. While lower echelon organizations sometimes underestimate the costs of program changes, my observations indicate that upper echelons almost invariably overestimate them. Often the costs of making any changes in a particular configuration are made to seem astronomical, even before a single piece of metal has been bent. The benefits of flexibility are underestimated typically because the range of contingencies the decision-makers regard as reasonable is much smaller than the range that should be taken into account. Whether or not large size itself makes the tendency inevitable, I suggest that large organizations are commonly highly intolerant of ambiguity.

Finally, another major obstacle to the conditions that would make for more rapid progress in our military capabilities is our system of incentives. In the past, the method used for rewarding defense contractors has made the reward more or less independent of their performance. At the present time, incentive contracts are being substituted for cost-plus contracts in an attempt to rectify this situation. But I wonder whether the incentives embodied in these contracts will be strong enough to make a real difference in contractors' behavior. If the government wants to impose a much stronger system of incentives, it should insist that prototype models be built before full-scale development contracts are awarded, and that production contracts will not be let until the system in question is well in hand. In other words, I suggest that winning or losing a 500 million dollar contract might prove a stronger incentive to most contractors than a possible variation of from 4 to 10 per cent in the profit rate of that contract.

Quite as serious a problem as that of the sellers' incentives is the lack of a much better system of incentives on the *buyers'* side of the market. Long-established rules of the game within the Defense Department often lead to types of behavior which the uninformed may find hard to understand. I don't mean to imply that these rules are unique to Defense, for they prevail in many other public organizations and agencies and are not unknown within the business and academic worlds. Each new proposal for an R&D program will, of course, have its proponents, who will in turn naturally strive to convince others of the virtues of their projected systems. Under the rules of the game, as I understand them, it would not be wise for the proponents of a proposed system to draw attention to the merits of other possible systems, for the latter may be used against them in higher courts. In other words, there is a pressure to suppress alternatives. Secondly, once plans have been drawn up and submitted to higher echelon agencies, it is difficult to change them since changes might well be regarded as a sign of weakness in plan and uncertainty of will. Third, when and if the development program is started, the rules as they exist reward a strategy of getting the program underway with sufficient steam that it will be terribly difficult to stop. Economists can iterate and reiterate that past investments should not be considered in making future decisions, but they will be.

One can say, of course, that those who obey these unwritten rules of the game act irresponsibly. To do so indicates a willingness to judge them that implies the game itself is poorly understood: no individual in the organization is more responsible for the kinds of rules of the game that result in such behavior than is an individual in a corporation whose rules result in other kinds of strange behavior.

Some argue that the only way to get around these problems is to set up a centralized system for both procurement and research and development. But I myself would not want to see such a solution adopted. Without attempting to go into the reasons, let me say only that one thing that weighs heavily in my judgment is the experience of the British Ministry of Supply. Though the Ministry did very well during World War II—when apparently there was not time to get things really well organized—in the postwar period what the ministry did to improve efficiency in the small was far overshadowed by the conservative influence it had on military research and development as a whole.

To date, very little work has been done by social scientists on the crucial problem of getting better rules of the game. But there is no problem facing the Defense Department that is more important—or more challenging—than removing these and other obstacles to a more effective set of R&D policies.

Improving the Efficiency of
Military Research and Development

Carl Kaysen, formerly Professor of Political Economy at Harvard University and Deputy Special Assistant to President Kennedy, is now Director of the Institute of Advanced Study. This article is taken from his paper in Public Policy, *published in 1963*

THE SUGGESTIONS that follow . . . are attempts to sketch some of the major ways in which change in the system [of military research and development] may be expected to work for improvement. This expectation is, of course, a prediction and, like all predictions in the social-economic world, surrounded with a considerable measure of uncertainty. The changes discussed are essentially a matter of degree in the use of devices which are already known and have been used to some extent in the past, not all-or-nothing substitutions of entirely novel arrangements for the present ones. Accordingly, the most optimistic and positive attitude toward these proposals which their author can adopt, and the only one he can recommend to his readers, is an experimental one: the problems of our present system are sufficiently serious to justify some movement in directions which promise improvement; let us try them and see.

The central point of our recommendations is a greater emphasis on research and development activity aimed at the discovery and utilization of new ideas, a lesser one on the procurement of new weapons systems as integrated packages. This, in turn, means more separation between research and development activities and production and a great increase in the proportion of the research and development effort not tied directly to a particular procurement program. The aims of this change would be the more rapid development and early testing of new components and new subsystems; and the earlier testing, in terms of the whole procurement cycle, of new weapons, rather than the commitment to procure on the basis of the system design that now operates.

The first step in securing these results is the redirection of a large proportion of the research and development activity to organizations more suited to perform it than the present major contractors. Their first requirement is that they be organizations devoted to research and development and divorced from production responsibilities. Their second is that they operate under financial arrangements which permit fairly steady programs with long-term aims, rather than gearing income to a succession of projects, and requiring a substantial effort of salesmanship to keep up the flow of projects. In general, it is doubtful that the ordinary business enterprise is a suitable vehicle for this task. The nonprofit research institute or the government laboratory both provide more appropriate means. The best industrial research laboratories are themselves organized in a way which comes closer to a non-profit institute than to a business operating department: they are given a budget basis which permits long-term planning, rather than one which is tied to specific projects; they are not expected to show a profit on their activity in any narrowly defined accounting sense; they are, within the framework of the nature of the business which supports them, fairly free to define their problems and they have a high degree of managerial autonomy within the enterprise. What is widely agreed to be the best example of an industrial research laboratory operating in a business context—Bell Laboratories—comes much nearer in its essential arrangements to being a non-profit corporation with a high degree of income security than a business firm.

Among the most successful devices for organizing research and development laboratories of this type is the use of a university as a contractor. The Los Alamos and Livermore laboratories of the A.E.C., for which the University of California at Berkeley is the contractor, and the Instrumentation and Lincoln Laboratories of the Air Force for which M.I.T. is the contractor, all of which have weapons development tasks of just the sort we have been considering, provide the leading cases. In addition to providing the initial organizational framework, the university connection has been important as a source of continuing assistance in recruitment for these laboratories, thus helping to ensure a flow of good scientists to their staffs and also, but to a much smaller extent, as a source of scientific advice and a stimulus. The independent nonprofit corporation, such as RAND or Aerospace Corporation, provides another possible mode for the creation of such organizations.

While the independent contract laboratory has many advantages over the government laboratory, it seems undesirable to remove all research and development from the government. Each service should operate some research, development, and testing facilities of its own, simply in order to maintain within the service the kind of technical competence that is necessary to the whole process of acquiring new weapons in the context of present technology. There is some reason to believe that the difference in relation to the government of a contractor—even a nonprofit research contractor—and a government laboratory is significant for the decision-making process. The essence of this difference involves the question of delegation of function and the extent to which the government must be able to provide within its own structure the kind of technical personnel whose advice is necessary to an intelligent exercise of the powers of delegation. If the government is to succeed in maintaining its laboratories at a high level of capability, it must face problems of pay scale and working arrangements which are now not capable of holding the best people against the bids of private contractors. Some further comment on this question appears below.

In considering the possibility of moving a substantial share of military research and development to specialist laboratories, the possibility of using the atomic energy laboratories such as Los Alamos and Livermore directly should be examined. The demands on them for military research and development are declining and a formal nuclear test ban might lower them further. These laboratories represent an important resource and equally good ones would be difficult to create in a short time if they are allowed to disband or shrink substantially.

The movement described above would pose a readjustment problem of some proportion for the existing suppliers, especially those specializing in weapons production. If our judgment about the effects of present arrangements is correct, this readjustment may well involve a diminution in the total demand for engineers in this sector. The kind of shift suggested could not, of course, take place immediately, or all at once, so that some time would be available for the job shifts required. Further, part of the response of the present suppliers to such a change might well be the reorganization of their own R and D operations along similar lines, so that they would be qualified to participate under the new arrangements. Their participation should take the form of contracts supporting a certain level of activity in a defined area of R and D, rather than the kind of project support tied to the development of specific weapons they now get. This is not to say that there will not continue to be development and even research problems arising in connection with production contracts, which the R and D departments of such firms will be required to solve; but rather that these departments should continue to function on a large scale only if their major activity is not of that type.

When a large proportion of research and development is carried on in specialized organizations and not connected with procurement contracts, it will become more readily possible to reap the benefits of competition in this activity. Competition in this connection means simultaneous and independent efforts to deal with a problem, where possible in terms of different approaches. The most effective way to speed up the solution of problems is by the multiplication of parallel efforts. There is, of course, a budget constraint which must limit the process; but, in general, the use of parallel efforts will be cheaper per unit of achieved progress than attempts to determine best paths of solution *a priori*, and then to make development follow the predetermined course. This again reflects the fundamental character of the whole R and D process as a learning process, which must ultimately rely on experimental evidence to determine what will and will not work well. Of course, the use of parallel efforts implies a routine of test procedures, which can evaluate the results of an approach at the earliest possible stage, so that promising developments are pushed and unpromising ones abandoned.

There is sometimes a tendency to view "duplication" as inherently wasteful, whether in research and development or in any other activity, and to cry for "coordination" of centralized decision making. This view ignores the essential character of the learning process involved. Its appropriateness to the problem can be seen by examining either the "natural" organization of science as it develops in the university world, or the "natural" organization of the process of innovation in management method as it develops in the market. In either case, we observe many independent centers of efforts, dealing with closely related or similar problems; making no explicit attempts to coordinate their efforts; relying on, in one case the criticism of the body of scientists, in the other, the "criticism" of the market place to test what is successful and select it out from what is less so; and, by wide agreement, succeeding better than would any centralized effort at "coordination." The problems of military research and development are, in general, closer to those of academic science, with which they overlap considerably, than to business management, but what all three share is the fact that there are problems, solutions to which must be found by an experimental learning process.

Once the intimate connection between R and D and production contracts has been broken, the services will be much freer in their choice of suppliers and their use of contract instruments for production contracts than they are now. It will be possible to offer much larger parts of a total weapons procurement program to more numerous suppliers than now is the case. While formal advertising procedures and competitive bidding would still be inappropriate for most production contracts, a kind of competitive negotiation with more than one source might be usable on a wide scale. Further, under these circumstances it might prove desirable and feasible to procure components and subsystems from more than one supplier, using fixed-price-incentive-type contracts in which rewards depended on the cost performance of the lowest cost producer, and thus gaining some of the competitive incentives to efficiency even though formal competitive bidding is not possible. Further, the breaking-up of procurement into smaller pieces would increase the number of firms not specializing in weapons production which could participate in military business; this in itself is a desirable result, as well as one which diminishes the difficult political problems caused by large cuts in the activity of firms specializing in weapons production. Nonspecialists would be willing to participate in this kind of production, assuming they could do so without taking on the development burden it now involves. Among the incentives from the firms' viewpoint which would lead to this result, other than the direct one of getting business, is the advantage of learning new technologies while they are still young and getting part of the cost of this education paid by the Department of Defense. From the public point of view, of course, the more widely these new technologies can be spread among firms that are not specialists in weapons production, the greater the likelihood that these technologies will be applied to ordinary output, with the corresponding extra return to defense expenditure.

It is perhaps worth laboring the obvious point that business organizations and competitive markets are superior instruments for securing efficiency in production, whatever their unsuitability to the organization of highly risky and expensive research and development activities. To the extent that the research and development portion of the task of new weapons supply can be separated from the production portion, competitive incentives and market forces can be relied on to do a much better job in guiding the production portion than they now can.

A final step in moving to a greater reliance on market incentives wherever possible is to abolish profit renegotiation. Even now, the effect of averaging contractor performance on all contracts is to dull whatever incentives to efficient performance there are in any particular contract. It might be argued that, as procurement is presently organized, the absence of competitive incentives and checks justifies renegotiation in spite of this. But any attempt to move to a wider reliance on market and profit incentives, and to a greater degree of competition in order to make them effective, would logically call for the end of a system which in fact undercuts the market incentives to efficiency. A further disadvantage of renegotiation, which present contract negotiation procedures are also not free of, is its focus on profit levels. These are not unimportant, but the problem of cost levels is many times more important: excessive costs, rather than excessive profits should be the center of concern. It is natural, of course, that, in the absence of a market and the presence of so much novelty and uncertainty, profits are examined so closely, because there is often little basis on which costs can be examined.

SOME FURTHER PROBLEMS

If all the changes proposed above were effected, and in general the results lived up to expectations, there are some new problems which the proposed reorganization would raise. Two, at least, can be foreseen with sufficient clarity to deserve some comment. The first is the question of what happens to the integrating role; the second, the problems of expanding the capabilities of the government itself to perform in this field.

While the importance of the design and technical integration problem is greatly overemphasized under present arrangements, it is a genuine problem which will continue to exist. At present, the responsibility for dealing with it is divided between prime contractor and the buying service. In the case of the Air Force ballistic missile program, that responsibility has been contracted out, originally to Ramo-Wooldridge and its successor, Space Technology Laboratories, and now to a newly organized nonprofit corporation, Aerospace. Problems are presented when a prime contractor bears the responsibility. Both the remaining solutions—the nonprofit corporation with no manufacturing activities or the Service organization—are free of the problems of conflicting incentives that beset contractor-subcontractor relations between potentially competing profit-making firms. The experience of Aerospace is still too limited to provide any basis for deciding whether it provides a model that should be followed. In the Navy, the function has been carried out by service organizations, as for example, the Special Weapons Project Office for the Polaris submarine project. In any event, a shift to either pattern would mean a further reduction in the demand for the services of the major aircraft-missile producers, with consequent readjustment problems.

If reliance for this function as well as for a considerable part of the R and D activity is to be placed on service laboratories, some attempt has to be made to deal with the problems of pay scales, organization, and flexibility in government laboratories. It seems that pay scales are too low for the government to compete in attracting technical and scientific staff with private laboratories, whether or not they are profit-making organizations, as long as they operate under cost-plus contracts. It is clear that Ramo-Wooldridge, for example, was staffed substantially by hiring away, at considerably higher pay scales, engineers and contractors from Redstone Arsenal and other government laboratories. Both a change in the cost-plus method of contracting for R and D, and a change in government pay scales are necessary to meet this situation. Further, the whole hierarchical structure of the Civil Service, and its inflexibility in dealing with scientists are inimical to the kind of recruitment policy necessary to build up and maintain a good laboratory. In particular, rank and pay must not be correlated with position in a hierarchy of authority to the extent that they still are in government service. Although special legislation enabling the Defense Department to pay extra-high salaries to scientists and engineers has been passed, the number of positions that fall within its scope is too small to deal with the problem. Finally, the rigidity of Civil Service rules with respect to travel expenses, procurement of small items, working hours, and the like, all have a somewhat inhibiting effect on the flexibility of a government laboratory and the ease with which its professional staff can work, as compared with circumstances in competing outside laboratories. To be sure, the changes in contracting practices recommended would do much to curtail the capacity of independent laboratories to bid away government staff, but more is probably needed.[1]

The staffing problem is not limited to professional personnel connected with R and D. It is equally important to the effectiveness of procurement that managerial personnel in the service agencies and procurement negotiators be of the highest possible capability. Here again, government salary scales are such as to make the competition for men between government and contractors a very unequal one. To deal with these problems goes far beyond the scope of this essay, of course, but their importance must be recognized.

If the government were able to compete on more equal terms with private contractors in attracting managerial and technical personnel, there would be much to be said in favor of introducing the arsenal system in the Air Force, at least to the extent that it now functions in the Navy and Army. The existence of some production capacity, if only on a relatively small-scale basis, would enhance greatly the Air Force capacity to choose among alternative suppliers. There is more to be said for explicit government enterprise in the form of arsenals or shipyards than for the kind of quasi-government enterprise which arises when the Air Force supplies three-quarters or more of the capital of a

1. [Since this was written, the Defense Department has decreased its use of cost-plus-fixed-fee contracts.—*Editor*.]

"private" enterprise and purchases 90 per cent of its output. If an increase in government-owned and operated facilities for production were possible, the capacity of the services to perform for themselves the technical integration function would be greatly enhanced.

It may be that the kind of change in the relative attractiveness of government and private employment required by these proposals is highly unlikely. In that event, another possible line of innovation in this area is the conversion of two or three of the major weapons producers into limited-dividend corporations, with government holding some of their stock and having power to name some of their directors. These quasi-arsenals would have three main functions: to deal with the assembly and testing portions of weapons production; to provide technical integration services for these programs; and to carry on R and D activity in appropriate related fields. They would be prohibited from backward integration into the production of any subsystems which the private market could supply, but they would be free to engage in R and D activity in these areas whenever it seemed appropriate to their managements to do so. The services might treat them as preferred contractors for assembly, test, and integration tasks, but not to the point of abandoning reliance on other organizations for performing them, or failing to take competitive performance into account. This is clearly a wide departure from current practice, but, again, it does no more than recognize that the specialized weapons producers are not now operating as competitive private enterprises in any meaningful sense. If this fact is faced, then it seems more appropriate to ask what kind of organization is adapted to the tasks and circumstances than to do battle under the slogan of "free enterprise vs. socialism." To ask of business firms that they perform functions to which they are not well adapted under incentives which point away from rather than toward socially desirable results is to undermine free enterprise, not to support it. To see the problem of the relative roles of profit-making firms, independent nonprofit organizations, and government agencies in the tasks of developing and procuring new weapons as an issue of principle rather than a question of balance and emphasis is the end of relevance rather than the beginning of wisdom.

Kaysen on Military Research and Development: A Comment

PAUL W. CHERINGTON

Paul W. Cherington is James J. Hill Professor of Transportation at Harvard University. This comment first appeared in Public Policy, *1963.*

THE FUNDAMENTAL ARGUMENT of Carl Kaysen's paper appears to run as follows: (1) In the case of advanced weapons, R&D is a function distinct from production. (2) R&D cannot be conducted as effectively in business organizations as in nonbusiness organizations. (3) The merging of R&D and production in weapons, given other institutional factors, leads to gross inefficiencies. (4) More R&D should be done in nonbusiness organizations, including government laboratories. (5) The "systems approach" and concurrency (the second term is never mentioned specifically, but Kaysen seems to include it in what he calls the "systems approach") in weapons development are apt to be very wasteful and do not seem to buy much time. (6) The integration problem in weapons development is really not very serious.

Obviously, these short statements do great violence to a full development of the concepts in the Kaysen paper; but they perhaps serve to highlight the thread of his thinking. I take exception both to some of his premises and to some of his conclusions.

RDT&E IN NONBUSINESS ORGANIZATIONS

The Kaysen argument in favor of having government, university, or nonprofit groups (as contrasted with the business groups) conduct the RDT&E [research, development, test, and evaluation] functions is essentially two-fold. In the first instance, he believes that the hierarchical and functional structure of business is "inimical" to the development task. In the second instance he believes that business organizations are too production-hardware oriented. We shall leave this second point for later consideration.

123

The RDT&E task for a large modern weapon is an enormously complex one, inevitably calling for a high degree of organization, planning, and management, as well as for technical and scientific competence and virtuosity. The integration task, the collection and analysis of test data, and numerous other functions can no longer be handled by a few imaginative scientists working in an informally organized laboratory. Scientists can be, frequently have been, very helpful, but the idea that they can do the weapon system development job alone in a quasi-academic setting is simply naive nostalgia for the good old days. Such an organization may prove effective in research, but not in the development of a large system. It will perhaps provide answers to perplexing problems within the system, and may be optimal for developing some components or even test models of subsystems. But for the full development and the integration of the system (a problem that Kaysen treats rather lightly), some form of essentially hierarchical and functional organization and a considerable amount of management control are clearly needed. This is true, not only with respect to the weapon itself, but also with respect to its integration into the physical and logistics environment of the services. For example, among the most difficult tasks in the missile programs have been ground support equipment and the site activation problems. When Kaysen indicates that hierarchical and functional organization structures are "inimical" to the development task, he appears to be reverting to his experience with scientific research groups and applying it to weapon system development.

At one point Kaysen refers to the Bell Telephone Laboratories as the outstanding example of a successful nonprofit laboratory in the development field. It should be pointed out that BTL is a wholly owned nonprofit subsidiary of AT&T and Western Electric, the manufacturing arm of AT&T. Thus BTL is "nonprofit" in a fairly specialized sense of that term. I would certainly share Kaysen's high regard for BTL, but if one examines the way in which BTL handles system development projects, in contrast to its extensive basic and applied research, it appears to behave much more like a business than a university. This is true both in the way it decides to proceed with a project, the way the project is controlled as it progresses, and particularly the way in which BTL development people work closely with the development and manufacturing people in Western Electric and with the users in the AT&T operating companies and its long lines department.

Even the government and nonprofit laboratories which have developed successful weapon systems (such as Huntsville, the Naval Ordnance Test Station [NOTS], etc.) have a considerable hierarchical organization and have departed substantially from the straight research laboratory concept as described by Kaysen.

But essentially the question of who can do the best job on the RDT&E functions, business or nonbusiness groups, seems to resolve itself into two questions—(1) Which type of organization can get and retain the better management and scientific-technical personnel; and (2) Is there anything lost by having separate groups do the RDT&E and the production tasks? Of course, if it is assumed in connection with the latter question that government should take over the production work (which not even Kaysen suggests) then the second part of this question is of little importance.

In terms of the first question, it must be stated that some good weapons have been developed in nonbusiness organizations. Sidewinder at NOTS, Redstone and Jupiter at Huntsville, are only examples. But the principal weapons in the U.S. arsenal today have been developed in large part by business organizations with varying levels of technical direction provided by the government. It can scarcely be said, therefore, unless one is willing to state that our arsenal is a poor one, that business organizations have failed to do the job. The question really is whether nonbusiness organizations could have done the job better or equally as well for less money. The answer here keeps coming back to the question of personnel.

Given present government pay scales, the answer on personnel is clear. The government can neither attract nor hold *enough* high quality management and technical people to do the entire RDT&E job on weapons development. It will be fortunate if it can hold enough good people in uniform and in civil service to do an adequate job of "buying" systems plus doing a certain amount of basic and applied research in its in-house laboratories. (We will ignore the numerous intangible factors which militate against government service.) Of course, it is true that the government is paying all (or the bulk) of the salaries and fringe benefits that at-

tract good people to industry. With a drastic upward boost in top
military and civil service salaries, the government might be able
to attract and retain the right people. But such an argument says
too much. It admits the obvious fact that government is excep-
tionally sluggish about correcting blatant flaws in its way of doing
business, in this case the recruitment and retention of personnel.
The patchwork of super grades and special compensation for
scientists and engineers has fallen far short of an adequate solution to this problem. (It should be pointed out that the foregoing statements appear to apply essentially to the top echelons
of personnel. Government pay scales and salaries for middle and
lower grades are more nearly comparable to those paid by industry.) Thus far, the substantial up-grading of top government
managers and technical people has proven politically impossible.
In consequence, the government has drastically limited its market
for this type of talent. Whether they are less dedicated or more
manna-minded or for some other reason, a considerable proportion of management and technical talent likes to receive compensation at the going rate in the civilian economy in which they
live.

One solution to the problem of attracting and retaining talent
to the government would be to freeze top salaries for industry
personnel. Unless it were possible, however, to apply the freeze
to nondefense management and technical talent, such a freeze
would have the effect, over a period of time at least, of driving
many of the better technical and management personnel into
nondefense work. A solution better designed to bite off your nose
to spite your face cannot be conceived.

One answer to the problem has been the independent or university nonprofit group. Here it is necessary to differentiate between nonprofit groups that have stayed exclusively in the study
or research area from those that have gotten into various phases
of system development. Among the latter are Cornell Aeronauti-
cal, Applied Physics Laboratory, Lincoln Laboratories, Jet Propulsion Laboratory, Mitre, and Aerospace, the latter two in a
restricted way. Many of the problems of adequate pay and al-
lowances that seem to baffle the federal government can be met
through the nonprofit. On the other hand, the nonprofit groups
which have been the longest in the development area appear to
have difficulties in keeping themselves energized, and they begin

to take on some characteristics peculiarly their own. These include an enormous range of fringe benefits for employees, plush offices, increasing nervousness about continued contracts and hence a continual eyeing of "diversification" possibilities. Personnel turnover tends to increase as the nonprofits move through their life cycle. Often tied essentially to one service and completely dependent upon it for continued existence, the nonprofit finds it hard to avoid settling into a sort of super-bureaucratic rut, breaking up, or diversifying. None of these alternatives improves its usefulness to the government in the development area. In addition, the nonprofits of late have come under a substantial amount of criticism from Congress as being a subvention of civil service pay scales, and more importantly, for exercising unwarranted policy making authority which should have been exercised by government officials.

It should be noted that government laboratories and nonprofit organizations can, should, and do make numerous important contributions in the form of basic and applied research. They undoubtedly will continue to do so. But this is not the area about which Kaysen is primarily talking, that of weapon system development, which is a good deal broader set of functions.

The foregoing has been primarily a negative argument against removing business from its primary role in the RDT&E field. Is there anything positive to be said about primary reliance on business organizations for the RDT&E function? Somewhat greater flexibility and adaptability for the development job appear to be prime qualities of business in contrast to many government and nonprofit groups. The radically changed nature, organization, and focus of numerous defense firms over the past five years attest to this quality of adaptability and flexibility. It may be that some firms have not changed fast enough, and it must also be said that some government and nonprofit groups have demonstrated a high degree of adaptability to new RDT&E tasks. Those who favor the government or nonprofit groups for the RDT&E task point with pride to the adaptability of such groups as the Jet Propulsion Laboratory, Huntsville, and NOTS. They tend to ignore the numerous other government and nonprofit laboratories which have not kept pace in this connection.

The reason for a high degree of adaptability and flexibility on the part of business firms to changing demands in the RDT&E

area is not hard to find. It has its root in the competitive pressures which force business organizations to adapt. Business firms must adapt to new tasks or they lose business. While only a few firms have actually exited from the systems development field, several are mere shadows of the status they formerly enjoyed in this area, as even a casual reading of the financial pages will indicate. Since change, adaptability, and flexibility are all painful processes, there is usually considerable resistance to them on the part of any organization, business or nonbusiness. The competitive pressure which can be brought to bear on business to make these adaptations is believed to be stronger than any which can be brought to bear on government or nonprofit organizations, although in the past these competitive pressures have not perhaps been well utilized by the government. This is perhaps the single most compelling reason for believing that business firms should be relied upon primarily in the RDT&E field as against primary reliance on government and nonprofit groups. Again it should be stressed that there will probably always be room for a limited number of outstanding government and nonprofit groups in this field, and that government and nonprofit laboratories should be encouraged to continue activities both in the area of basic and applied research and in the area of giving technical assistance in the "buying" of RDT&E work.

THE RELATION OF RDT&E TO PRODUCTION

Let us now examine Kaysen's second basic conclusion: That RDT&E should be divorced from production and that the commitment to production should be held off until as long as possible, certainly until the RDT&E task is largely completed. After so doing, we can return to his contention that business firms are too production-hardware-oriented to do a good job on development.

Another, and perhaps extreme, way of stating this Kaysen conclusion is to the effect that systems should only be put together from fully developed components and subsystems. This would mean that the development phase of a system project would be devoted entirely to integrating the various subsystems and testing the whole weapon. It assumes a very large shelf-stock of advanced components and subsystems in a sufficient variety so as to minimize the integration and testing task permitting an early decision on production. Such a procedure runs the risk either of having an enormous arsenal of components and subsystems (but no modern weapons) or of excessive time delays while one or another subsystem catches up. If all components and subsystems were developed at the same technical pace, then this approach might be feasible; but in fact, they do not. For example, guidance may be well ahead of reentry vehicles or vice versa. And propulsion systems may lag both. Simply to combine existing subsystems will almost certainly result in a weapon which will be quickly outmoded.

In the "systems approach" which Kaysen rejects, existing art is projected a short way into the future and component and subsystem development projects are instituted so as to yield a weapon that will not be obsolete on delivery. This may not be as "conservative" an approach as utilizing only proven and existing subsystems, but it may well be more economical in terms of getting effective, modern weapons with some lasting value. Nor is it by any means as reckless as it might seem if the program is properly conducted. The technical reach into the future is carefully studied and limited, so that the probabilities of success are high. There are, of course, instances where we have tried to reach too far, but there are many more instances of notable success.

This does not mean, of course, that we should not devote more attention and resources to the development of advanced components and subsystems which have no immediate application to a specific system. But to say this is not to say that we should abandon the systems approach as our principal way of obtaining new weapons.

In addition the arguments which Kaysen uses against the systems approach appear to underestimate substantially the problems involved in the redesign and the integration even of off-the-shelf componets and subsystems. The interface problems in marrying subsystems have been among the most difficult in weapon developments, as for example in circuitry compatibility and feed-back in electronic systems.

In any event Kaysen's conclusion with respect to the separation of RDT&E from production appears to ignore three recent developments in the field of weaponry: (1) the much more rapid state of technical change that is going on; (2) the much greater urgency which applies to many weapons, partly due to technical change and partly due to increased enemy capability; and (3) the changing complexity and basic character of weaponry, particularly the increasing capability of each individual weapon unit and the reduction in total numbers needed.

These three trends have greatly blurred the old line between RDT&E and production. The increased pace of technological change has become virtually a truism and need not receive extensive consideration here. It is sufficient merely to call attention to the fact that the increased tempo of change means that there is a substantially higher risk of developing and putting into production weapons that will soon be obsolete. This calls for a delicate balancing between the pitfall of reaching too far in the state of the art versus the equally unpleasant consequences of an arsenal composed of obsolete hardware. It places a substantially increased premium on shortening development-production lead time. Many of our current weapons, particularly in the missile field, have substantially contracted this lead time through various devices, primarily through a partial merging of the development and production cycles. But changing technology has a different impact. It often requires the furnishing of essentially new test or industrial facilities and capacity. The lead time for the establishment of such facilities is often as long as the development of the weapon itself. This tends to force relatively early decisions on numerous production items unless extensive delays in producing the weapon are to be accepted.

The need for extensive testing, furthermore, calls for the availability of quasi-production facilities even back in the development cycle. A test program of several dozen or even a hundred missiles cannot be satisfied with a laboratory model shop. This may not mean that a complete production line has to be established, but the difference between the required facilities and tools for test missiles and production missiles is much smaller than that between the facilities to turn out three or four hand-built prototype aircraft and a 3,000 aircraft production line. For example, Redstone appeared to have what was virtually a production line at Huntsville for the Jupiter, even though Chrysler was the producing contractor. We have previously mentioned the difficulties of integration on advanced weapons and subsystem contractors and vendors; systems engineering or integration must be performed at the outset of the development process if the test vehicles are to be useful. The need to build up a substantial integration organization in the RDT&E stage makes it quite difficult and costly to turn over the production function to another organization. This is especially true when the production run may be only a few dozen or a few hundred weapons. All of these factors tend to go to the point that the line that used to exist quite sharply between R&D (now broadened to RDT&E) and production has now become blurred, and that it is increasingly difficult to say with assurance where the RDT&E function ceases and production takes up.

We can now return briefly to Kaysen's charge that business is too production-hardware-oriented to do a successful job on development. This may have been true some years ago when R&D was a very small part of the acquisition of a new weapon. But with the increasing size (and cost) of the RDT&E task, relative to the weapon cycle (RDT&E, Production and Operation), companies have been forced to pay more attention to the development phase of their work. It is undoubtedly true that companies would like long production runs of frozen design weapons. Increasingly companies are aware of the fact that in order to have any production at all their reputation and actual performance as good and efficient managers of RDT&E functions are crucial in their selection. Competitive pressures are driving them inexorably in this direction.

The foregoing comments do not mean, of course, that there are not many things wrong with the current system in weapons acquisition, nor do they mean that we should not take radical steps to try to improve performance, both business and government, in the weapons acquisition field. Some of the things that can be done constructively in the direction of improving our performance in this area include strengthening the government's role as a "buyer" (not as a developer) of advanced systems, providing stronger incentives to and controls over the performance of business, and improved decision-making in the selection and timing of programs. But the solutions to these problems which Kaysen proposes—the complete divorcement of the RDT&E function from production, the maximum delay in commitment to production, and the performance by government labs and nonprofit corporations of most RDT&E work seem to lack appeal in terms of weapons acquisition as it is apt to exist over the next ten years.

Weapons Acquisition and Public Policy

MERTON PECK and F. M. SCHERER

Merton Peck is Professor of Economics at Yale University. Currently he is on leave as a member of the President's Council of Economic Advisors. F. M. Scherer is Associate Professor of Economics at the University of Michigan. This piece is taken from the concluding chapter of their book, The Weapons Acquisition Process, *published in 1962.*

UNCERTAINTY AND THE WEAPONS ACQUISITION PROCESS

SUBSTANTIAL uncertainties permeate the weapons acquisition process. Two major classes of uncertainties . . . [are] internal uncertainties, which originate largely in the technological character of weapons development; and external uncertainties, which originate largely in the strategic environment. Furthermore, the vast size and extended duration of major weapons programs mean that the risks involved in each program are great. These uncertainties and risks mark the weapons acquisition process as unique.

These points, we feel, will not be disputed. But their implications for the organization and conduct of weapons acquisition are more controversial. In our view, the substantial uncertainties and risks vitiate the use of familiar economic and administrative concepts borrowed from established institutions.

The notion of a market system is one such inapplicable set of concepts. Still much of the public discussion of weapons acquisition problems proceeds as if the terms "competition," "price," "buyer," and "seller" had the meanings they do in a market system. Consider, however, the difference. Payments to contractors are on the basis of cost incurred rather than competitive prices, and yet competitive prices are an essential feature of a market system. In weapons acquisition the buyer exercises control over sellers through the auditing of costs and other activities that involve the government in the internal management of its contractors. Yet another essential element of a market system is that

132

buyers exert their control only by distributing their patronage among competing sellers. Similarly, while in a market system the initiative for product decisions rests upon sellers, the government rather than its contractors decides what weapons are to be created through its program decisions. Program decisions are in turn implemented by scores of optimization decisions, some made by government agencies, some shared between the government and its contractors, and still others made by contractors. At this more detailed level the decision-making roles of government and contractors become intertwined in a manner foreign to a market system's rigid distinction between buyers and sellers.

Thus weapons acquisition is characterized by a form of economic organization quite different from the market system found elsewhere in the U.S. economy. The shift of weapons making from arsenals to private firms is sometimes said to have involved the desocialization of a traditional government function. Yet the nonmarket character of the relationship between the government and its weapons vendors implies in many ways the arsenalizing or socialization of private firms. Given the uncertainties and risks that pervade weapons acquisition, the development of such a nonmarket system was inevitable. Consequently, the concepts of a market economy are not a fruitful point of departure for formulating weapons acquisition policy.

A second set of inapplicable concepts is much simpler: the idea of applying the practices and procedures of commercial product development to weapons acquisition, rather than attempting to apply the market system in its entirety. Both before and after Sputnik, there was much testimony that if commercial practices were imposed upon the weapons acquisition process, substantial improvements would result.

This proposition is less abstract, and hence more subject to empirical verification than the market system notion. To test it we compiled case histories of seven commercial product developments. These situations were atypical, since the great proportion of commercial activity does not involve technically advanced undertakings. Yet even in this sample, selected to match as closely as possible the technical and financial characteristics of weapons programs, the comparison was uneven.

In general, we found that the compulsions in weaponry for rapid state of the art advances on a broad front had little counterpart in the normal activities of commerce. When occasionally advanced and complex commercial products were developed on a compressed schedule in response to competitive or other pressures, weaponslike problems appeared. Cost overruns were experienced, schedules slipped, and performance goals were not met. Likewise, weaponslike procedures were often used. The commercial development most nearly matching a weapons program in both technical characteristics and organization was [an] . . . atomic power plant development. The business practices in this situation reflected not the normal arm's length relationship between buyer and seller, but rather were strikingly similar to those of a weapons program.

Thus, commercial product developments seldom involve the technical advances, complexity, and urgency of weapons development, and when they do, they encounter weaponslike problems and use weaponslike procedures. For this reason we would conclude that commercial practice affords little in the way of proven precedent that can be transferred bodily to the weapons acquisition process.

A third set of concepts applied to the weapons acquisition process, especially by persons of academic orientation, is drawn from the field of basic research. Basic research, so the argument goes, also is conducted in the face of substantial uncertainty. But despite the uncertainties, basic research has been enormously productive over the past hundred years. The institutional arrangements within which basic research has flourished are characterized by extreme decentralization of decision making, considerable duplication of effort as diverse investigators conduct parallel experiments, the relatively small scale of individual projects, and the absorption of only proven ideas into the main stream of scientific thought. By analogy, then, weapons development ought to be highly decentralized, with considerable duplication and competition at the relatively inexpensive subsystem and component level. Weapon systems would then be put together from a stock of subsystems and components in advanced stages of development.

But even though this set of concepts does recognize that uncertainty is an important factor in the weapons acquisition process, we believe it is as inapplicable as the other two concepts discussed here. To be sure, we agree that the United States could profitably conduct more component, materials, and subsystem development work unfettered by the immediate requirements of weapon system programs. Furthermore, there are certain conditions under which multiple technical approaches are desirable. Nevertheless, we think the basic research analogy misinterprets the technical nature of weapon system development.

The spectrum of research and development is divided into four steps, Step I being (roughly) basic scientific activity and Step IV product engineering. We hold that most advanced weapons development efforts belong to Step III (the identification, modification, and combination of feasible or existing concepts, components, and devices to provide a new application).[1]

In this Step III kind of activity, the uncertainties concern not so much whether the basic technical problems can be solved as whether the outcome—quality, time of completion, and cost—will be such as to make the effort worthwhile. The scientific analogy attempts to ignore the need for choice by relying upon duplicate and competing projects. But as a rule, managerial decisions involving the choice of projects, approaches, and resource levels are unavoidable. Furthermore, the technological uncertainties in weapons development are typically local rather than general, permitting (and indeed demanding) the exercise of managerial discretion. Many areas of potential technical difficulty can be foreseen in a competently conducted feasibility study, and management can then decide to develop around the problem areas (perhaps by making performance sacrifices) or to employ multiple approaches in those narrowly defined areas. The appearance of technical problems which could not have been foreseen again requires decisions on the employment of technical resources and possible modifications in performance goals. The scientific analogy also fails to recognize that many of the uncertainties connected with weapons development concern the functional interrelationships of diverse components and subsystems, and that these uncertainties can be eliminated only through the testing and modification of prototypes closely resembling the contemplated operational weapon system config-

1. [Step II is, according to the authors, the search for knowledge about specific means of using the phenomena of nature to practical advantage. —*Editor.*]

uration.

Finally, the basic science analogy ignores the nature of weapon system innovation and evolution. That is, when advances in one or a few bottleneck areas of conceptual or component technology make it possible to meet previously unfilled weapon system needs, those advances will generally form the basis for a new weapon system development even though other (nonbottleneck) components or subsystems have not been developed. At the same time, recent history indicates that the Soviets have reacted quickly to such advances. If the United States accomplishes an important conceptual or component advance, it is likely that it will soon be exploited by the Soviets. As a result, there is seldom time to accumulate a well-stocked inventory of concepts, components, and subsystems. As soon as something significantly new and useful appears on the horizon, the armaments competition requires that it be utilized in a weapon system development long before it can be perfected and "put on the shelf." The creation of radically new concepts and components is itself the prime mover of weapon system technological advance.[2]

For these reasons, we believe that organizational and administrative concepts borrowed from the field of basic science are not very helpful precedents for the weapons acquisition process. Similarly, we reject the market system and commercial product development analogies. In our view the weapons acquisition process is unique, without the salient characteristics of commercial activity on one hand or of scientific activity on the other. Ideas and concepts relevant to the weapons acquisition process are difficult to come by, for what is needed is not something borrowed, but something new.

2. Indeed, given this relationship between basic conceptual and component technology advances and man's propensity to build weapon systems of greater destructive ability, it can be argued that work in the more basic areas of science relevant to weaponry ought to be de-emphasized rather than emphasized, as many atomic scientists apparently held at the outset of the atomic and hydrogen bomb developments. Cf. Robert Jungk, *Brighter Than a Thousand Suns* (New York: Harcourt, Brace, 1958). Yet as long as the fear exists that a potential aggressor will secretly achieve and exploit important basic advances, such de-emphasis is virtually impossible.

THE INSECURITY OF NATIONAL SECURITY CONTRACTORS

The weapons contractor's lot is not an easy one. To be sure, he has a customer who agrees to pay his costs during the development period, whatever the outcome may be. The cost reimbursement contract is a distinctive feature of the weapons business with few commercial counterparts.[3] Yet he deals with a bureaucratic maze for a customer. Some of the occupants of this maze may be less than fully qualified for their demanding jobs. Second, the nonmarket character of weapons acquisition brings the customer into his internal operations in a way that restricts his freedom to manage his own business. Third, the crucial resources of a weapons vendor are technical talent rather than the more conventional factors of production. Directing technical talent requires a high degree of management skill.

But a more fundamental problem of the weapons contractor is the insecurity of his market position. The rapidly changing requirements of military technology force firms to shift their product lines rapidly—rockets instead of piston or jet engines, complex electronic gear instead of large quantities of airframes, and so on. By and large the weapons firms have adapted well to these changing requirements, even though one can point to firms about which it is said, "They were dragged screaming into the missile age." A further factor has been the relatively easy entry of new firms into the weapons industry. The advent of newcomers, however, has meant that some older firms have lost their relative market positions. Some measure of the relative instability of a market position in the weapons industry is provided by an analysis which showed that membership in the group of the 100 largest defense contractors was about twice as unstable as membership in the 100 largest industrial companies in the U.S. economy.

Even though the necessary shifts in the weapons industry have occurred, there are problems in the way they have been accomplished. Individual firms have made the decision to enter or to diversify upon their own evaluation of the future. This is, of

3. [In recent years, the Department of Defense has reduced its use of cost-plus-fixed-fee contracts.—*Editor*.]

course, normal business behavior. The exceptional aspect is that the government has paid most of the entry or diversification bill of weapons makers in the context of individual weapons program costs.

Government subsidy of entry and diversification was probably inevitable. The rapidly changing nature of weaponry requires the creation of new capability at a rate beyond what private financing might sustain. The costs of these changes are properly, we think, borne by the government.

The problem has been that firms have emphasized the development of weapon systems in such a way as to enhance their capability for new projects at the expense of good performance on current projects. This phenomenon is most apparent in make or buy decisions, although we have also drawn attention to the conflict between present efficiency and future capability in the allocation of technical talent. Some of this loss in current efficiency may be worth the gain in future capability. And yet the preoccupation of firms with their future positions has on the whole put an excessive drag on the conduct of weapons programs.

Furthermore, some of the capability created in this way has been redundant. To convert an aircraft firm into an electronics firm may simply create excess capacity in established electronics firms and in the industry at large. This overcapacity situation magnifies the insecurity of national security contractors and injects several additional problems into the weapons acquisition process. For one, the stickiness of overhead in a cost reimbursement environment leads to inefficiency in firms with declining sales, and hence to poor utilization of defense resources. Second, excess capacity in technical groups encourages the "goldplating" of weapon systems, increasing costs and possibly reducing reliability due to overcomplication. Third, excess capacity exaggerates the propensity for unrealistic bidding in competitions for new development contracts, increasing the difficulty of obtaining reliable data for program decisions.

[There are] several possibilities for meeting this insecurity problem. One is some form of industry planning by the government. Yet the planning would have to be most astute, for the changing requirements of weaponry require planning for change and flexibility. Planning for change is almost a contradiction in terms. The common notions on industry planning relate largely to obtaining efficiency in producing well-established products, so that little experience is available to guide planning for change.

One example of industry planning in a weapons context is provided by the 1960 reorganization-by-merger of the British aircraft industry. Although this was accomplished by private merger actions, the consolidations were at the "suggestion" of the government. The objective was to prevent the dissipation of resources on an excessive number of projects. Yet differences in size and national security environment between Great Britain and the United States preclude using this experience as a direct precedent.

Whatever form industry planning takes, it must provide for both new and old firms. New firms have an impressive record of innovation, and so their emergence should be permitted and encouraged. At the same time, the preceding discussion suggests that some assurance of continuity is necessary for the older firms in order to moderate their preoccupation with the next program rather than with the existing one. Yet this assurance cannot be so complete that existing organizations are perpetuated in their present size and form without regard to effectiveness. Just as a mechanism is needed to bring in newcomers, so a mechanism is needed to displace the older firms which have lost their vitality.

This displacement mechanism might also provide incentives for good performance on existing projects. It is clear that contractors are concerned primarily with maintaining and improving their long-run positions, rather than with immediate profits. More explicitly, contractors are concerned with developing a weapon system in such a way that their capabilities for future projects will be enhanced, rather than with making an extra 1 per cent or 2 per cent of additional profit on the current project. Consistently rewarding good performance on all dimensions (quality, time, and cost) of current projects with new business would capitalize upon powerful incentives to motivate contractors. At the same time, if poor performance led to decreased sales, the displacement of the less effective contractors would be accomplished.

Such a proposition raises two fundamental questions. Is it possible to distinguish between good and bad performance in weapons programs? Is performance on past programs a reliable predictor of performance on future programs?

To answer the first question, we have attempted to establish through a survey of knowledgeable persons in government and industry the extent to which program performance can be evaluated. The results of that survey indicate that programs can be ranked on the basis of overall contractor performance. Admittedly, this was only a pilot experiment, but it suggested strongly that knowledgeable persons can distinguish consistently between good and poor performance.

This ability to evaluate contractor performance might well provide a basis for awarding future business. To be sure, the success of a weapons program depends to a considerable extent upon factors outside the contractor's control, but in this respect the weapons maker is in no worse position than the firm in other industries, where the course of the business cycle, competition, or even international events influence its success and profits.

Perhaps a more fundamental problem is posed by the relationship between past performance and future capability. We cannot assume that good performance in the past will necessarily mean good performance on future projects. Partly for this reason and partly because the award of weapons contracts has broader economic and political implications, source selection typically involves multiple and possibly conflicting objectives and criteria. As a result, the rewarding of good past performance and penalizing of poor past performance as a means of providing incentives may have to yield to other more expedient objectives in source selection actions.

THE PROGRAM DECISION

We have examined the broad tradeoffs among time, quality, and cost that can be made in planning, scheduling, and budgeting weapons programs. From this analysis it is clear that there is no one best way to run a program. Rather, the optimal approach depends upon the range of possibilities afforded by the relevant technology and upon the military value of alternative technical possibilities (which depends in turn upon strategic and tactical considerations). To illustrate how variations in these factors influence program decisions, let us consider four highly simplified general cases:

1. The strategic situation is such that a weapon system of cer-

tain technical characteristics is urgently needed; very high military value is associated with possessing the system. The required performance can be obtained for the most part using known concepts and components and subsystems which have been demonstrated at least in early prototype form; thus, major state of the art advances are not required. In this case, program decisions should emphasize a high level of technical effort, the sacrifice of marginal performance features to utilize known technology, early commitment to an expected operational weapon system configuration, and calculated-risk investment in long lead-time production items and tooling.

2. The strategic situation is such that a weapon system affording high military value is urgently needed, and major state of the art advances must be achieved for it to perform the required mission. Here a high level of effort should be maintained and multiple technical approaches should be pursued in uncertain component and subsystem areas. When there are substantial uncertainties at the system level, two complete weapon system developments should be undertaken. If possible, the over-all system configuration selected should be flexible, to permit the ready incorporation of alternative subsystems. Commitments to an operational configuration and to long lead-time production items should begin as soon as major subsystem uncertainties are eliminated.

3. If significant state of the art advances are desired on a less-than-urgent timetable, emphasis should be upon low level of effort approaches in crucial areas of uncertainty. Detailed configuration decisions can be postponed until critical subsystems are proven. For example, if propulsion or airframe concepts are especially uncertain, these should be tested in simple prototype form before the development of electronic systems is permitted to continue past breadboard demonstrations. If the military value of the system is low or doubtful, it may be desirable to emphasize applied research rather than more expensive subsystem and prototype testing.

4. If the need for a weapon system is not urgent and if major state of the art advances are not required, the emphasis should be upon the use of proven concepts, subsystems, and components, relatively early configuration decisions, and prolonged prototype testing to ensure reliability before production commit-

ments are made.

To be sure, these four cases are oversimplifications. Several possible subcases can be distinguished within each broad category, and the military value and state of the art advance variables used to distinguish the cases are continuous, rather than two-valued (high or low) as suggested here. There will undoubtedly be future weapons program situations in each of these four major categories and indeed in all categories of some more complex classification scheme, and so program decisions and development approaches must vary widely to suit the particular circumstances.

Still it appears that U.S. weapons programs may tend in the future more and more toward Case 2—high military value (and hence urgency) and ambitious state of the art advance. This is so for two major reasons: (1) It is clear that, barring some agreement on armaments limitation (which presently appears unlikely), the United States is locked into a qualitative arms race with the Soviet Bloc. Moreover, the history of events since 1949 indicates that the Soviets are extremely proficient at exploiting advances in technology for military purposes. The United States is therefore forced to make equivalent advances in the state of the weapons art to maintain qualitative parity. (2) The United States is in a distinctly inferior position with respect to intelligence on military technology. As the Soviets take the initiative in weaponry, the United States will find itself forced more and more into crash programs to catch up with Soviet efforts which have proceeded unnoticed for several years.

Since Case 2 programs are by far the most difficult and expensive to conduct, and since the considerations affecting the choice of weapons programs and development program approaches are in general extremely complex, sound program decision-making assumes special importance. The program decision, however, can be little better than the information upon which it is made. The various forms of source selection competition—management, design, and prototype—yield increasing quantities of program decision-making information, but at the expense of increasing cost and time. Emphasis upon management competitions in the late 1950's has meant a great reliance upon "paper" information. And for all three types of competitions, the inherent uncertainties of weapons development give rise to substantial errors.

Still there are significant man-made errors in existing information-gathering processes. Most of the data used for program decisions are supplied by the participants in weapons programs—contractors and the government program management agencies. As a result, there is a self-serving optimistic bias in cost estimates, projected availability dates, and technical performance predictions.

Another difficulty lies in the significant interactions among program decisions for different projects. These interactions usually cut across traditional service boundaries. For example, an Atlas program alone might be of extreme urgency. But if some kind of Polaris or Jupiter will perform essentially the same functions, the importance of minimizing time in the Atlas development may be altered. Program decisions which do not take these interactions into account cannot be very rational, and it appears most difficult for the individual services to define the interactions of their proposed weapons with the weapons of the other services.

Thus, two things are needed for sound program decision-making: good, fairly dependable data; and a thoroughgoing analysis of the data which recognizes the interactions among time, quality, cost, and value variables for any given weapon system program and the interactions among programs. It therefore appears essential to develop improved methods of obtaining for the Office of the Secretary of Defense the information it needs for effective program decision-making by bolstering its in-house competence, ferreting out the data possessed by other organizations, and developing improved analytical capabilities and methods of analysis. Although its capability has been enhanced in recent years, the OSD Weapon Systems Evaluation Group still appeared in 1961 unable to provide the degree of analytical support required to make major improvements in U.S. program decisions.

Indeed, the establishment of a top-flight data gathering and analysis organization is one recommendation we propose very strongly here. Given the problems of recruiting and holding government personnel, creating such an organization would be difficult. Yet an investment in talent at this point in the weapons acquisition process would, we believe, lead to considerable improvement in the overall process.

THE CONDUCT OF WEAPONS PROGRAMS

As we read the record, the conduct of U.S. weapons programs has on the average been fairly good on the technical performance dimension and somewhat less favorable on the development time and reliability dimensions. But the most notable deficiency has been the failure to hold development and production costs to reasonable levels.

Weapons program costs have been high partly because of inadequate attention to the efficient utilization of technical, production, and administrative manpower—areas in which major cost reductions are possible. High costs have also been due to the development of qualitative features and increments of technical performance not worth their cost.

There are several more fundamental reasons for the high cost of U.S. weapons programs. For one, the services have placed much greater emphasis on time and quality considerations than on cost reduction, especially in the higher priority programs. Even when they have tried to do so, the services have not been especially successful in stressing cost reduction because they lacked the technical competence to evaluate contractor costs in detail. Moreover, contractors have recognized that a record of meeting schedules and delivering high-quality products is much more important in obtaining new contracts than a reputation for efficiency. Finally, the cost reimbursement character of weapons development and initial production has meant that contractors' profits have been roughly proportional to total cost, so the normal commercial incentives for cost reduction have been lacking.

The excessive cost of weapons programs is a most serious deficiency in the weapons acquisition process. It is not merely that money is wasted. It is rather that money costs reflect the scarcity of talented engineers and scientists, competent managers, and skilled production workers. Therefore expenditures on any one program are always at the expense of other existing or potential programs. Thus it is essential to hold the cost of any single weapons program to reasonable levels, freeing unnecessary resources to meet other pressing national security requirements. Nevertheless, eliminating excessive costs in weapons programs poses extremely difficult problems.

PART FOUR

Basic Research,
Civilian Technology,
and Public Policy

The Scientific Estate

DON PRICE

Don Price is Dean of the Graduate School of Public Administration at Harvard University. This article is taken from his book, The Scientific Estate, *published in 1965.*

DURING THE EARLY 1960's, it was a rare scientific meeting that failed to discuss two pronouncements on the relation of science to politics. The first was Sir Charles Snow's vivid story about the wartime rivalry of Tizard and Lindemann as scientific advisers to the British government. That "cautionary tale" warned us that democracy was in danger from the great gulf in understanding between the Two Cultures of science and the humanities, and from any possible monopoly on scientific advice to high political authority. The second was the farewell address of President Eisenhower, warning the nation that its public policy might "become the captive of a scientific-technological elite."

It is easy to appreciate why President Eisenhower felt as strongly as he did. His administration had started out to cut back on expenditures for research and development, but had ended by quadrupling them. This increase was by no means for defense alone; during his eight years in office the Congress multiplied the appropriations for the National Institutes of Health more than ninefold, giving them each year more than he had recommended. Science seemed clearly to be getting out of hand. It was almost enough to make one try to apply to the budgeting process the theory of Henry Adams that science, as it becomes more abstract, increases in geometrical progression the physical power that it produces.

The President's statement was a great shock to the scientists, especially to those who had been working with the administration rather than criticizing it in the columns of the *Bulletin of the Atomic Scientists*. President Eisenhower, indeed, quickly explained that he was not talking about science in general, but only those parts allied with military and industrial power. Nevertheless, to the typical American scientist who still believed that science had helped to liberate man from ancient tyrannies, it was disconcerting to be told by a conservative president that he had become a member of a new priesthood allied with military power.

Yet it had begun to seem evident to a great many administrators and politicians that science had become something very close to an *establishment*, in the old and proper sense of that word: a set of institutions supported by tax funds, but largely on faith, and without direct responsibility to political control. The terms under which this support is now given to science do not seem to many politicians to fit into the traditional ideas of Jeffersonian democracy.

From the point of view of scientists and university administrators, on the other hand, the growing dependence of science on government brings a great many problems, especially the danger of increasing government control over universities. It is hard to turn money down, but more and more scientific spokesmen are beginning to worry about the conditions that come with it. From the point of view of government, the sentiment in Congress now seems to be considerably more critical of the terms on which money is provided for scientific research. Edward Gibbon summed up the cynical eighteenth-century attitude toward a religious establishment by remarking that all religions were "considered by the people, as equally true; by the philosopher, as equally false; and by the magistrate, as equality useful." And now, it seems that all sciences are considered by their professors, as equally significant; by the politicians, as equally incomprehensible; and by the military, as equally expensive.

So we are beginning to observe in the Congressional attitude toward science some of the symptoms of friction between an establishment and a secular government. The symptoms showed up, for example, in Congressman L. H. Fountain's investigations of the National Institutes of Health, wherein he sought reform by uncovering abuses in the administration of the cloistered but tax-supported laboratories. And they showed up in Congressman Wright Patman's attacks on the tax-exempt foundations—institutions which by a modern kind of *mortmain* give science a range of political initiative outside the control of politics.

These attacks do not get at the main issues. They have so far been only a minor nuisance to scientific institutions, with an effect measured mainly in the time taken to fill out accounting forms. But they are a threat because they may reflect a more fundamental uneasiness in the intellectual as well as the political world. This is an uneasiness not merely about the terms of the financial relationship between government and science, but about the question whether the growing influence of science can be kept compatible with representative government. It is, in short, the same question asked by Dr. Rabinowitch [editor of the *Bulletin of the Atomic Scientists*]—can democratic government cope with problems raised by the scientific revolution?—but from the opposite point of view.

These attitudes, as yet, may have very little to do with the way most American scientists think, either on or off duty, and practically nothing to do with the amount of money their laboratories get in government grants. They are only a small cloud on the intellectual and political horizon of the United States. But they correspond to a much greater intellectual disturbance, over the past century and a half, in Europe, where the political faith in the alliance of science and reason with free government that was characteristic of the Enlightenment gave way in the late nineteenth century to various forms of scholarly despair. In America, a faith in the political rationalism of the Enlightenment tended to persist in the political thinking of scientists, even after the depression shook their confidence in the inevitability of progress. Right up to the present, American scientists have shown singularly little interest in either the conservative political theorists who tell them that scientists cannot deal with basic values or solve the major human problems, or the radical theorists who tell them that science can do so if it will only join in a political system, like Marxism, that will give it real power over society.

Even the strongest critics of the government and its scientific policies—for example, many of the contributors to the *Bulletin of the Atomic Scientists*—are surprisingly traditional in their approach to the political system. They may question the capacity of our representative institutions to cope with the scientific revolution, but they tend to propose as remedies, more international good will and cooperation, adequate scientific education of political leaders and the electorate, and unbiased scientific advice for members of Congress.

It is hard to quarrel with any of these ideas. But they are a little like the remedy that was most often proposed for corruption in government during the late nineteenth century: more good men should go into politics. That exhortation surely did some good, but probably less than the effort to adjust our political and economic institutions to the realities of the industrial revolution. That adjustment required a great many changes, by Congress and the judiciary and administrators, but it did not follow the prescriptions of any of the single-minded political prophets. It came instead from a new way of looking at the problem: we gave up thinking about politics merely in terms of the formal Constitutional system, which had been based on an analogy with Newtonian thought—a mechanistic system of checks and balances. In the latter part of the nineteenth century, students of politics (if they had not given up their interest in science) might have noted with interest a new analogy: as science penetrated the structure of the molecule, and identified its elements, politicians were becoming preoccupied with the elements of politics—with parties and economic classes and pressure groups—as well as its mechanistic Constitutional balances.

The scientific revolution in nuclear physics and in such fields as genetics is carrying us into a third stage of complexity. That revolution seems certain to have a more radical effect on our political institutions than did the industrial revolution, for a good many reasons. Let us note three of them.

1. *The scientific revolution is moving the public and private sectors closer together*—During the industrial revolution, the most dynamic economic interests were more or less independent

of the political system. They might depend on it, as many American corporations did by relying on tariff protection, and they might try with some success to control it, but they were not incorporated into its administrative system, they did not receive support from taxation, and the main directions of their new enterprise were controlled by their owners and managers. Today, our national policy assumes that a great deal of our new enterprise is likely to follow from technological developments financed by the government and directed in response to government policy; and many of our most dynamic industries are largely or entirely dependent on doing business with the government through a subordinate relationship that has little resemblance to the traditional market economy.

2. *The scientific revolution is bringing a new order of complexity into the administration of public affairs*—The industrial revolution brought its complexities, and relied heavily on new forms of expertise, but it did not challenge the assumption that the owner or manager, even without scientific knowledge, was able to control the policies of a business. And the same general belief was fundamental to our governmental system: the key ideas, if not the lesser details, could be understood by the legislature and debated before the public, and thus controlled by a chain of public responsibility. In one sense this was never true; in another and more fundamental sense, I think it is still true. But it is much less apparently true today than it was, and a great many more people doubt it. The great issues of life and death, many people fear, are now so technically abstruse that they must be decided in secret by the few who have the ability to understand their scientific complexities. We were already worrying about the alleged predominance of the executive over the legislature; now we worry lest even our elected executives cannot really understand what they are doing, lest they are only a façade that conceals the power of the scientists—many of whom are not even full-time officials, but have a primary loyalty to some university or corporation—who really control the decisions. If (as I believe) this is not really true, it is nevertheless true that the scientific revolution has upset our popular ideas about the way in which policies are initiated and adopted, and in which politicians can control them and be held responsible for them.

We have to reconsider our basic ideas about the processes of political responsibility.

3. *The scientific revolution is upsetting our system of checks and balances*—From a moral or ethical point of view, the industrial revolution raised problems that were relatively simple. Everyone admitted that it was possible for economic interests to control politics, but the remedy seemed to be clear: regulate business to prevent abuses, and keep selfish business interests out of the political process. This seemed clearly the basic formula for dealing with the obvious conflict of the public interest with the special interests of business. And the formula of separation of business and government was analogous in a comforting way to the formula for the separation of church and state. A church that was not dependent on government support was able to provide an independent source of moral judgment which could help to control the ethical standards of our politics and our business. As the problems began to seem a bit complex for unaided theological opinion, the universities began to provide an additional source of more scientific, but equally independent, advice to the public on the basic value judgments that should govern our policies. This was the fundamental system of checks and balances within our society: the check on practical political affairs imposed by sources of utterly independent criticism, based on a system of values that was not corrupted by the political competition for wealth or power.

But the scientific revolution seems to threaten to destroy this safeguard in two ways: First, it has gradually weakened the moral authority of religious institutions by the critical skepticism that it has made predominant in Western intellectual life, most notably in the universities. Second, it has made the universities themselves financially dependent on government, and involved them deeply in the political process. Thus, after helping to disestablish churches and free most universities from ecclesiastical control, science has now made those universities dependent on a new form of establishment, in the guise of government grants, and allied them more closely with a military power that is capable of unlimited destruction.

These three developments make some of our traditional reactions—our automatic political reflexes—unreliable in dealing with our present problems. We are automatically against socialism, but we do not know how to deal with an extension of governmental power over the economy that technically leaves ownership in private hands. It is almost an instinct with us to distrust the political bosses who, by controlling the votes of the ignorant masses, seek personal profit or power without accepting official responsibility. But we do not know how to deal with irresponsible influence that comes from status in the highest sanhedrin of science, untainted by any desire for personal profit. And we are fanatically against the public support of any institutions that might impose religious values on public policy, but when the institutions of organized skepticism tell us what science believes or how much money science needs, we have no reliable procedure for questioning their infallibility, or even for criticizing their budgets.

Science has thus given our political evolution a reverse twist. It has brought us back to a set of political problems that we thought we had disposed of forever by simple Constitutional principles. These are the problems of dealing not only with territorial subdivisions of government, and not only with economic interests and classes, but also with various groups of citizens which are separated from each other by very different types of education and ways of thinking and sets of ideals. This was the problem of the medieval estates.

The three estates of the realm, whose customary privileges grew into constitutional functions, were the clergy, the nobility, and the burgesses—those who taught, those who fought, and those who bought and sold. In our impatience with privilege at the time of the American Revolution, we abolished the estates in our political system so thoroughly that we have almost forgotten what the word meant. To abolish the first estate, we disestablished the church and provided secular education through local governments. To abolish the second, we forbade titles of nobility, made the military subordinate to civil authority, and relied on a popular militia rather than a standing army. To abolish the third, we did away with property qualifications on voting and exalted freedom of contract and competition above legislative interference.

But now the results of scientific advance have been to require federal support of education and the appropriation of a tithe of the federal budget for research and development, to set up the most powerful and professional military force in history, and to make free competition a minor factor in the relationship to government of some of the major segments of the economy.

Thus we are left to face the second half of the problem which we were afraid to face during the depression, and tried to escape at the end of the Second World War: the necessity for discovering a new basis for relating our science to our political purposes. We learned half of our lesson from the scientists: the lesson that we could not have a first-rate scientific establishment if we did not understand that first-rate science depended on fundamental theoretical work and required the support of basic research for its own sake, and not merely as a by-product of applied science. Now the outlines of the second, or political, half of our problem are becoming more clear. Basic science as such became steadily more powerful as it freed itself from the constraints of values and purposes. As an institution in society, it had to free itself in an analogous way from subordination to the applied purposes of the industrial corporation or the government bureau or the military service. And in the unpredictability of its progress it challenges the old notion that in matters of public policy the scientist must be controlled completely by purposes defined by politicians. So we must face the possibility that science will no longer serve as a docile instrument toward purposes that are implicit in a system of automatic economic progress, or even toward purposes that are defined for scientists by business and political leaders. In short, we can no longer take it for granted that scientists will be "on tap but not on top."

Accordingly, we need to consider not only the practical relation of scientific institutions to the economy and the government, but also the theoretical relation of science to political values, and to the principles that are the foundation of the constitutional system. Only with the help of scientists can we deal with the great issues of war and peace, of the population explosion and its effects in the underdeveloped countries, or of the dangers to our environment from our technological advances not only in weaponry but also in civilian industry and agriculture. But before we are likely, as a nation, to let science help us solve such problems, we are sure to want to know the full terms of the bargain. For although some of the political reflexes that we have acquired by several centuries of constitutional experience may be out of date, one of the most automatic is still useful: we want to know not only whether some political pronouncement is true, but why the speaker said it, having a healthy suspicion that we need to know whose interests it would further, and what its effect would be on our capacity to govern ourselves, or at least to hold our governors responsible.

The scientific community in the United States is not an organized institution, or a group with definite boundaries. It is not a hierarchical establishment. But its existence as a loosely defined estate with a special function in our constitutional system is becoming apparent, and we would do well to assess its political significance. If we do, we may find that a deeper understanding of the basic relation of science to government will help us to give it the kind of support it needs for its own purposes, as well as use it more effectively for the practical ends of public policy. And if we are willing to renounce the utopian hope that science will solve our problems for us, we may find that science by its very nature is more congenial to the development of free political institutions than our anti-utopian prophets would have us believe.

Research, Development, and the Federal Budget

WILLIAM D. CAREY

William D. Carey is Executive Assistant Director of the Bureau of the Budget. He delivered this paper at the 17th National Conference on the Administration of Research, Estes Park, Colorado, September 11, 1963.

I TAKE FOR MY OPENING TEXT the observation of Malcolm Muggeridge that human beings suffer more as a result of being unduly serious than of being unduly flippant; their worst blunders arise out of their solemnity, not out of their mirth.

The relationship of government to science in the postwar years is a case in point. Without very much visible deliberation, but with much solemnity, we have in little more than a decade elevated science to a role of extraordinary influence in national policy; and now that it is there, we are not very certain what to do with it. We have evolved a variety of rationalizations for what we have done and for what we doubtless will continue to do: science for national security, science for a better life, science for a growing economy, and science as a cultural end in itself. What we have done less well is to employ research support as an effective agent in upgrading higher education not just for a few leading institutions but at its broad base, provide safeguards against expediency in influencing career and vocational commitments, and establish a truly competitive market place within which science and technology must justify itself and its costs in fair competition with other social priorities and preferences.

We have gone through a whole generation of science administrators and political executives who developed ulcers in bringing science and technology to its present dimensions. Now we are inducing ulcers in another generation of scientists, administrators, economists, and politicians who are trying to solve the problems left by their predecessors. Is big science and technology for space

154

and defense in fact bleeding the private economy of the incentive and capability for innovation and creativity? Where is the high-grade intellectual manpower coming from to make good the commitments we are so freely entering into for the next decade? How are we to make certain that rising expenditures for research and development are not lost by dwindling productivity and quality in research? Can some way be found to ensure an adequate spin-off from space and defense research for the benefit of civilian technology? Have we approached the time for a healthy shaking-down of our federal science and technology for purposes of taking stock and consolidating our efforts where the priorities lie?

In short, reaction is at last setting in. It is apparent in the scientific community, perhaps because of fears lest major programs and enormous hardware costs will push less exotic science to one side. It is apparent also in the Executive Branch of the federal government, where the budgetary pinch is becoming acute. And it is perhaps most spectacularly apparent in the Congress, where a mounting wail of frustration and uneasiness is being reflected in a rash of proposals to bring science and technology to heel, possibly reflecting a thought uttered by the quotable Mr. Justice Holmes, who said "We need education in the obvious more than investigation of the obscure."

The point I want to make is that government's part in the research and development business has now reached the point where it commands attention because of its sheer size and propensity for growth. From here on, we will have to be more choosy in what we do, and better prepared to supply answers to questions about marginal costs and benefits. The budget this year for research and development is a husky $15 billion. Its growth potential dwarfs anything else in the budget. Someone has figured out that the doubling time for R & D as a fraction of national income is only seven years, and that if this continued for thirty years research and development would rise to one-half of the national income. Dr. James Killian estimates that on the basis of present trands, total national expenditures for research and development could exceed $40 billion by 1970, with the federal government tagged for most of it.

In my judgment, without for a moment discounting the talent of the R & D community for finding new and expensive frontiers, these trends are not realistic. In absolute terms, I expect the level of federal support for R & D to rise, but at a diminishing rate which could produce a leveling-off of the budget for science and technology over the next few years. Nevertheless, even a moderate upward trend is not to be taken for granted. Funds for R & D have come so easily during the past decade that in some quarters of the scientific community we find a state of mind that assumes that the miracle of the loaves and the fishes will go on indefinitely, and that the mere assertion of a valid scientific need will suffice to turn on the financial gusher once more. I should like to make it plain that the justification for the sixteenth and seventeenth billion will have to be very different from the justification which sufficed for the first billion. We have arrived at the point in the government's budget where the trends of the past are meaningless. A budget which quadrupled in the forties and doubled again in the fifties is extremely unlikely to behave in that style in the sixties, even for science and technology. And so that next billion dollars will come under both executive and legislative scrutiny of a kind previously unknown. And the scientific community will have to take a major responsibility for being sure that government chooses to put its dollars behind the best of many choices.

I would further hazard the view that this tightening of the federal pursestrings will cause some convulsions in the scientific community. When dollars for Big Science become scarcer, the science community can be expected to break ranks and form clusters of opinion and dissent to a greater extent than is the case to date. If a massive program for high-energy nuclear physics costing six to eight billion dollars, or a development program for a supersonic commercial air transport costing even one billion dollars, has the effect of heralding the displacement of other urgent claims for federal support, we can expect the fur to fly and the issues to be illuminated with far more pungency than we have seen thus far. And this is precisely as it ought to be. This is the competitive market place at last.

To be sure, with this comes a new hazard, and one which is already visible. This is the danger of injecting the technique of the "pork barrel" into the area of science and technology. While I run some risk of excommunication for even bringing the matter up, it is a risk someone needs to take. We are talking about large sums of money, highly attractive physical plant, research tools to tantalize any self-respecting scientist with a forgivable eye on a Nobel Prize. We are speaking of national prestige science and technology which can be vital to the intellectual standing of a university or a group of universities. Where the tools are located, where the facilities are built, how funds are disbursed to equalize research opportunity among the various sections of the country—all these are very real issues in the era of Big Science. Scientists and educators with all this at stake are already learning how to bring pressure on their political representatives on their behalf, first for the approval of the programs and then for the location of facilities and the disbursing of operating funds. As new thresholds of research and experimentation materialize requiring highly sophisticated hardware, this phenomenon will become a force to be reckoned with. If I may say so, we can expect to face this not only in the area of applied science and technology, but even within that cloistered and rarefied world concerned with basic research. But if I am right about all this, and I think I am, one result will be to make science somewhat less luminous and otherworldly than it has been to date, and add a slight tinge of green to its halo.

As a more or less living example of the type of people who work on the federal budget, I should like to venture some general observations about that operation insofar as it touches science and technology.

To begin with, the budgetary process is the closest thing we have in government to a systematic effort at resource planning. Imperfect as it is, we would probably have to invent it if it did not already exist. What it provides is a round-the-year examination and re-examination of needs and resources in a changing society, in a setting of economic purposefulness and a Presidential program of political action. It is a process which stresses challenge and the evaluation of responses to that challenge. It reaches for rational criteria against which to sift competing claims and demands, and it aims toward a workable synthesis of goals within a financial and economic plan. In our framework of government, the budget process is the President's chief tool for facing up to the issue of what must be done now and what must wait. Underlying the exercise of this process there must, of course, be some basic strategy, and this will vary with Presidents and their public philosophies. One President may view the budget as a built-in Maginot Line against further extension of the arc of public action and intervention, while another will recognize it as an opportunity to advance our society purposefully in many fields of action important to both internal and external progress.

The Bureau of the Budget has never agreed with suggestions that it should establish within its structure a Division of Science, staffed with qualified scientists and engineers, to review R & D proposals. We prefer to do our work by using a broad approach which examines program issues in the field of science and technology from the standpoints of public policy, soundness of justification, the availability of money and manpower, and the balance of financial effort as among alternative program commitments. To be sure, our analysis frequently requires inputs of sophisticated professional judgment as to technical feasibility, state of the art, and possible alternatives to a proposed line of development, as, for example, in the moon program or in the missile field. In recent years, however, we have been able to obtain this kind of judgment through the Office of Science and Technology and the President's Science Advisory Committee. We have also arranged each year to undertake an overview of selected fields of science with the objective of relating levels of effort and support in particularly vital areas of science and technology to our general budgetary planning. This year, for example, we selected the areas of atmospheric science, oceanography, water research, high-energy nuclear physics, basic science, and science information for special review, and we conducted this exercise jointly with the office of the President's Science Adviser. I might say that the budget review process is not slanted toward exposing the weaknesses and follies of science proposals, although at times it has that result. But the process we employ is also calculated to bring out situations where we feel that there are distortions and imbalances in the government's support of science and technology and education, and in such instances we look for corrective solutions even though this might actually run the totals up.

I would like to be able to assert that the budget process employs an ideal combination of criteria which guarantees a fully rational exercise in decision-making where we are dealing with science and technology. The truth is that we have a long way to travel before achieving that Utopia. There are still too many variables, too many unknowns, to leave us comfortable. We have no way to measure satisfactorily the potential yield to civilian technology from military and space R & D. We lack dependable data to judge whether we are approaching—or have already reached—the point where government-supported science and technology is displacing or impeding private investment in the R & D which feeds economic growth and creates the new products and markets needed for an economy on the path to full employment. Our crystal ball is still very foggy in forecasting what all this scientific and technical exuberance may mean in accelerating automation with all its implications on the mix of skills and utilization of our basic labor force. After twelve years of the National Science Foundation, we are as far away as ever from any clue as to how much basic research should be supported, year in and year out, as a national purpose, and we continue in that area to depend too much on the oversimplified formula of budgeting for some rough percentage of the worthwhile acceptable research proposals that are expected to roll in. We have found no absolute answers to the dilemma of priorities when we are faced with a well-reasoned but vastly expensive long-range program in high-energy nuclear physics and, simultaneously, programs for major outlays for oceanography, supersonic aircraft development, and the moon program; how does one assign relative values to the spectrum of opportunities to advance knowledge? James Reston of the *New York Times* has seen fit to draw attention to the dilemma of priorities in a piece entitled "Kennedy and the Scientists: the Quiet War." It is not a war at all, but an abundance of opportunities which government itself has invited and which only government can seize for the benefit of its people. The problem is that government today cannot take the easy way of recognizing them all and endowing science and technology with an unlimited drawing account. As I said earlier, the sixteenth and seventeenth billion are harder to come by than the first. Our problem is an embarrassment of intellectual riches which is not matched by the affluence to employ them fully. While Mr. Reston is entitled to his doubts about the adequacy of the government's method for reaching sound choices, it is my view that the difficulty here is not one of inventing more super-authorities but rather one of organizing "research about research," of developing more adequate insights into cost-benefit relationships, of illuminating our value analysis so that we can with greater confidence strike a balance between being "first" in high-energy accelerators and being first in education and in decent living and job opportunity. I do not think that government alone can reach these answers, but perhaps government can—and indeed I believe it must—be as proportionately lavish in stimulating this kind of intellectual inquiry as it has been in endowing science and technology.

Federal Support of Basic Research: I

Carl Kaysen is Director of the Institute of Advanced Study in Princeton. His paper is taken from Basic Research and National Goals, *published in 1965.*

THE FUNDAMENTAL JUSTIFICATION for expending large sums from the federal budget to support basic research is that these expenditures are capital investments in the stock of knowledge which pay off in increased outputs of goods and services that our society strongly desires. However, the nature of the payoff is such that we can appropriately view these investments as social capital, to be provided in substantial part through the government budget, rather than private capital to be provided through the mechanism of the market and business institutions. Broadly, the payoff of basic research in the aggregate to the whole of society is clear. However, the fruits of any particular piece of research are so uncertain in their character, magnitude, and timing as to make reliance on the market mechanism to provide an adequate flow inappropriate. The market mechanism operates on the principle that he who pays the costs gets the benefits, and vice versa, and relies on an anticipation of benefits that is certain enough to justify the outlays required to realize them. The benefits of the kind of knowledge that basic research seeks are usually difficult or impossible to keep for a particular firm or individual. Indeed, the knowledge is often useful as it can be added to the general stock of scientific knowledge that is held in common by the community of those technically proficient in the relevant discipline. Thus a business firm which paid for a particular piece of basic research work could not, in general, prevent its result from being used by others. Further, the uncertainty as to just what would result, and when, and as to whether the useful purpose to which it could be applied would in fact be one that was relevant to the activities of the firm, would in general make expenditure in support of this work an unattractive investment. Finally, several of the kinds of payoffs from basic research relate to outputs that are already the product of government activity, rather than of business operating through the market mechanism.

None of the arguments that justify federal support for basic scientific research provide in themselves a measure of what level of expenditure is necessary or desirable. Indeed the nature of the arguments themselves is such as to make it impossible for any precise payoff calculation to be made. In sum, they say expenditure on basic science is investment in a special kind of social overhead—knowledge and understanding—that contributes directly and indirectly to a wide variety of vital social purposes. It is in the very nature of an overhead that a nice calculation of the "right" amount to expend on it is difficult. While we could conceive a level of research activity so small that education and applied research began visibly to suffer, and equally, we can conceive a flow of funds so generous that they would obviously be wastefully employed, the limits between the two are very wide.

In the absence of more specific bases of calculation, the usual method of budgeting for an overhead item is to allocate to it some share of the total to which it seems most relevant. In this case, we might assign to basic research some fraction of the total expenditure on applied research and development, on the ground that this is the major item to which basic research is an overhead. In fact, the past growth of basic research figures as reported by the National Science Foundation has been closely parallel to the growth in total expenditures for research and development. The share of basic research in the total has fluctuated between 8 and 10 per cent. Thus one method for solving the problem is simply to continue to allocate about 9 per cent of the total expenditure of research and development to basic research, and continue to provide the same proportion, or about 55 per cent of this amount, from federal sources.

An alternate method is to look to the fact that it is ultimately brains, and not money, that is the limiting factor on the size of the useful national research effort. The budget for basic research could then be set in terms of the level required to support the research activity of all those with proper training and an appropriate level of ability, with the share provided out of federal resources again to be determined on customary grounds. Let us put aside for the moment the thorny question of what is the appropriate level of ability, and the equally thorny one of who determines its presence or absence in particular cases. It is worth noting that the intimate tie between research and advanced training means that the results to which this method would lead would not be unrelated to those arising from the previous one. Any given rate of growth in the total applied research effort requires a corresponding rate of increase in the pool of scientists and engineers who perform it. If these are trained at the institutions that do a major part of all basic research, as they are now, and in such a way that training and research are complementary, then the size of the basic research effort required to finance the activity of the teacher-researchers is related to the rate of flow of the scientists and engineers they are called upon to train. But, as a practical matter, this approach does not provide an easier way to calculate the proper level of federal support for basic research than the "overhead" method suggested above. The problems of defining the levels of competence and training that qualify a man for support are great. Teaching and research are not strictly complementary, and there is no fixed ideal ratio between them that can be applied to every institution and every branch of science. Finally, future demand for graduates with scientific training is necessarily uncertain, and basing present basic research budgets on projections of these demands may tend to introduce an element of inflation in the estimating process.

For these reasons the overhead approach appears more useful. In applying it, two kinds of problems must be borne in mind, which will make it necessary to review the appropriateness of the particular overhead percentage from time to time. First is the fact that at any moment, the composition of total expenditures on basic research in terms of investment in large new facilities, their operating and maintenance expenditures, and expenditures on personnel and current support may be such as not to permit maintenance in the future of both the particular total and the particular composition. The creation of large new facilities may build in a requirement for operating and maintaining them of such magnitude as to require either more expenditures or a cutback in actual research effort. Second, the overhead ratio appropriate to a rapidly rising level of total expenditures may not be the one appropriate to a more slowly growing one. This caution is especially relevant to the situation we may face in the middle future, as the rate of growth of expenditures in applied research and development slackens off. At that time, a part of the adjustment process to such a change may well be a temporary increase in the overhead ratio for the support of basic research. Since it is my aim to sketch general principles and indicate how they might be applied, rather than to formulate detailed programs, I leave further discussion of these points, both of which are important, and potentially complex in detail.

Federal Support of Basic Research: II

Harry G. Johnson is Professor of Economics at the University of Chicago. His paper, from Basic Research and National Goals, *suggests a different procedure from that described in the preceding article.*

A GREAT DEAL OF STRESS IS LAID, in current arguments for federal support of basic scientific research, on the importance of scientific progress to the improvement of productivity and the standard of living. Since the findings of economists on this question, such as they are, are easily subject to misinterpretation, it seems useful to provide a brief outline of their nature before turning to the economic argument for government support of basic science.

Broadly speaking, economists concerned with economic growth conceive of the total output of the economy as being the resultant of various inputs of productive services into the production process, and seek to explain the measured growth of output by reference to changes in the quantities of inputs over time. The term "measured growth of output" embodies a limitation important in the present connection, since the methods of measurement of output largely fail to catch improvements in the quality of the goods and services produced, and such improvements are an important part of the contribution of progress in knowledge to human welfare. The procedure involves specifying both the inputs and the value of their contribution to output; any residual growth of output not explained by changes in input quantities is a measure of the contribution of factors not taken into account in the formulation of the relationships assumed to determine output. In the early stages of this type of research there was an unfortunate tendency to describe the residual as the increase in productivity of the inputs, and to identify it positively as the contribution of the advance of knowledge to increases in output—particularly unfortunate as the early studies worked with very simple models of the production process and an extremely crude measure of labor input in terms of labor-hours without reference to skill, and for this reason among others produced residuals that were extremely high in relation to the total growth of input. Subsequently, the residual has come to be regarded as simply "a measure of our ignorance" and to be described as "the residual" rather than as "increase in productivity." Correspondingly, research on economic growth has aimed at improving the model of production and the specification and measurement of the inputs so as to increase the proportion of measured growth explained and to reduce the residual.

The most comprehensive study of this kind is Edward F. Denison's *The Sources of Economic Growth in the United States and the Alternatives Before Us,* which attempts in particular to estimate the effects of changes in the quality of labor inputs associated with increased education and other changes, and to apportion the residual increase in output per unit of input among various contributing factors. Since it is the most comprehensive, it arrives at one of the lowest figures for the residual that economists have produced. Denison's figures ascribe approximately 20 per cent of the growth of real national income from 1909 to 1929, and approximately 32 per cent of the growth from 1929 to 1957, to the increase in output per unit of input. For the latter period, somewhat over half of the increase in output per unit of input (just under 30 per cent of measured growth) is ascribed to Denison's residual category labeled "Advance of Knowledge." This label is, of course, misleading, since the category is a residual that incorporates both any errors in the estimates of the influence on the growth of real income of changes in the factors explicitly taken into account in Denison's analysis and the influence of all the factors not so taken into account. It is not a direct estimate of the contribution of "advance of knowledge," in any concrete sense of the phrase, to measured economic growth. Moreover, as previously mentioned, the measured growth of output fails to catch improvements in the quality of output, to which advances in knowledge make an important contribution. Nevertheless, imprecise in meaning and unreliable in magnitude as it is, the residual figure is the most careful estimate available of the portion of past growth that might be attributed to the growth of knowledge.

The growth of knowledge in question is the growth of all knowledge relevant to efficient production, managerial and organizational as well as technological and scientific. Denison further estimates that about one-fifth of the contribution of "advance of knowledge" to growth in the period 1929 to 1957 can be attributed to organized research and development; and he calculates that the social rate of return on organized research and development is about the same as on investment in nonresidential capital. This in turn implies that the contribution of increased expenditure on research and development to measured economic growth would be small, and, more important, that there is no social benefit to be obtained from governmental measures to increase research and development activity. Denison's calculations are, however, no more than educated guesses; they do not include improvements in product quality, to which much of research and development is directed; the calculated rate of return on research and development could be much higher if research and development yielded its contribution only with a substantial lag; and there are reasons, elaborated below, for believing that resources are not allocated to research and development as efficiently as they could be.

Though the importance of the advance of knowledge to improved living standards is difficult to quantify, and the magnitude of the contribution of basic scientific research to the advance of productivity is still more obscure, and though both may easily be exaggerated in carelessly formulated argument, there is no disputing that basic research has played a significant part in the growth of the U.S. economy. This fact by itself, however, does not constitute a case for government support of basic scientific research, though scientists frequently write as if it did; the argument that it does is equivalent to arguing that, because part of the growth of output is attributable to population growth, the government should subsidize birth and immigration. In order to establish a case for government support, it must be shown that basic research yields a social return over its cost that exceeds the return on alternative types of investment of resources. Alternatively, it must be shown that the amount of basic research that would be carried on in the absence of government support would be less than what would be economically optimal. It is, incidentally, important to recognize that even without government support some basic research would be carried on, as in the past—and probably on a much larger scale than in the past, owing both to the growth of interest in science and to the growth of wealth and the capacity to support scientific research through the universities and through privately supported research organizations. It is also important to recognize that government cannot create additional resources for the economy, with which to support basic research; it can only take resources away from private individuals, who might prefer to use them for some other purpose, but would probably contribute some of them to the support of science if science is deemed socially beneficial. Government support means the difference between more and less, not between all or nothing at all.

From the point of view of economic analysis, research is conceived of as one form of investment of resources, the investment involving the use of human and material resources to acquire knowledge and the return resulting from the application of that knowledge to increase human welfare in one way or another. Normally a free-enterprise economy depends on the exercise of private decisions operating in the marketplace to decide on the total investment of all kinds and its allocation among alternative forms of investment. The market will arrive at a socially efficient allocation of resources provided that the risks undertaken by and the prospective returns open to the private decision-taker coincide with the risks and returns to society as a whole. These conditions are not fulfilled for private investment in research, and particularly for private investment in basic scientific research. The risk to the private investor in the creation of scientific and technological knowledge is greater than the risk to society, because the knowledge that results from the research may be useful to someone else but not useful for him, and the return to the private investor is likely to be less than the return to society as a whole, because the benefits to society cannot be fully appropriated by charging for the use of the knowledge. These divergences of private and social risks and benefits are by definition greater for basic scientific research than for applied scientific research; they are also smaller for the large diversified research organization or industrial corporation than for the small specialized research organization or company.

In consequence, there is good theoretical reason for expecting that, left to itself, the market would not only tend to allocate too few resources to research in general, but would also tend to bias the allocation against basic scientific research as contrasted with applied scientific research, and toward research in scientific areas related to the technology of industries dominated by large multi-product corporations. This expectation seems to be substantially confirmed by the facts, especially those on the industrial distribution of research and development expenditure. A further relevant point is that, insofar as private appropriation of the benefits of successful research requires concealing the new knowledge from other potential users, the social gain from research is reduced correspondingly.

These defects of the market mechanism with respect to the allocation of resources toward and among investments in research imply that the market needs to be supplemented, and perhaps, with respect to basic scientific research, entirely replaced by social provision and allocation of resources for the support of scientific research. Our society does not, however, in fact depend exclusively on the market mechanism for decision on the amount and allocation of resources to be invested in. Instead, large amounts of money are channeled into basic research through the universities, through local and state governments, through private contributions, and through the federal budget. The question then becomes, not whether the market system needs supplementation, but whether the degree of supplementation provided through existing nonmarket channels is adequate, too large, or too small, in relation to the economically optimum, and whether the resulting allocation of resources among rival fields of scientific inquiry is reasonably efficient.

To provide satisfactory answers to these questions, and therefore some firmer basis for answering the House committee's questions, would require calculations of an extremely difficult sort, probably impossible to effect with any reliable degree of accuracy —calculations that have so far not been attempted on any substantial scale. The difficulties are suggested by some of the questions that need to be asked: What have been the social rates of return on past investments in basic scientific research, for particular research projects, and on the average? How likely are particular proposed lines of research to produce new contributions to knowledge, and how valuable to society are these contributions likely to be in relation to their cost? (The assessment of the returns on specific projects requires an estimate of the likelihood of success, as well as of the value of success and the prospective cost.) How likely is it that if a particular project is not undertaken in the United States it will be undertaken somewhere else, and what net loss, if any, would there be to the United States from relying on [foreign] scientists to carry it out?

These and similar questions relate primarily to the allocation of resources among research fields. With respect to the total allocation of resources to basic scientific research, questions of a different nature arise. One concerns the extent to which increased allocations of scientific personnel and supporting resources to basic scientific research would reduce the quality of the average research product; in other words, how rapidly do returns to research diminish?

The second concerns the relative extent to which increased expenditures on scientific research is reflected on the one hand in increased research effort and on the other hand in higher money costs; in other words, how far does increased expenditure on scientific research increase the quantity of research results produced, and how far does it merely bid up the salaries and raise the operating expenses of research personnel? Economists who have considered these questions (such as Machlup and Denison) seem to believe that the returns from increased expenditure on scientific research diminish fairly sharply for both reasons; more concrete evidence on these economic questions would be extremely useful.

A final question, of considerable relevance to policy making, concerns the extent to which government support and private support of basic scientific research are substitutes for one another, in the sense that larger-scale government support for science tends to reduce the private support forthcoming, and conversely a reduction in government support would elicit larger-scale private support. It is quite conceivable that the interest of the public (including business firms) in science, and its faith in the ultimate usefulness of contributions to scientific knowledge, together with

the competition for excellence among the universities, would furnish the resources required (or a large part of them) on the
alternative basis of private donations and fees. (Raising the funds
for basic research in this way would, of course, involve substantial
institutional changes.) Moreover, private support of science might
have certain advantages over governmental support, in that it
might tend to produce a more flexible adjustment of support to
the changing frontiers of scientific advance. That is, in science as
in the production of commodities, a decentralized decision-taking
process might produce a closer adjustment of supply to changing
needs or opportunities.

The foregoing questions illustrate the kind of information that
is necessary to judge the adequacy of federal support of basic
scientific research, from the economic point of view. In the absence of hard information or reasonably reliable estimates, any
such assessment has to be an exercise in informed judgment and
inference from scrappy evidence. In this connection, Richard
Nelson has advanced an argument to the effect that the United
States is probably not spending as much as it profitably could on
basic scientific research. He reasons as follows:

. . . if basic research can be considered as a homogeneous commodity,
like potato chips, and hence the public can be assumed to be indif-
ferent between the research results produced in government or in
industry laboratories; if the marginal cost of research output is assumed
to be no greater in nonprofit laboratories than in profit-oriented
laboratories; and if industry laboratories are assumed to operate where
marginal revenue equals marginal cost, then the fact that industry
laboratories do basic research at all is itself evidence that we should
increase our expenditure on basic research.

The key to the argument is the assumption discussed earlier, that
the social benefit from industry research exceeds the benefit
to the firm conducting it; the assumptions stated imply that the
social benefit exceeds the cost in industry research, and that the
same situation is true of nonprofit research. Nelson admits that
the factual assumptions are extremely shaky, particularly with
respect to the comparability of the research output of nonprofit
and profit-oriented laboratories; and some doubt is cast on the
argument by carrying it to its logical conclusion, which is that
government support of basic research should be extended to the

point where no profit-oriented laboratories have any incentive to conduct basic research.

How much federal support should be provided for basic scientific research, and how should it be allocated among fields of scientific endeavor? The previous discussion has illustrated the difficulty of providing any firm guidance on these questions by drawing on economic analysis. In principle, the "scientific culture" type of argument for federal support of basic scientific research requires that public opinion, as expressed through Congress, must decide at what point to strike a balance between supporting the scientific culture and using its resources for other desirable forms of expenditure. The economic argument, on the other hand, would require allocating resources among scientific fields so as to equalize the prospective social rates of return from marginal expenditure on each field, and fixing the total of resources allocated to the basic research at the level yielding a marginal rate of return on all investment in basic research comparable to what is earned on other forms of investment, or else equal to the rate of interest at which the community is willing to forego the alternative of consuming the requisite resources. But since the information required to perform these exercises is absent, the principles can serve at best as a way of formulating decisions on the questions.

In the absence of any firm knowledge about the relation between the level and allocation of federal support for basic science research and the magnitude of the social benefits obtained therefrom, there is a strong temptation to attempt to evade the issue by resorting to rule-of-thumb procedures based on the situation of the present or recent past. One such is the attempt to establish normative percentages tying expenditure on basic research to gross national product or to government expenditure on major applied-science projects. The difficulties with this procedure are, first, that the percentages are usually derived from some base period, and there is no reason to expect the level in the base period to have been the right level; and second, that there is no reason to expect the correct relationship to be a constant.

An alternative is to ignore the question of benefits, and to approach the question from the science side: This is exemplified by the recommendation that adequate support should be provided for all qualified talent in the category of "little science" research, while political decision on priorities should be taken in the light of prospective cost in the category of "big science" research. This recommendation essentially amounts to taking the consumption view of scientific research: In little science, support everyone who demonstrates talent according to the scientific standards of his fellow scientists, and, in big science, decide how much society can afford to spend.

As regards little science, the approach just outlined evidently trusts the scientific community and the process of educational selection to produce a total and an allocation of expenditure not wildly out of line with governmental capacity to pay and the rough requirements of efficient distribution of scientific effort (efficient, that is, in scientific but not necessarily economic terms). Ultimately, it relies on the self-equilibrating processes of the intellectual market in ideas and the commercial market in scientifically trained labor to prevent serious misallocations. It should also be noted that the approach depends on a particular assumption about the supply of scientific talent: that there is a limited and fairly readily identifiable group in the population that is capable of acceptable scientific performance, and a sharp difference in ability between this group and the rest. This assumption does not make economic sense in any long-run perspective: One would expect the supply of potential scientists, like the supply of any other kind of skilled labor, to vary in response to the income and career opportunities offered. (Even if scientifically talented people were a fixed proportion of population, it would still be possible to increase the number available in the United States through immigration.) Consequently, any attempt to fix the total level of support on this basis implies a judgment that the present level of scientific activity (or something near it) is the correct one. Alternatively, if the principle is to offer support to everyone of competence who offers himself for a scientific career, the level of scientific activity will be left to be determined by the attractiveness of alternative occupations.

In conclusion, it seems desirable to draw attention to a facet of policy toward basic science that is important but tends to be overlooked by scientists. This is the implication of the geographical distribution of science support for the pattern of growth of the U.S. economy. The location of scientific research activity in a particular city or region generally constitutes a focal point for the development of science-intensive industries in the surrounding area, and this should be taken into account in deciding on the location of such scientific activity. There is a natural tendency for scientific activity to agglomerate around established centers of scientific accomplishment; and this is probably the most efficient way of conducting scientific research from the point of view of science itself. From the economic and social point of view, however, and perhaps even from the longer run scientific point of view, there is a strong case for encouraging the development of scientific research centers in the more depressed and lower income sections of the country, as a means of raising the economic and social level of the population in those sections. Much of the poverty problem is associated with geographical concentration of high-income industries in certain areas and their absence from others, which makes migration the only feasible route to economic improvement. A deliberate policy of locating scientific research in the backward areas of the country to encourage their industrial development could in the long run provide a socially and economically more attractive attack on the poverty problem than many of the policies now being applied or considered.

This point, it should be emphasized, is independent of whether the nation is spending too little or too much on the support of basic research, that is, of whether the beneficial effects described are worth their cost.

The Technology Gap and the Brain Drain: I

HUBERT HUMPHREY

The selection by Vice President Humphrey comes from his speech before the Symposium on Technology and World Trade, November 16, 1966.

THE SO-CALLED "technological gap" between the United States and other nations—particularly our Western European friends—can hardly be escaped these days. Each day there seems to be a new proposal—and some of them have been good ones—toward closing that gap. If there is a technological gap, there is no gap in the information about it. Therefore, rather than enter into any technical discussion this evening, I would simply like to leave behind a few general observations and ideas.

First, although some people deny it, I do not dispute the fact of a technological gap. I know that all the statistics indicate that we in the United States have commanding leads over Western European nations in many fields—especially in computer technology and utilization.

But we have advanced technology in large part simply because our industry, which exists in many cases on a far larger scale than European industry, has had the need for it. Supply *does* follow demand.

I think by far the most promising proposals for closing the American-European technological gap have been those such as Prime Minister Wilson's for a European Technological Community. If Europe—which has already seen the benefits of a European Economic Community, a Coal and Steel Community, and an Atomic Energy Community—were to pool her technology in a similar way, I have no doubt that the gap would already be a long way toward being closed.

The very fact of entry into the European Communities by Britain and her EFTA partners—and eventually perhaps by others—would help create an even larger European market and larger industry able to finance and sustain advanced technology, along with the necessary research and development. And from the general need for such technology, I feel sure it would follow.

This leads me to my second observation: Namely, that economic integration and the creation of larger, continental markets —all over the world—can be a powerful force for closing any technology gaps.

It seems obvious, but too often overlooked, that small and poor nations stand little chance for economic sustenance if they do not seek economic integration—or at least, close economic cooperation with their neighbors. This is beginning to happen in Latin America, Asia, and Africa, but not nearly rapidly enough.

Long after any North Atlantic technology gap is closed, it will be the business of the Atlantic nations to try to close the far more dangerous rich-poor nation gap. We in the rich nations must begin taking more active steps now to help the poorer nations build their economies, create broader markets, and develop their own technologies.

I do not mean that each developing nation, and its economic partners, will need the capacity to produce and market sophisticated IBM systems. I do mean that, without trained manpower and the ability to enter the technological age, the developing nations will not only be unable to compete in world markets but that the resulting political and social unrest in these nations will be a threat both to their own security and ours.

And this leads me to my third general observation: That we all ought to do a little more thinking about what technology is *for*. If technology is used just to construct more impressive pieces of hardware—without resulting human benefit—then it will be wasted.

I believe that today we have the technological capacity already at hand: to rebuild the decaying central cores of large cities all over the world; to provide decent and reasonable housing on a wide scale; to lift primitive agriculture into the modern day; to compress the time scale for nations with catching up to do; to master our physical environment before it masters us; to end the coexistence of starvation and abundance on the same planet.

In my view, the real "technological gap" is between our technological capacity and our application of it to social needs. These needs—such as education, public health, recreation and transportation—exist in every part of the world. Meeting these group needs, however, is quite different from meeting individual needs such as for automobiles, clothing, or electrical appliances.

Old ways of doing things simply won't do the job. We need new mechanisms, new ways and means for bringing technology into the market place of public needs.

Technology moves in the form of products and services that nations exchange. It moves through patent royalties and licensing arrangements. It also moves in textbooks.

I have noticed that while a breakthrough in science flashes quickly around the world, a breakthrough in technology may take years to find its way to a place of need. What we should seek, therefore, are rules and practices to help speed the flow of technology, not slow it down or stop it.

I know the argument that technology carefully gained should not be easily shared, lest hard-earned competitive advantage be lost. The argument against sharing of technology, it seems to me, is not unlike the argument against liberalized trade. But in technology, as in trade, the benefits of openness and free exchange would seem to outweigh any loss of temporary, protective advantage.

I should think that an *international* patent system, for instance, would go a long way toward safeguarding ownership of valuable technological processes without burying each nation under paper.

And it seems clear to me that the United States' own long-term economic interest dictates that our trading partners should develop strong, technologically based competitive economies.

Technology also moves in the minds of people who travel from one country to another. Some travel to teach, and some travel to learn.

When students have been trained in another country and then remain there to fashion their careers, we are faced with one element of what is the now-famous "brain drain."

There are thousands of young scientists and engineers working in the United States who came here to learn, but have stayed to earn.

If it is any comfort to those nations which have lost the services of their talented citizens, they should know that we have experienced a comparable situation in the United States. Some of our states and regions graduate more Ph.D.'s each year than they employ. There is a "brain drain" from our Midwest to our East and West Coasts. We deplore this. But from a broad, national point of view, we can at least take some comfort from the fact that the United States as a whole is richer for this new talent.

There is no comfort at all for the developing country desperate for trained manpower when that manpower is' swallowed up here. These are precious human resources they cannot afford to lose.

How do we reverse this flow?

First of all, I take it for granted that good, technically trained people do not turn away from their homelands for money alone, or for better living conditions alone. Any good man wants to be where the problems are and where he has a fair chance of solving them. He also wants to utilize the most modern equipment and facilities.

There are some things we can do. I believe a great part of the problem lies in the educational systems of the *industrialized* countries. Too often, we offer discipline-oriented—rather than problem-oriented—education and training. Quite properly we emphasize the "ics"—physics, optics, nucleonics. I believe we must emphasize, too, the "tions"—education, transportation, nutrition, communication, irrigation—the things needed in developing countries—so that both our own citizens and those of developing nations can acquire the useful skills of nation-building.

I think, too, that we can help draw these valuable people homeward by making available to their own nations equipment and facilities that they have become accustomed to here. Our government agencies, our universities, and private industry are all topheavy with equipment which is perfectly satisfactory for skilled use, but which has been superseded by the next-generation model. As chairman of the Aeronautics and Space Council, I have made it my particular business, for instance, to see that equipment which has served its purpose in our advance research and application in space has been put to good use elsewhere.

We can help by working with the developing countries to insure that too high a percentage of their students do not come to the United States to acquire skills which have no relation to the priorities at home. We can also, quite practically, do what we can to help establish institutions in their home countries which will give these young people the skills they need without leaving home in the first place.

There is the across-the-board need to help build the technologies of the have-not nations so that their talented people will have sufficient daily challenge. It is clear that unemployed or underemployed scientists, even if they do not leave their country, pose political and social problems. In all we do to raise technological capabilities around the world, and to use those capabilities for human benefit, I am convinced that we should not become bound by doctrine, dogma, or ideology.

The Technology Gap and the Brain Drain: II

RICHARD MORSE

This paper by Richard Morse, former Director of Research of the Army, is taken from the 1967 Industrial Management Review.

THE public press, politicians, economists and industrialists in Europe are currently examining the United States in an effort to explain the role of science and technology as an aid to industrial development. Proposals have been advanced for a Technological Marshall Plan on the theory that some magic formula may exist to employ technology as an open sesame to solve the many problems of both highly industrialized and less developed areas of the world.

In general, Europeans incorrectly believe that "size" is the solution to effective competition. Mr. Anthony Benn, the new British Minister of Technology, was recently reported to say, "The giant American corporations are so strong that they can spend a lot on research, development, marketing and management skills." The problem is not that simple.

Our universities, industry, and the federal government are making substantial efforts to develop a better understanding of the increasingly complex nature of research and development. The "innovation process" is an essential and unique characteristic of our free enterprise system, and as a matter of fact may be one of America's most valuable national assets.

Technically oriented industrialists, here and abroad, may well understand this subject. Nevertheless, certain misconceptions regarding the "technological gap" should be reviewed. A number of fundamental differences between the European and American environment can then be identified. No pretext is made to present quantitative research findings, but the philosophy discussed here can be well documented by experience within our technically based industrial community.

Many of the misconceptions probably stem from the fact that

discussions about the "technological gap" are often undertaken by individuals who understand neither science and technology nor the problems associated with its application. A detailed analysis of the real problems relating to the effective utilization of modern science and engineering know-how in Europe would probably lead to conclusions somewhat different from those often quoted.

We have comparable discussions between representatives from different states and regions of varying degrees of industrialization within the United States. The "technological gap" between North Dakota and New Jersey is far greater than that existing between the United States as a whole and *any* major European country.

The term "technological gap" as used by Europeans suggests a wide discrepancy in available technology between the United States and the rest of the free world. The United States undoubtedly has a greater total capability in advanced technology than any other country, but there is little evidence that such technology, per se, is solely responsible for its economic growth rate or standard of living.

Figures are often quoted regarding the tremendous U.S. expenditure for R&D. Several European countries have comparable R&D efforts in the civilian sector of their economy, on a per capital basis or as a percentage of gross national product. Contrary to European opinion, our large, government-funded programs in space and defense may be detrimental to our ability to compete in world trade with new technical products. Two-thirds of our technical-professional manpower is now associated with federally sponsored R&D programs, and as a result, our capability to design, develop and market competitive products may have been reduced rather than enhanced in terms of our national effort. Scientists and engineers who have been associated solely with government work seldom have the necessary qualifications to develop and design commercial products in a highly competitive market-oriented economy.

The United States aircraft industry sells commercial aircraft, and some aerospace companies have developed new markets via corporate acquisitions. Almost without exception, however, no predominantly space-or defense-oriented company has successfully developed and marketed new commercial or consumer products on a substantial scale. The management and marketing capabilities for successful government contract work are not suitable for use in the highly competitive civilian economy.

There is no doubt that a vast amount of advanced technology evolves from our large defense and space programs. The technological gap, insofar as this relates to the civilian sector, assumes that so-called spin-off will occur automatically from these federally funded activities. In fact, many misconceptions exist regarding this process of technology transfer. The dissemination of patents and technical data does not in itself implement the innovation process. The receipt of a thousand technical reports dealing with science and technology by a person incapable of their ·appraisal, interpretation or commercial application accomplishes nothing.

New ideas are implemented by a "people transfer process." Technical people do move from space programs into new commercial enterprises. In this new environment the experience and background of the individual can be applied to the solution of specific problems and the attainment of commercial objectives. People in the civilian sector of the economy also may find technology within the space and defense programs that can assist in the solution of their problems. The impetus for the use of new technology must be generated by identifiable need or the requirements of a mission-oriented program. It is very seldom that a new development in government-sponsored research will find a ready path to the market place unless some enthusiastic individual serves as a coupling mechanism for the process of technology transfer. This individual may be an entrepreneur employed by a small or large company or a government contractor who sees a commercial application for some new piece of space technology and wants to do something about it.

It is people, and highly skilled, motivated people, who must take ideas arising from science and technology and move them through development and manufacturing into the market place. Without competent people operating in the proper environment with high mobility, technology transfer will not take place effectively in any city, region or country.

Certain programs involving the application of new technology on a large scale obviously can be undertaken only by a large, highly industrialized country with adequate scientific, engineering, production, and management talent. For instance, in the area of computers, or in the development of a supersonic transport, there is in reality a technological gap. This calls for the effective allocation of total technical resources and scientific, engineering, and management personnel within a country. Nations should develop plans and programs for economic growth in the same sense that corporate plans are developed by progressive business enterprises on the basis of available assets and objectives. Unfortunately, such factors as emotion, politics, and national prestige dominate the development programs of many countries. Several illustrations come to mind.

The Soviet Union and the United States are both committed to a gigantic space program, a large portion of which has little military or civilian justification. Nearly ten years ago four significant uses for space were clearly identified: communications, weather, reconnaissance, and navigation. No new, economically justifiable applications have evolved, outside of science for its own sake. The often quoted concept that new products evolving from our space program justify the expenditure is an interesting argument. If in fact the current NASA funding of five billion dollars per year were considered "research" in the industrial sense, this might suggest a corresponding sales volume of some 150 billion dollars of products per year. This assumes a 30:1 ratio of gross sales to R&D, a ratio that is common for a technical commercial enterprise. The 150 billion dollar figure is based on some unreasonable assumptions, because a relatively small portion of the NASA budget is in the area of pure product development or research. Nevertheless, it is clear that the space program cannot be justified in terms of resulting commercial products.

The French and British are committed to the Concorde on the basis of national image rather than a technical, economic evaluation of its operation in competition with other planes that will be available during its period of operation. France, India, and Israel have all elected to devote substantial technical resources to the field of atomic energy. This may be sound national policy, but it should be implemented with better recognition of the impact of such activities on the economic growth and the standards of living of countries with limited resources.

One final misconception relative to the technological gap is that all foreign enterprises operate at a disadvantage in technical areas. This is certainly not the case. The business records of such technically based companies as Philips in Holland, Imperial Chemical Industries in England, and Volkswagen, as well as chemical and steel organizations in Germany, confirm the ability of well-managed foreign organizations to compete against the United States. Both Sony and Honda in Japan prove that individual entrepreneurs can launch new enterprises and, by innovative procedures in the use of science, technology, management techniques, and marketing, invade the United States with competitive products. As a matter of fact, these two Japanese companies demonstrate selling methods more ingenious than famed Madison Avenue itself. In shipbuilding Japan has assumed a position of world domination, not because of its reputedly cheap labor but because of innovative management and production methods. No other country in the world, including Britain, had the initiative or ability to adopt such techniques.

In summary, the tremendous level of federal funding of U.S. expenditures for R&D is not in itself responsible for the rapid applications of advanced technology in the civilian sector of our economy. The use of government-sponsored technical programs as a mechanism to promote economic growth depends upon a more complex process than is generally recognized and the effectiveness of so-called spin-off is probably greatly overemphasized. Although it is doubtless true that the United States has an advantage because of size, resources, and markets which do contribute to a technological gap, these facts do not automatically insure over-all civilian benefits from large federal R&D programs. While the U.S. is investing vast sums in defense and space, a great majority of the science and technology evolving from these activities is generally available at no charge on a worldwide basis. Thus it would seem that if there is some gap between the U.S. and Europe to which Europeans should direct their attention, it is not the *technological gap*, but rather a *management gap*. In fact, even within the U.S. itself there exist wide variations in management capabilities. Many companies, due to lack of initiative or innovative methods, find it increasingly difficult to compete with more enlightened corporations willing to utilize new technology for competitive purposes.

The Technology Gap and the Brain Drain: III

The paper by the University of Chicago's Harry G. Johnson first appeared in Minerva *in 1965. It is concerned particularly with the case of Canada.*

LET US FOCUS ATTENTION on the migration of educated and professionally trained people, the category of international migration to which the concept of "brain drain" refers. To bring out the issues that concern those who have expressed alarm about "brain drain," let us consider an extreme case, in which a large proportion of a region's or a country's trained young people continuously emigrates; this case has been exemplified over a long period by Scotland, certain countries in Southern Europe, and within Canada, by the maritime provinces.

Such a case of continuous emigration is the consequence of the poverty of the region in natural resources, or in locational advantages for high-income lines of productive activity. From the standpoint of the emigrant young people, migration is their means of escape from the local poverty. From the standpoint of the individuals, their parents, and their community, education is often the only way in which the opportunity for such escape can be provided. This is frequently recognised explicitly, especially in the regions of long-term emigration; but often those who live in such a region regard the outflow of trained people as a loss to the region.

The emigrants obviously do not lose; by migrating they gain. To the extent that the presence of trained people gives rise to unpaid-for benefits of some kind to the other people among whom they live, their migration merely transfers these benefits to another location but does not destroy them. Any loss there may be, therefore, must be a loss incurred by the remaining residents of the region. In what sense, if any, can there be such a loss?

There is one directly obvious way in which the residents of a region may lose by the emigration of trained people. If education is financed wholly or partly by general taxation of the resident population, every emigrant takes with him a gift—in the form of the education he has received—from the place he leaves to the place he goes to. To put the point another way, the region of immigration gets the right to tax the high income made possible by an educational investment it has not paid for, while the region of emigration loses the opportunity to recoup by taxation the cost of the educational investment it has made. This loss is a consequence of two special features of our social arrangements governing educated labour—the free or subsidised provision of education and the freedom in deciding the type of education and what use to make of it that is allowed the individual student. It could be prevented in a variety of ways: by providing education free only when the individual so educated will remain in the region, by requiring that individuals oblige themselves to repay their education costs to the community out of future income, or by obliging the migrating individual, or the country or region to which he emigrates, to pay over to the region of origin a capital sum or income stream equal to the cost of his education or the loss of tax revenue his emigration occasions.

This kind of loss, however, is not the type of loss that excites the most discussion, except possibly among economists. Moreover, there may be little or no real loss involved. For one thing, a region of emigration may be quite happy—or might be quite happy if it thought the matter through—to incur the costs of free or subsidised education of its youth, precisely because education provides the opportunity for its youth to emigrate and so escape the poverty of its parents. For another, the loss may be recompensed in part or wholly by compensating gains. These may range from such obvious and calculable compensations as emigrants' remittances, which play an important part in the balance of payments of some countries, to such intangibles as the political benefits from having native sons in positions of influence on the national scene or in large neighbouring countries, or the region's own share in the benefits of the contribution the emigrants may make to general world progress in science, technology, and the arts, contributions which they could not have made had they not left their native region.

The usual arguments about the loss from emigration of skilled people see that loss instead in the mere fact that the emigrants are not present in the local economy and society; and, this alleged loss raises some complex questions. To discuss these, it is necessary to distinguish between the services rendered by trained people that are sold in the market and any benefits conferred automatically on others by the mere presence of educated people among them.

So far as the marketable services are concerned, the allegation of loss is implicitly a complaint that these services are not available cheap to the residents of the region of emigration, instead of being sold dear to the residents of the region of immigration. This must be so—at least for opportunity-motivated migration—because if the services could be sold at a higher price in the region of emigration, emigration would not be advantageous to the emigrants. Thus the loss to the residents of the region of emigration is precisely the gain to the emigrants from emigrating; and the allegation that the region incurs a loss from emigration is implicitly an assertion that the gains to the emigrants from emigration should not be counted as a gain to the region. To put this point another way, the claim that there is a loss of trained people from emigration implicitly asserts that people born and brought up in a region should stay in the region no matter how little they are paid for doing so and no matter how much they could earn elsewhere. This is, of course, the ultimate in nationalism. And it makes no difference to the argument whether it is asserted that the emigrants ought not to emigrate, i.e., that people who could raise their incomes by emigrating ought to sacrifice the potential increases in their incomes to benefit those who cannot gain by emigrating, or that those who cannot gain by emigrating should bribe those who can gain by emigrating not to emigrate by paying them more. In either case, the fundamental assertion is that someone should incur a sacrifice of income he would otherwise enjoy in order to prevent a loss of population from a particular geographical territory.

Furthrmore, it is not true that the services of emigrants are not available to a region if they are needed to the extent that the region is prepared to pay the market price for them. On the contrary, given the cheapness of modern transportation and the international mobility of professional people, these services are available when demanded. Also, they are probably available more cheaply on this basis than they would be if provided on a permanent residential basis; for emigration means that the region to which the migrants go bears the normal overhead or support costs of maintaining the stock of professional people. In the words of the old adage. "Why keep a cow when you can buy milk by the bottle?" Several recent Canadian royal commissions dealing with economic problems have been staffed, and ably staffed, by Canadian economists normally teaching in and supported by American universities.

With respect to the non-marketed benefits that accrue simply from the presence of educated people, it is necessary, to begin with, to call attention to two common fallacies in the contention that "brain drain" involves serious losses. The first is the tendency to argue as if the problem is one of all or nothing and to ignore the fact that some proportion of its educated professional talent does stay in the region of origin.[1] The second fallacy stems from the tendency to look only at the most conspicuously successful of the emigrants, in assessing the loss from "brain drain." The vast bulk of emigrants are ordinary people, just like the ones who stay behind; and in some cases the region of origin is lucky to be rid of them. In fact, many Canadians in American academic life are there precisely because no Canadian university has considered them as good as the people it already has.

The nature of the non-marketed benefits from the presence of educated people—more accurately, of more educated people than would be retained by natural market forces—is of course difficult to define precisely because they are not marketed. In the analysis of these matters, it is helpful to distinguish between con-

---

1. If I may permit myself a personal reference, I am frequently embarrassed by being held up as an example of "brain drain," when I know perfectly well that at least a half-dozen Canadian resident economists could present my subject with equal knowledge, perception, and style. In fact, one of the main services I perform free for my fellow Canadians, from the University of Chicago, is to call their attention to resident economic talent they do not know they possess.

sumption and investment benefits—that is, between benefits that take the form of an increase in the current welfare or satisfaction of the region or country and benefits that take the form of an increase in the future level of its production or satisfaction above what it would otherwise be. To make this distinction concrete, consider two contemporary arguments for supporting more scientific research. The consumption argument is that a great nation ought to be in the forefront of the pursuit of knowledge for its own sake; the benefit here is prestige, which has to be bought by sacrificing economic resources to support the researchers. The investment argument is that scientific research repays the society in future increases in productivity and real income: the benefit here is increased future well-being, to be bought by investing in the support of research. The non-marketed benefits alleged to follow from the presence of educated professional people, and to be lost by their emigration, can similarly be divided into those that stress the contribution of such people to the quality of cultural life and those that stress the contribution of such people to future income and growth.

So far as the consumption benefits are concerned, the following may be said: if you believe that a larger proportion of professional people makes for a better society, you are welcome to spend your money on supporting them. It should be pointed out, however, that such arguments are usually asserted most vigorously by professional people themselves and that, whether the alleged benefits are real or not, the consequences of accepting the arguments are very much to the private benefit of these people and to the private cost of the rest of the community. One of the things that impresses me most about the contemporary Canadian scene is the extent to which professional people, especially in the communications industries and the universities, have been able to exploit nationalistic feelings for their own economic advantage.

The investment arguments, however, are the ones that receive the most weight, especially among the professional people themselves; they have become extremely popular in recent years, to the point where education, research, innovation, etc., have become panaceas for all kinds of economic and social ills. Few if any of these arguments have been substantiated; little effort has been made to prove that such investments yield a reasonable profit after allowing fully for costs. Nor do we have any validated procedures for determining how much money should be spent, and in what ways, on this kind of investment.

To return to the problem of "brain drain," the question is, how significant are the benefits of these two types lost through emigration of professional people? In the nature of the case, the question is really unanswerable—though there are any number of volunteers prepared to assert that they are incalculably large. Here I would merely point to some of the fallacies involved in the common assumption that emigration of educated professional people means a loss of these non-marketed benefits to the country. First, many of the benefits of both types are such as to accrue to the world in general, regardless of where the individual lives— this is certainly true of great writing and of basic scientific research—and in those cases, emigration means that the foreigner bears the costs and risks of providing the non-marketed benefits for everyone. I would guess that Canada gets a substantial flow of non-marketed benefits from the writings and research of Canadians resident in other countries, notably the United States and the United Kingdom. Secondly, and of considerable importance, many of the non-marketed benefits conferred by emigrants on the region of immigration are conditional on the fact of their migration and would not be enjoyed by the region of emigration if the people in question did not emigrate. As already mentioned, new ideas and new discoveries are frequently generated by the confrontation of an individual with a new and different culture. Also, and this is particularly true of modern scientific research, accomplishment may depend on the availability of finance for a long period of training and the purchase of extremely expensive research equipment, facilities that can only be provided in a large and wealthy country that can afford this degree of specialisation. Thirdly, emigration of trained professional people confers certain non-marketed benefits on the residents of the region of emigration. For example, the emigrants carry with them a knowledge and understanding of the characteristics and problems of their region of origin that they diffuse in their new environment, which diffusion may lead to favourable effects on the policies adopted towards their region; I have no doubt that both

United States and United Kingdom policies towards Canada have been influenced in this way. Also, emigrants are often prompted to think seriously, or re-think, about their country's problems; and in so doing, they have the advantages of non-involvement, detachment and, especially, of independence.

Before leaving the general economics of "brain drain," I should mention one aspect of the activities of professional people that is sometimes brought into the argument—the possibility of what economists call "economies of scale" in these activities. The notion here is that the presence of a larger total number of professional people will have the effect of raising the average quality of such people, or of their work, through such routes as increased stimulus and competition and greater specialisation and division of labour. This is a non-marketed benefit of a different type from those previously discussed, since it rests on increased efficiency due to larger numbers rather than on the larger numbers themselves, and would be additional to the others. As applied in the context of an alleged loss from "brain drain," the argument of scale economies must assert that "brain drain" makes a significant difference to the size of the professional portion of the population; that this size difference makes a significance difference to the quality of its performance; and that the benefits to the country from this improvement are not outweighed by any losses from the reduction in the scale of professional activity elsewhere that would result from less emigration. These assertions may seem plausible if one looks only at the comparison between the United States and Canada and neglects to make adequate allowance for the tenfold difference in population and thirteenfold difference in national income between the two, instead of comparing Canada with countries of more nearly similar size. But my own judgment is that there is probably very little, if anything, in this argument, if it is confined as it should be to changes in scale within the realm of reason.

The Allocation of Research and Development Resources: Some Problems of Public Policy

Richard R. Nelson is an economist at the RAND Corporation. This paper first appeared in Economics of Research and Development, *published in 1965.*

ONE OF THE MAJOR CONTRIBUTIONS that economic analysis can make in the discussion of science policy is to point out that there is an allocation problem; allocation makes a difference. Often the discussion of the need for more R&D funds for one purpose or another tends to ignore that the human and material resources which comprise our scientific and technical capability are scarce and valuable. Less than one and a half million scientists and engineers carry the major burden of the application and advancement of science and technology. The supply of these resources is not very elastic in the short run. If they are utilized in one job, they cannot be used in another.

Only about one-third of the working time of the scientists and engineers of the United States is spent in R&D. Two-thirds is spent in teaching, management, operations, and other functions. There are some important and complicated problems of public policy involved in the allocation of scientists and engineers among these functions. There is the closely connected, and extremely important, set of problems relating to how to increase the supply of scientists and engineers. But in this paper the concern will be predominantly with the allocation within the research and development function.

The fact that there is a real problem of choice has been somewhat blurred by over-reaction to the fact that the benefits from R&D often diffuse far beyond the area of intended application. It is true that the areas of potential practical application of the results of a basic research project are uncertain, that research on plastics can lead to better paints, and that the civilian economy sometimes can make considerable advantage of the by-products of military or space R&D. This fact is extremely important and its implications will be considered later. But certain kinds of R&D are not all that uncertain, and obviously the particular R&D projects to which the talents of scientists and engineers are applied most certainly influence the type of payoffs society can expect from their work. If R&D is aimed at creating information needed to build a better rocket engine, it is likely to do just that and precious little else.

Perhaps the best evidence that the allocation of R&D resources really matters is provided by the Minasian[1] and Terleckyj[2] studies. The Minasian study found that, within an industry, there was a significant correlation (.70) between R&D spending by a firm and subsequent productivity growth.

The Terleckyj study found that between industries there was a significant correlation (.62) between R&D spending (and scientists and engineers employed) by the industry and its productivity growth. The correlations are not spectacularly high, but they are significant. While the historical record is clear that many of the most important technical advances affecting the productivity of an industry originate from research done in other industries, or in universities, or in government laboratories, or by individuals working alone, apparently where the research is done (a good indication of what practical problems the research is designed to illuminate) does matter.

It is interesting that much of the discussion of the likely economic impact of our defense and space R&D efforts has tended to ignore that the allocation of R&D resources among sectors and industries strongly affects the sectoral composition of technological progress. There seems to be a widespread belief that the rapid growth of space and defense R&D will revolutionize the civilian economy. Actually, if their allocation effects are considered, it would seem likely that our military and space R&D pro-

1. J. Minasian, "The Economics of Research and Development," in National Bureau of Economic Research, *Rate and Direction of Inventive Activity* (Princeton, N. J., 1962).

2. N. Terleckyj, "Sources of Productivity Growth" (Unpublished Ph.D. thesis, Princeton University, 1961), cited in J. Kendrick, *Productivity Trends in the U.S.*

grams may be holding down the pace of technological advance in the civilian economy.

While between 1954 and 1961 total R&D spending tripled, the rate of growth of R&D financed by the DOD, AEC, and NASA was almost twice the rate of growth of other R&D. In industry, the number of total R&D scientists and engineers financed by government agencies (over 95 per cent by DOD, AEC, and NASA) increased from 36 per cent to 55 per cent of the total. While the number of total scientists and engineers engaged in R&D in industry grew at approximately a 10 per cent annual rate, the number financed by private industry out of their own funds and, presumably, involved principally on civilian programs grew at only one-third that rate.[3]

The limited data suggest that, in small part at least, the very rapid growth of demand for scientists and engineers for defense and space R&D was met by a more rapidly growing supply.[4] However, a large share of the increase in scientists and engineers in defense and space R&D was achieved through the bidding away of talent from civilian industry. Between 1957 and 1960, beginning salaries of engineers increased 19 per cent. There is considerable feeling among R&D laboratory directors that defense and space companies are snapping up the lion's share of the really good graduates. If anything, the market should get tighter over the next few years. The projected increase in space R&D alone is likely to absorb one-third to one-half of the expected increase in the number of available scientists and engineers.

The Terleckyj study suggests that R&D performed to advance the nation's space and defense programs contributes far less to the advance of productivity in civilian industry than R&D concerned more directly with civilian problems. Further, the bulk of military R&D is not of the sort we would expect to generate

3. These figures are obtained by assuming that if the government finances x per cent of the R&D done in an industry, x per cent of the scientists and engineers are working on the government's problems. There are many difficulties with this assumption, but it is not clear whether it is an overestimate or an underestimate. The data are from the National Science Foundation.

4. For example, between 1954 and 1960 the number of college degrees in engineering, mathematics, and physical science increased from 13 per cent to 17 per cent of the total.

knowledge of much relevance to civilian problems.

The degree of general purpose relevance of the results of R&D tends to be relatively great toward the basic research and technical experimentation end of the R&D spectrum. Toward the applied research and product development end of the spectrum, the results of R&D tend to be principally of relevance to the particular problems and hardware configurations which are the focus of the work. Of the DOD's total R&D budget, almost 90 per cent is for hardware development, less than 5 per cent for basic research. With NASA and the AEC the percentage of development expenditures to total R&D expenditure is significantly smaller, but for the three agencies taken together, more than 75 per cent of their total R&D spending was aimed at creating information relevant to a specific end item, and probably created very little knowledge of general purpose to the economy as a whole.

The civilian economy does gain some by-product advantage from the research and development financed by the DOD and NASA. But military and space research and development increasingly are exploring areas far away from those of clear relevance to the civilian economy. While it is very difficult to measure the degree of civilian relevance of defense R&D programs, clearly research on mildew resistant fabrics for military use in the tropics is much more likely to have obvious civilian applications than research on nose cones. A very large percentage of the civilian applications of military R&D listed in the Operations Research Office study [5] are of the "mildew resistant cloth" type, and this type of research probably is a much smaller percentage of military R&D today than before the missile age.

However, while direct product adaptation is not likely to be particularly important, the long-range benefits to the civilian economy from some of the sophisticated defense and space R&D programs may turn out to be substantial. Whole new technologies, of great potential civilian utility, are being opened. However, the translation to civilian uses will not be easy. Considerable further R&D will be needed. Yet the military and space programs are drawing away the lion's share of the people who are capable of doing the work of adapting the new technologies to civilian use.

5. Striner, Sherman, and Karadbil, *Defense Spending and the American Economy* (Washington, D.C., 1959).

The purpose of the preceding discussion was not to argue that we are spending too much on defense and space R&D. We may be spending too much or we may be spending too little. Nor is this to argue that our defense R&D programs are hindering economic growth by drawing R&D resources away from the civilian economy. By creating the knowledge which enables the capital and labor engaged in defense work to meet defense needs more effectively, defense R&D contributes to increased productivity in defense industries.[6] This has permitted a given quantity of resources engaged in defense work to produce a greater defense capability, and has reduced the quantity of resources needed to produce a given level of defense capability. Obviously, technical change in the defense industries has contributed to economic growth. But it is clear that to the extent more R&D resources applied to the civilian sector would have contributed to the creation of better products and processes, the opportunity costs of defense and space R&D probably are lower productivity, higher costs, and poorer products in the civilian sector. Allocation has made a difference.

SOCIAL CRITERIA FOR R&D ALLOCATION

Economic analysis also can contribute to an evaluation of R&D allocation by suggesting what are the relevant criteria. An optimal allocation in terms of economic analysis means an allocation such that resources cannot be transferred from one use to another in such a way as to increase welfare. Economic analysis must point out that some R&D (or a considerable amount of R&D) going on in a particular area is not sufficient evidence that enough is going on. The relevant question is: Are the marginal returns from increasing R&D in that area greater or smaller than the marginal returns from the R&D resources in other uses?

In order to deal with this question at all effectively, there must be a relatively clear understanding of the types of returns that society can expect from R&D.

The output of R&D is information; information as to what results when certain chemical compounds are mixed together; in-

6. That growth measured in terms of the gross national product does not account this "productivity" improvement adequately is another matter.

formation that a virus causes a certain disease; information that a particular theoretical model explains quite well the properties of metals; information as to the properties of a particular metal at high temperatures; information whether or not a metal will fail when used for a particular engine part under specified laboratory conditions; information that a particular engine design will work.

Research and development has economic value because the information it creates permits people to do things better, and sometimes to do things that they did not know how to do before. Put another way, the information created by R&D expands the perceived·choice set and enables better informed choices to be made within the set. The information created by R&D throws light on the most fruitful next series of researches in a certain field of chemistry, or whether or not it is worthwhile to try to find a vaccine to prevent a particular disease, whether or not a particular engine should be designed and what metal should be used for a part, whether or not to produce the engine for practical use.

There is no simple way to evaluate the benefits society can expect from the knowledge created by different kinds of R&D aimed at illuminating different kinds of problems and questions. The importance of the added national prestige we may obtain if we allocate more R&D resources to finding out how to get to the moon, the value of obtaining better information on the causes of cancer, and the value of obtaining information which will permit the development of a silent home air conditioner somehow must be compared.

Often it is possible to translate the value of the likely fruits of new information into dollar terms, as when there is a good market for the product involved, or where there are alternative (non-R&D) ways to achieve the objective which would be taken if the R&D project were not undertaken. The economist should stress that, where possible and relevant, these dollar value comparisons should be made. But he must also point out that for some of the kinds of benefits new knowledge can yield, the market is very thin and imperfect.

Yet the fact that the market is thin and imperfect, and that therefore it is difficult to attach a dollar value to the information created by a particular research and development project, is no reason for assigning it a low value. It is extremely difficult to place a dollar value on a successful cure for cancer. Surely the total value would dwarf any measurable contribution to economic product resulting from the increased size and vigor of the work force. It would reflect a distressing confusion of means with ends if basic scientific research had to be justified solely in terms of future economic product. Surely we want a stronger economy in part because then we will have greater room for undertaking cultural pursuits, of which basic research is one.

Returning to the question of whether or not we are allocating too large a quantity of our R&D resources to defense, clearly it is impossible to place a dollar value on the additional defense capability a particular defense R&D project is likely to yield. Economic calculations, however, are applicable to choices among alternative military R&D projects which are likely to have the same effect on defense capability. And economic calculations are applicable to decisions as to whether to increase defense capabilities by R&D or by spending more on existing weapons systems (developing Minuteman rather than building more Atlas missiles). Indeed, economic analysis might suggest that to the extent R&D resources are underprices on the civilian market relative to the values they produce, a military R&D project must be significantly less costly than the non-R&D alternative which can do the same job before it is socially desirable to choose the military R&D alternative.[7] However, the market can provide very little guidance with respect to the level of military security we should strive for.

While it often is extremely difficult to do so, the attempt to measure and compare the gains to society from better understanding, better information, of the sort which is likely to result from R&D is the proper approach to making R&D allocation judgments. Essentially, R&D must be evaluated in terms of the kind of information it is likely to produce, the increased ability to solve certain problems or make certain decisions which will result from that information, and the value to society of solving the problem or making the decision better. If we focus on R&D likely

7. This assumes, of course, that the external economies from civilian R&D are likely to exceed the external economies from military R&D. To the extent that the military R&D project is aimed at a particular weapon system far removed from civilian analysis, this is likely to be the case.

to lead to technological progress (to more efficient production techniques and better products), we must ask the questions: Where is R&D most likely to lead to technological advance and where are technological advances likely to be of most value to society in terms of resources saved or wants better met.[8]

THE MECHANISM OF ALLOCATION—PUBLIC POLICY AND THE MARKET

What are the mechanisms which guide the allocation of R&D resources? How can these mechanisms be controlled so that they will allocate R&D resources to the areas where the social returns are greatest? These are questions on which economic analysis can shed some light.

In the United States we have established a reasonably well-working division of labor and responsibility between public and private agencies, between agencies whose goals are the general welfare and organizations whose goals are those of the controlling individuals.

In general, the federal government must take direct responsibility for seeing to it that for these areas of our political economy where it has major decision-making responsibilities, the investment in R&D is of adequate size and quality, given the returns and the costs. While defense, space, and the development of atomic energy dwarf quantitatively the other governmental R&D programs which are conducted' out of a responsibility to manage

8. As a footnote, it might be added that solving the unemployment problem of sick industries is not a proper criterion. The reasons are obvious. And the data confirm the theory. While R&D growth and productivity growth are related (as Terleckyj's data show), and the productivity growth and output growth are highly correlated, there is little relation between productivity growth and employment growth. (Another way of saying this is that the elasticity of demand is, on the average, equal to one.) If we eliminate the Korean and post-Korean years where the correlation between defense employment (which increased substantially) and R&D spending in the defense industries results in an extremely misleading correlation between R&D and employment growth, Kendrick's data show that productivity advance in an industry and employment increase in that industry have only a very low positive correlation. For the 1899 to 1953 period, the coefficient of correlation was only +.32. However, rapid growth of output and declining relative price of an industry's product were quite strongly related to rapid productivity growth. The coefficients of correlation are +.69 and −.87, respectively.

efficiently a "public function," there are many other areas as well. The government has major responsibility for research to improve weather forecasting, public health, public roads, schools, hospitals, and other urban facilities, to name just a few. This does not mean that the government must do all of the work in its own facilities or that it must finance all, or any, of the work. But since public agencies have direct responsibility for managing these areas of our political economy efficiently, they have an implied responsibility for seeing that the appropriate R&D is done, in one way or another.

In addition, fundamental scientific knowledge itself can, and should, be considered a public good; for the total benefits which accrue from a fundamental advance in knowledge far exceed those which can be traded on a free market. In recent years, the federal government has acted to sponsor basic research generally and has established major programs in certain key areas, such as peacetime atomic energy and space technology, on the grounds that the advances which might result would be very important and sufficiently widespread in their impact to be treated as public goods.[9]

These are the traditional areas of governmental responsibility for R&D: R&D relevant to the public sector, and fundamental research. For research and development aimed at advancing technology in the private sector, the United States has, with limited exceptions, relied on the workings of the market.

However, both the character of the research and development activity and of the commodity it produces—information—tend to make the market work imperfectly. Since it often is difficult to know, in advance, just what practical problems the information generated by a particular R&D project will shed light on, and since the range of illuminated practical problems may be extremely wide, an organization with a relatively narrow range of interests may be able to use, itself, only a fraction of the potential value from the information created by the R&D it sponsors. Since information is a very difficult commodity for which to establish property rights, many organizations other than the one which sponsors the R&D may be able to benefit, without compensating

9. For a discussion of these points, see R. Nelson, "The Simple Economics of Basic Scientific Research," *Journal of Political Economy* (1959).

the organization which paid for the work.

These characteristics—uncertainty, widespread potential use, and inappropriability—usually are not particularly serious for R&D on product improvement and new product development. A business firm, feeling the needs of the economy as expressed through the market and stimulated to meet these needs by the lure of profit and the spur of competition, can engage in this kind of R&D reasonably sure that, if successful, it will be well rewarded. The information created by this type of work is likely to be directly relevant to the firm's problems. The firm is likely to be able to make private property of the information through a suitably written patent. And this patent is quite likely to enable the firm to share in any economic benefits created by the information for activities outside the range of the firm's market interests.

However, there are good reasons to believe that market incentives tend to cause business firms to spend much less than is socially desirable on research and experimental development exploring advanced concepts and designs. This work is risky—in most cases the information created will not be sufficient in itself to permit the design of a marketable product or process but rather will suggest additional R&D, or may prove a blind alley. In all save the largest and most secure firms, the time horizons are too short and the possibilities of spreading the risk too limited to give a firm strong incentives to do much of this kind of work. But society's interests are very long run, and for society as a whole risks are spread over a very large number of projects. This difficulty is compounded by the tendency of many (though certainly not all) business firms to think in terms of their existing product line instead of the functions these products serve, woven cloth instead of clothing materials, brick instead of building materials. Thinking in terms of limited market horizons is not necessarily irrational. Often it is a very rational reaction to the facts that the firm has technological competence, market experience, and organization in certain fields and not in others, and that the costs of learning to deal with new technologies and invading new markets may be considerable. Thus there is a bias toward marginally improving old ways rather than experimenting with radically new ways of meeting needs. Yet society scarcely has a vested interest in existing product lines and ways of satisfying needs. The very rapid development of military technology, where the incentives have caused us to devote a considerable effort toward developing and testing new concepts and designs, suggests that the returns might be very great if there were considerably more R&D aimed at creating and testing prototypes of radically new civilian products and processes.

Our enterprise system also tends to fail badly in situations where one company takes the risks and covers the costs but many companies share widely in the benefits. The whole areas of process improvements not subject to patenting (a major source of productivity growth), of testing and evaluation techniques, and of analysis of materials and methods are cases in point. Research on standards, and user safety, also is unlikely to yield a private firm profits commensurate with the benefits to society.

Another problem area is R&D which cuts across the market interests of firms and industries. For example, the analysis and development of integrated production systems is not easily forthcoming where there is no equipment supplier who produces a full range of equipment for a particular production sequence. This problem, as well as those discussed above, is likely to be particularly serious in industries comprised principally of small firms. Small firms often find too little use for highly trained engineers to hire them and often are unable to attract and hold them even when an effort is made. They thereby tend to be cut off from keeping up with the innovations of others as well as from innovating themselves.

These problems of allocation of research and development resources resulting from the properties of the R&D process and of the commodity produced (information) have as their counterpart some serious problems with respect to the dissemination of information. Not only is it true that often the information created by research and development in one organization is of significant value primarily to another organization, but often the two organizations, one which has the information and the other which can use it, are not aware of this fact.

It is clear that many business firms have far less than full information as to the technological possibilities open to them.[10] This

10. While the technical information services in the United States, public and private, have expanded tremendously in recent years, so has the pro-

problem is not so serious for technical information which is clothed in an industrial product, a machine, a material. The companies which produce the product or machine have a strong incentive to advertise the new development; for, in a very real sense, they have been able to make private property out of the information their R&D has created, and thus are able to sell that property on the market.

But for new information which is not so embodied in a product, the market generates very little incentive for dissemination of that information. As Kenneth Arrow has pointed out,[11] the value of information is not known to the potential purchaser until he knows what the information is, but then he has, in effect, acquired it (or a significant part of it) without cost. The producer of the information loses his control of the information the minute he transmits it. Often the alternative to ability to make private property of information is industrial secrecy. Further, even when the information is readily available in the scientific or technical literature, a firm without a strong technical staff often is unable to understand or use the information.

Thus the same problems which suggest that the federal government should take an active role in support of certain kinds of R&D also suggest that the federal government should take an active role in the dissemination of the information that R&D creates.

SOME GENERAL CONCLUSIONS ON NEEDED CHANGES

As long as our research and development resources are limited, we never shall be able to do all the things it would be nice to do.

---

duction of new technical and scientific information. Further, the problem of classifying new scientific and technical information in a form convenient for the many and diverse potential benefiters has intensified as a growing share of R&D of possible benefit to the commercial sector of the economy is performed in connection with defense, the AEC, and under NASA contracts with firms with little interest in civilian markets. At present we have only begun to experiment with policies and institutions designed to evaluate results of defense and space research for their civilian applicability, and the task of providing potential users with the new information in an understandable form grows increasingly complex as the scientific component of technology increases.

11. See his "Welfare Economics and Inventive Activity" in National Bureau of Economic Research, *The Rate and Direction of Inventive Activity* (Princeton, N.J., 1962).

Over the long run, our total research and development capabilities will depend on the number of new scientists and engineers provided by an educational system. But over the shorter run, it is doubtful that public policy will be able to affect strongly, one way or another, the rate at which the supply of scientists and engineers is increasing. Thus, at the same time that we are proceeding with policy in the field of education, the shorter-run problem will be to encourage the most efficient and effective allocation of a given time path of supply.

We will have to face some very important decisions. We will not be able to increase very significantly the scientific and technical resources allocated to one area of technology without a parallel decision, explicit or implicit, not to advance another as rapidly as we might like. In particular, it should be noted—or better, stressed—that the decision to allocate a large and rapidly growing quantity of scientists and engineers to the NASA program seriously constrains the expansion we can achieve in the more mundane areas of civilian technology.

Focusing then on what appear to be desirable reallocations, there are several things that can be done to increase the value that society gains from its research and development resources:

First, aside from the fields of defense and space, it is likely that we are relying too much on the workings of private incentives as stimulated by the market to generate R&D relevant to the public sector. Very little is being spent, for example, on research to improve urban transportation systems, or educational technology. While it is not obvious that more research in these areas would yield considerable results, it is clear the the government is only beginning to look into the question carefully. But if the government does not take responsibility in these areas, no one else will. The Bureau of the Budget and the Federal Council for Science and Technology should, each year, be responsible for evaluating the quantity and quality of research going on that is of relevance to the needs of the public sector.

Second, the federal government has not as yet recognized adequately the role that it must play in helping to allocate private sector R&D effectively in those instances where the market does not work well. This does not mean that the federal government should get into the business of developing new products and processes for the civilian economy, save in very unusual circumstances in which private organizations are too small or weak to do a job (as in agriculture). But it does mean that the federal government should support, conduct, or provide special incentives for R&D of the sort which creates information of widespread use to industry but which cannot be readily traded on the market and for the expansion of the system which disseminates that information.

Federal activities in support of agricultural technology suggest a wide spectrum of policy possibilities.[12] The Department of Agriculture conducts some research in its own facilities and, through Hatch Act and other funds, supports research at the agricultural experimenting stations of colleges and universities. TVA has contributed to productivity growth in agriculture by research and development work in fertilizer, an industry which traditionally has not supported much R&D out of private funds. The federal-state cooperative extension service has acted to accelerate the diffusion of the results of research in a form particularly well suited to the needs of farming. The Department of Agriculture itself publishes considerable information. The Griliches [13] study of hybrid corn and other agricultural advances suggests that we, as a nation, have benefited greatly from this work.

The suggestion here is not that the federal government apply to industry exactly the programs in support of technology it has applied to the problem of agriculture. Rather, it is that there are many possible programs, and the agricultural programs provide some basis of relevant experience. The British experience in the government-aided industry research institutes provides another possible approach, the German technical and scientific institutes still another.

Obviously a developing program of support of research and technical information services for the civilian economy—both private and public sectors—should be pragmatic, experimental, and flexible so that we can learn as we go along. The type of relevant programs are likely to differ from sector to sector. However, the

12. For an excellent discussion see V. Ruttan, "Research on the Economics of Technological Change in Agriculture," *Journal of Farm Economics* (1960).

13. Z. Griliches, "Research Costs and Social Returns," *Journal of Political Economy* (1958).

experience with programs in support of civilian technology suggests that the programs should be defined broadly enough so as to avoid industry and product-line provincialism and political pressure and to attract scientists and engineers of varied backgrounds. At the same time, it is essential that there be good lines of communication with those who will utilize the results of research.

To the extent that R&D resources are underallocated to research concepts and designs, to process research not likely to lead to a patent, and to other work where the benefits diffuse widely, it is in the public interest that there be a reallocation in this direction. One possibility would be to provide government grants or contracts for work of this sort to the engineering experimentation stations of the universities or to other university-affiliated facilities doing research on problems of civilian technology.

A second, and complementary, possibility, would be to provide a tax credit, or matching dollars, for industry funds contributed to cooperative research associations or to other nonprofit research institutions (including universities). To assure that firms would not have incentive to finance under this arrangement product development work and other R&D that they would have done otherwise in their own facilities, all results would be published and any resulting patents available for nonexclusive licensing to any American business firm. Several of these institutions presently are doing outstanding work. But in many cases the research is mundane (particularly in the industry association), and in others the work is of little use to industry (particularly in the other nonprofits). The incentives provided by a tax credit or matching funds mechanism would provide these institutions with more funds and, by providing a strong interest for industry, help to orient the work toward real problems. However, to relieve the institutions from industry pressure to work on short-run problems, some other mechanisms, like government grants and contracts, are needed.

The recent appointment of an assistant secretary for science and technology at the Department of Commerce should provide a natural focus for a considerable extension of programs in support of civilian technology. A considerable portion of the budget for these programs could be contracted or granted to various nonprofit organizations. The success of these programs would depend on the imagination and competence which went into selecting the research areas and organizations. Experience suggests that a strengthening of the in-house R&D competence of the federal government is a prerequisite for obtaining this competence.

To provide a major part of the needed in-house competence, the National Bureau of Standards might significantly expand its role. A set of broadly oriented research groups might be associated with the Bureau, the mission of each group defined in terms of a broad functional area, like materials, transportation, and housing. The research objective of these groups would be to explore the technological problems and opportunities of its area including experimentation with radically new ways of doing things.

It is clear that effective and imaginative support of nongovernment research and the strengthening of in-house R&D competence are complementary objectives. The proper division of research between in-house and contract certainly would differ from case to case, and will have to be worked out through actual experience. The objectives of the overall program would be to generate information as to the technological possibilities open to industry by exploring the feasibility and technical problems of advanced concepts and designs and of ways to increase productivity. Development of new products from this information would remain the responsibility of private enterprise. The major question relating to the value of the program is: Will the quality and relevance of the work supplied by the program be greater than the quality and relevance of the work the same resources would have done in the laboratories of private companies? The analysis of the preceding section suggests that it indeed should have a higher marginal value. But this will not be the case unless the program is well conceived and managed, the nonprofit laboratories are competent and imaginative, and the information created by the research is relevant to industry, and industry is well informed of the research results.

As a complementary program in support of civilian technology, the Office of Technical Services (OTS) could develop a much more effective program. One of the recent proposals of the Department of Commerce is for a pilot program of support of engineering extension services at the engineering colleges. The objective of the program is the strengthening of the scientific and technical competence of management and supervisory personnel in small and medium-sized firms and to bring to their attention the technological possibilities open to them. At the local level the extension program would be complemented by an expanded program of applied research on technical problems of relevance to the industry of the state or region. The program would include both experimentation and demonstration under pilot-plant conditions at the experimentation stations or in cooperating firms.

The extension centers would be able to call on the OTS for studies and reports on problems which have general applicability or which they are unable to solve in their own facilities. OTS would contract for these reports with the organizations presently associated with OTS in the foreign-aid technical-information program. One of the major benefits of this program would be a feedback to the government of information as to the important technical problems facing American industry.

Of course, the Department of Commerce will not, and should not, have sole responsibility in the civilian technology area. The Departments of Health, Education, and Welfare, and Agriculture, the HHFA, and other government agencies clearly should continue to have prime responsibility within their own areas.

As the government's role in civilian research expands, there will be some difficult problems of coordination which the Bureau of the Budget and the Federal Council for Science and Technology will have to deal with.

Third, it is of major importance that the federal government, principally the Bureau of the Budget and the Office of Science and Technology, be more aware of, and concerned with, the effects of its actions on the allocation of R&D and the effects of changes in the allocation on the achievement of various national objectives. The federal government is, after all, a semi-monopolist in the field of R&D, supporting nearly 65 per cent of the total work done in this country.

In general, we economists should be delighted when a monopolist, be it a private firm or the government, does not behave as one. But in the case of R&D, there is reason to believe that the nation might be better off if the government acted more in awareness of its monopolistic position and of the fact that it takes real resources, not money, to perform R&D. Indeed, the federal government often behaves in the field of R&D as if the right hand knoweth not what the left is doing, with the results that it cannot plan effectively and that it has difficulty in carrying out its mission efficiently. There sometimes seems to be little awareness that a sharply increased NASA research budget will, for example, reduce the quantity of real R&D resources a given defense budget will hire by bidding up salaries of scientists and engineers.

Yet if this fact is not considered explicitly, defense R&D plans and the budgets which are supposed to implement them may not match. While considerable attention has been paid to the fact that the effectiveness, from the point of view of the nation, of defense R&D is dependent in part upon the competence of the small group of scientists and engineers within the federal establishment who are responsible for analyzing and monitoring the contract programs, only recently has there been clear awareness that the government's difficulty in hiring such people results, in large part, from bidding against itself.

It is not the "bidding against itself" aspect which should cause concern nor the resulting increase in salaries of scientists and engineers. Rather, it is the lack of awareness and resulting frustration of plans. In order to manage public sector R&D efficiently, the government must do a better job than it has up to now of assessing the impact of its R&D programs upon the total allocation of R&D resources.

The government must look at R&D allocation as a whole, private sector as well as public sector. Without arguing that the decision to invest so heavily in the moon race was a mistake, it can be said that there is strong evidence that the value of alternative uses for R&D resources, particularly private sector uses, was not considered. The development of effective policy with respect to the allocation of scientific and technical resources requires that natural and social scientists join in a continuing effort to appraise priorities based on economic need and technical promise against the existing allocation of resources.

Civilian Technology and Public Policy

Edwin Mansfield is Professor of Economics at the Wharton School, University of Pennsylvania. This piece is taken from his book, The Economics of Technological Change, *published in 1968.*

FEDERAL SUPPORT FOR RESEARCH AND DEVELOPMENT
IN TRANSPORTATION, HOUSING, AND POLLUTION CONTROL

THERE IS A WIDESPREAD FEELING that as a nation we are underinvesting in certain types of research and development. For example, Nelson has stated that ". . . aside from the fields of defense and space, peacetime atomic energy, and perhaps public health, it is likely that we are relying too much on private incentives as stimulated by the market to generate R and D relevant to the public sector . . . [Also], aside from the fields of defense and space, there probably is too little research and experimentation aimed at exploring radically new techniques and ways of meeting needs . . . Surely we can do better than to rely so heavily on 'spillover' from defense and space to open up the really new possibilities in materials, energy sources, etc." Three areas frequently cited as needing more research and development are transportation, housing, and pollution of air and water.

Transportation · Our cities suffer from congestion, commuting to work is often difficult and time consuming, the accident toll is considerable, and delays in terminals are high. According to the critics, new transportation technologies point toward the solution of many of these problems, but their potential benefits are not being realized because of unresolved organizational, administrative, and financial problems, because of the failure to take a more integrated look at transportation as a whole, and because the resources devoted to far reaching R and D in this area are meager.

Housing · There is a feeling in many quarters that the industry is backward technologically and that more advanced technologies should be explored in an effort to reduce housing costs. The impediments to the development and use of new techniques are numerous, the typical construction firm being too small to carry out its own R and D, and the industry being fragmented into various types of trades and subcontractors. Moreover, outmoded building codes bar many types of innovation, the codes being protected by various special interest groups and the fragmented character of local governments.

Air and Water Pollution · There is considerable public concern regarding increases in contamination. The growth of urban populations has concentrated the discharge of wastes into a small sector of the atmosphere and resulted in increased air pollution. A similar pollution of water resources has taken place. "We have been unbelievably irresponsible in contaminating our water resources to the point where we are now faced with a problem of limited supply . . . As our population density has increased, the natural cleansing ability of streams has been exceeded." To combat air and water pollution, the President's Science Advisory Committee and the National Commission on Automation have recommended that an enlarged research program be carried out.

Two things should be noted regarding the alleged deficiency in R and D expenditures in these areas: (1) One cannot make any estimate of the adequacy or inadequacy of R and D expenditures in a given field by looking simply at society's evaluation of the importance of the activity. In addition, one must consider the probability and cost of achieving a significant improvement in the activity through research and development. No matter how important a particular goal may be, if more research and development are unlikely to help us achieve it, there is no reason to increase our R and D expenditures in this area. (2) There is a feeling in some quarters that a lack of promising, well-developed research ideas and of receptivity to change in these areas is responsible for the low level of R and D spending. According to the President's Science Adviser, "what we lack in many of the civilian problem areas . . . is not a consensus on their importance. Rather, it is a lack of solid R and D program proposals . . . We cannot buy and create progress in a field which is not ready to progress." Also, there is a feeling that the need is for use of techniques already available, rather than for more R and D. For example, Capron "would place federally supported R and D fairly low on the list of things we need in the fields of urban housing and urban transportation . . . Our problems in these areas are much more institutional and organizational."

FEDERAL SUPPORT FOR CIVILIAN TECHNOLOGY

Transportation, housing, and pollution control are not the only areas considered to suffer from an underinvestment in research and development. According to the Council of Economic Advisers, "in a number of industries the amount of organized private research undertaken is insignificant, and the technology of many of these low-research industries has notably failed to keep pace with advances elsewhere in the economy." Freeman, Poignant, and Svennilson, in their OECD report, conclude that, "in spite of the great increase in research and development activity, there are good reasons for believing that in many cases this activity is still below the level desirable for efficient and sustained economic growth."

In 1963 the Department of Commerce proposed a Civilian Industrial Technology program to encourage and support additional R and D in industries that it regarded as lagging. It proposed that support be given to important industries, from the point of view of employment, foreign trade, etc., which have "limited or dispersed technological resources." Examples cited by the department included textiles, building and construction, machine tools and metal fabrication, lumber, foundries, and castings. The proposal met with little success on Capital Hill. Industrial groups opposed the bill because they feared that government sponsorship of industrial R and D could upset existing competitive relationships. More recently, Nelson, Peck, and Kalachek have suggested that a National Institute of Technology be established to provide grants for research and development aimed at placing the technology of various industries on a stronger scientific footing and to test the feasibility and attributes of advanced designs. In their view, work of this sort, which falls between basic research and product development, is likely to be in need of additional support. In cases where a broad-scale systems view is required but is deterred by the smallness of existing firms and the fragmentation of market interest, the institute would also support work through the middle and later stages of development.

Unfortunately there is little evidence to prove or deny that the areas in question suffer from an underinvestment in R and D. Since we cannot estimate the social returns from additional R and D of various sorts at all accurately, it is difficult to make a strong case one way or the other. The proponents of additional government support for nondefense technology rely heavily on the argument that R and D generates significant external economies and that, consequently, private initiative is unlikely to support work to the extent that is socially optimal. However, this argument only suggests that the government or some other organization not motivated by profit should support some R and D in these areas; it does not tell us whether such support (which exists in many of these areas) is currently too large or too small.

Under these circumstances, perhaps the most sensible strategy, both in connection with the proposed Institute of Technology and some of the other proposals discussed above, is to view the relevant policy issues in the context of the theory of sequential decision making under uncertainty. To the extent possible, programs designed to change the amount of R and D in particular parts of the public or private sectors should be begun on a small scale and organized so as to provide data regarding the returns from a larger program. On the basis of the data that result, a more informed judgment can be made regarding the desirability of increased—or in some cases, decreased—programs of federal support. A strategy of this sort has been suggested by Nelson, Peck, and Kalechek, as well as myself. If this approach is adopted, it is important that proper attention be given to devising methods by which the results of the small-scale program are to be measured. Without such measures, the sequential approach will obviously be of little use.

THE INDUSTRIAL EXTENSION SERVICE
AND PERFORMANCE-BASED FEDERAL PROCUREMENT

In 1965 the State Technical Services Act was passed by Congress. It authorizes for industry a program somewhat analogous to the agricultural extention service—universities and technical schools throughout the country distributing technological information to local firms and serving as economic planning centers for their areas. The program, under the direction of the Department of Commerce (which proposed a similar plan in its Civilian Industrial Technology program), was expected to include about thirty states in its first year. The major purpose of this industrial extension service is to increase the rate of diffusion of new technology. Some firms, particularly small ones, are slow to adopt new techniques because they are unable to comprehend and evaluate technical information. The industrial extension service provides demonstrations, short courses, and conferences, as well as referral to specialized consultants and experts. In this way, it hopes to narrow the gap between average and best practice.

The industrial extension service faces problems that were absent in the case of the agricultural extension service. Whereas the latter could deal with a relatively homogeneous group of clients, the former cannot; whereas it was possible in earlier days for an agricultural extension agent to be familiar with most relevant aspects of agricultural technology, it is impossible now for anyone to be familiar with most aspects of industrial technology; whereas individual farmers seldom view each other as competitors, in manufacturing one firm's gain in productivity and sales may be partly at the expense of another. In addition, it is more difficult in the case of the industrial extension service to delineate the set of appropriate clients. The firms that are most eager to use the service and those that are easiest to persuade to adopt new techniques are not necessarily those for whom the service can do the most good.

According to the provisions of the Technical Services Act, each state has considerable latitude in drawing up its own program. The effectiveness of a program will depend on how well it can identify fields and types of firms where there is a technical lag and on how well it can get its message across. It will also depend on the extent to which it becomes a passive reference service, rather than a more active force in promoting new technology, as well as on the costliness of providing information of the right sort to the firms in need of it—and in such a manner that they will be persuaded to use it. Within five years after the approval of the Act, a public committee appointed by the Secretary of Commerce, will evaluate the impact and significance of the program.

Turning to another proposal to stimulate the use of new technology, it has been suggested that performance criteria, which specify the desired end-result without limiting the design to existing products, be substituted where possible for product specifications in federal procurement. Performance criteria of this sort have the obvious advantage of stating directly what the customer wants. For example, rather than specifying the chemical composition of paint, the government might specify how long the paint should last. Proponents of performance-based federal procurement claim that it will free industry to innovate, limited only by the requirement that it perform certain specified functions, encourage cost reduction for the government; and encourage the government to serve as a pilot customer for technical innovations in areas where it represents a big enough market or a market sufficiently free from local restrictions, codes, etc. to make it worth industry's while to innovate. Respecting its role as a pilot customer, one important consideration is to stimulate state and local governments to apply new technologies by demonstrating their successful application in federal programs. There is a feeling in some quarters that the diffusion of new technology in state and local programs is unnecessarily impeded by the desire of local officials to buy locally, the influence of labor unions on building codes, lack of information by local officials, fragmentation of local government, and the tendency to look for "product" rather than "functional" needs.

In evaluating this proposal, it should be noted that federal procurement is an important factor in many civilian markets; for example, the federal government accounted in 1964 for almost 15 per cent of all building and construction and 7–9 per cent of the sales of fuel and lubricants, construction equipment, and photographic services. Performance criteria are already being devised in a number of nondefense areas, such as roofing materials and data processing systems, the work being carried out by the National Bureau of Standards. Many observers believe that performance criteria should be used more extensively, although they recognize that several problems stand in the way. First, the various aspects and dimensions of a product's performance are often difficult to observe directly, the consequence being that performance criteria are relatively expensive to develop. Second, performance criteria are relatively expensive to administer. Whereas simple inspection may show that physical specifications are met, it may cost thousands of dollars to establish whether performance criteria are met. Third, to the extent that government purchasing is pushed in the direction of new products, political problems are likely to be encountered.

CHANGES IN THE NATIONAL SCIENCE FOUNDATION

In 1966, the House Subcommittee on Science, Research, and Development proposed a number of important changes in the operations and functions of the National Science Foundation. The Subcommittee's basic criticism is that ". . . the Foundation has functioned, and still does, in a manner that is largely passive. It has not itself put a sustained effort into developing substance, form, and direction of the programs it supports. Once granted its annual budget, NSF has to a large extent followed a practice of waiting for talented outsiders to suggest appropriate projects on which to spend it . . . The Foundation's input toward the evolution of national science policy, never strong, seems to have weakened further in recent years."

To improve the situation, the Subcommittee recommends the following three changes: (1) The Foundation's position within the executive branch should be upgraded. It should be held responsible for the nation's science resources, freeing the Office of Science and Technology and the President's Science Advisory Committee from their detailed oversight in this area. In particular, it should evaluate the state of the various scientific disciplines, evaluate the condition of our scientific resources, and direct some research, basic or applied, to help bring into being new technology required in the public interest. Moreover, the social sciences should be explicitly included. (2) The character of the National Science Board should be altered. Its functions should be streamlined to relieve it of routine administrative tasks, and both Congress and the Executive Office of the President should be encouraged to use the Board as a source of advice and independent viewpoint. (3) The authority of the Foundation's Director should be extended to allow him to pass on all proposals for NSF support, subject only to Board restraint in exceptional cases. His pay grade should be elevated and additional high-level managerial talent should be made available to him. His prestige and influence in the executive branch should be enhanced.

If the changes are adopted, the Foundation will become more clearly a part of the central machinery of government directed toward the achievement of national objectives. Besides evaluating projects submitted to it, it will actively select areas of research to be emphasized. Decisions will become more the responsibility of the director, and he will become more clearly accountable to the Congress and the President. These changes have much to recommend them. The most important dangers are that the Foundation's political vulnerability will increase and that applied research may be increased at the expense of basic research.

This proposal is by no means the only one in this area emanating from Congress. On the contrary, Congress is becoming increasingly important in initiating changes in science policy. This is different from the earlier postwar years when, except for atomic energy affairs, government science policy was generally initiated within the executive branch. Another proposal of the House Subcommittee on Science, Research, and Development stems from its concern over the dangerous side effects which applied technology is creating or is likely to create. For example, chemicals developed to reduce the insect population have polluted the soil, and human beings now have measurable quantities of these pesticides in their tissues. The Subcommittee has proposed an early warning system which might be established by the federal government "to keep tabs on the potential dangers, as well as the benefits inherent in new technology." Other groups, such as a committee of the American Association for the Advancement of Science, have expressed similar concern. One problem in the Subcommittee's suggestion is the difficulty in predicting the consequences of new technology. However, the Subcommittee is undoubtedly right in believing that more attention should be directed at the external diseconomies generated by technological change.

DUPLICATION AND COORDINATION

During the sixties, Congress has begun to look more closely at the management of federal R and D programs, there being the concern on Capitol Hill that these programs involve needless duplication and waste. For example, according to Congressman Carl Elliot of Alabama, "A suspicion that there may be unjustifiable duplication of effort arises from the fact that 11 agencies and departments perform research in health and medicine; 5 agencies perform space research, exclusive of aircraft technology; 7 are doing work in oceanography, 8 in water research and 16 in meteorology. Multiple-agency interest is also apparent in such broad categories as defense, environmental health, natural resources, nuclear energy, and the like." Partly in response to Congressional pressure, more attention is being given to the coordination of R and D that cuts across agency lines. For example, in the case of oceanography, the President's Science Advisory Committee recommended in 1966 that a new mission-oriented agency be established to encompass a great portion of the non-Navy oceanographic programs that are now scattered through the government. At that time, an Interagency Committee on Oceanography was charged with planning and coordinating the overall program. Also, the Environmental Science Services Administration was created in 1965 to provide a single national focus for a number of allied scientific diciplines, like meteorology, that are concerned with the weather and the physical environment.

In the mid-sixties, there has been considerable pressure from many sources to repeat the pattern of AEC and NASA and to create separate agencies to deal with specific technologies, like oceanography. According to the proponents of this approach, a new and emerging technology does not receive adequate attention unless the existing capabilities are assembled in one agency. Moreover, in the case of some technologies, like space technology, they are so complex and expensive that one cannot afford to develop them separately for each mission. The main argument against the creation of new agencies for new technologies is that the promotion of the technology tends to become an end in itself apart from the social goals which it serves. Thus, it is sometimes charged that atomic energy has been pushed more enthusiastically than it would have been if the decisions had been made on the basis of the advice of scientists with more general interests and in accord with the priorities of administrators and politicians who looked more closely at the contribution of a particular technological development to the ends of public policy.

Problems of coordination are bound to occur in any large enterprise. Unquestionably, they occur in the federal R and D establishment, and the critics are right to press for improvements. Nonetheless, there is sometimes a tendency to overestimate the problem of duplication of effort. In basic research, there is little unnecessary, conscious duplication because the results are freely published and the rewards for duplicating someone else's work are generally quite small. Where conscious duplication occurs, it is likely to be required to confirm previous experimental findings. This, of course, is a valuable activity. In development, it sometimes seems that there is unnecessary duplication of effort. However, in some of these cases, parallel efforts are deliberately mounted in order to assure the quick attainment of an important objective. This can be the cheapest way to proceed. Besides duplication, there is considerable concern that federal R and D programs are inefficient, one apparent indication of this being the fact that so few programs produce useful results. In the Department of Defense, for example, it has been estimated that, for every twenty ideas which are explored, only five are carried to advanced development, only one or two are carried through the engineering for service use, and "zero or perhaps one of them . . . [are] deployed for service use." Estimates of this sort can be quite misleading. Although there may have been considerable inefficiency, the mere fact that many projects do not succeed is no proof of such waste since, even if there were no inefficiencies, many projects would fail, because of the inherent uncertainties in research and development.

FEDERAL ALLOCATION OF RESEARCH
AND DEVELOPMENT RESOURCES

Congress has also been concerned about other aspects of the management of federal R and D programs. In 1966, Congressman Henry Reuss of Wisconsin pointed out that the allocation of federal R and D expenditures is a fragmented process, no one really having responsibility for the adequacy of the over-all allocation. He expressed concern "that in the great bulk of R and D manpower expenditures, there is no central authority which takes a look at them, before they are launched, to determine whether there is an adequate supply of scientists to do the job—or whether you would not be robbing Peter to pay Paul if you do start a given new program."

According to the current organizational and budgetary procedure, research and development is considered an aspect of each federal activity. Judgments are made about the relative importance of various federal programs (defense, agriculture, etc.), and decisions are made regarding the total amount that should be spent on each one. Then many of the basic decisions regarding the level and allocation of R and D spending are made in the individual agencies and departments where R and D needs and opportunities are evaluated in a mission context. This is different from the procedure favored by Reuss and others, whereby the executive branch and Congress would focus attention directly on the R and D components of all agencies' expenditures and attempt to reach an optimal allocation.

With regard to the present system, it is important to add that the existence of large programs which are science-oriented and devoted to means rather than ends, makes the tradeoff between R and D and other activities within some agencies rather artificial. It is also important to note that the sorts of tradeoffs within R and D proposed by Reuss are being made to some extent within the Executive Branch, particularly by the interaction of the Office of Science and Technology with the Bureau of the Budget. Although these tradeoffs within R and D may have little influence in any single budgetary year, their cumulative impact over many budget years can be significant. However, it is true, of course, that Congress continues to be much more oriented toward the agency tradeoffs than the tradeoffs within R and D.

Although it is generally acknowledged that somewhat more coordination would be a good thing, Reuss's proposal has not stirred up a great deal of enthusiasm, most observers being impressed with the difficulties involved in direct allocation of R and D resources. The customary cost-effectiveness techniques are of limited use, because there is no good way of measuring the relative importance of various federal objectives and because the outcome of R and D projects is so uncertain. Also, the problem is complicated by the fact that R and D resources are by no means homogeneous. Nonetheless, these problems cannot be avoided simply by keeping the present system. Whether or not they are made explicit, judgments of this sort are imbedded in any decision that is reached, regardless of how the budgetary and decision making procedures are organized. Despite the enormous difficulties, it seems likely that more attempt will be made in the future to compare the costs and benefits of various kinds of research and development. However, it does not seem likely, or desirable, that the government will attempt to program science and technology on the basis of a totally integrated science and technology budget.

During the late fifties, as well as in more recent years, there have been proposals of a cabinet-level Department of Science, which would include the AEC, NASA, NSF, the basic research activities of the DOD, the National Bureau of Standards, the Office of Technical Services, the Patent Office, and part of the Smithsonian Institution. Advocates of a Department of Science, led by then-Senator Humphrey, advanced the following arguments in its favor: (1) The Secretary of such a department, because of his cabinet rank, would assure greater status for science. (2) The Department would help to eliminate useless duplication and to promote a better allocation of scientific manpower. (3) It would constitute a policy link between Congress and the President. The proposal has been opposed by the scientific community, for what seem to be good reasons. The 1958 Parliament of Science (and numerous scientists who testified) opposed the proposal because they feared further centralization and because it seemed administratively and politically unwise. Since the agencies that would be merged have great status and importance, the department might well be torn by intramural dissension. Moreover, the merger of agencies with practical missions with NSF might well result in the neglect of basic research programs. Finally, since the new department could not hope to include all government scientific activities (because Defense, Agriculture, etc. would have to maintain research establishments), the new department would have to compete with existing departments and could not act as a coordinator of all scientific activities.

Suggested Further Readings

Benoit, E. and K. Boulding, *Disarmament and the Economy* (Harper & Row, 1963).

Brooks, H., "Science and the Allocation of Resources," *American Psychologist* (March 1967).

Bush, V., *Science, the Endless Frontier* (Government Printing Office, 1945).

Dubridge, L., "Policy and the Scientists," *Foreign Affairs* (1963).

Dupree, A., *Science and the Federal Government* (Belknap Press, 1957).

Enke, S., *Defense Management* (Prentice-Hall, 1967).

Enthoven, A., "Economic Analysis in the Department of Defense," *American Economic Review* (May 1963).

———— and H. Rowen, "Defense Planning and Organization," in *Public Finances: Needs, Sources, and Utilization* (National Bureau of Economic Research, 1961).

Freeman, C., M. Poignant, and S. Svennilson, *Science, Economic Growth, and Government Policy* (Organization for Economic Cooperation and Development, 1963).

Gilpin R. and C. Wright, *Scientists and National Policy-Making* (Columbia University, 1964).

Grubel, H. and A. Scott, "The International Flow of Human Capital," *American Economic Review* (May 1966).

Hall, G. and R. Johnson, *A Review of Air Force Procurement, 1962–64* (RAND Corporation RM–4500–PR, May 1965).

Hildebrand, G. and N. Breckner, "The Impacts of National Security Expenditure upon the Stability and Growth of the American Economy," in U. S. Congress, Joint Economic Committee, *Federal Expenditure Policy for Economic Growth and ,Stability* (Government Printing Office, 1957).

Hitch, C., *Decision-Making for Defense* (University of California, 1966).

———— and R. McKean, *The Economics of Defense in the Nuclear Age* (Harvard University, 1960).

Kaufman, W., *The McNamara Strategy* (Harper & Row, 1964).

Kaysen, C., "Improving the Efficiency of Military Research and Development," *Public Policy* (Harvard University, 1964).

Kendrick, J., *Productivity Trends in the United States* (National Bureau of Economic Research, 1961).

Klein, B., "A Radical Proposal for R and D," *Fortune* (May 1958).

Knorr, K. and O. Morgenstern, *Science and Defense* (Policy Memorandum No. 32, Woodrow Wilson School, Princeton University, February 1965).

Machlup, F., *The Production and Distribution of Knowledge in the United States* (Princeton University, 1962).

Mansfield, E., *Industrial Research and Technological Innovation* (Norton, 1968).

————, *The Economics of Technological Change* (Norton, 1968).

Marschak, T., T. Glennan and R. Summers, *Strategy for R and D,* (Springer-Verlag, 1967).

Moore, F., "Efficiency and Public Policy in Defense Procurement," *Law and Contemporary Problems* (Winter 1964).

Morgenstern, O., *The Question of National Defense* (Random House, 1959).

National Bureau of Economic Research, *The Rate and Direction of Inventive Activity* (Princeton University, 1962).

———, Conference on the Economics of Defense (April 15–16, 1966).

Nelson R., M. Peck, and E. Kalachek, *Technology, Economic Growth, and Public Policy* (Brookings Institution, 1967).

Novick, D., *Program Budgeting* (Harvard University, 1965).

Peck, M. and F. Scherer, *The Weapons Acquisition Process* (Harvard University, 1962).

Price, D., *Government and Science* (New York University, 1954).

———, *The Scientific Estate* (Belknap Press, 1965).

Quade, E., *Analysis for Military Decisions* (RAND Corporation, November 1964).

Schelling, F., *The Strategy of Conflict* (Harvard University, 1960).

———, "Controlled Response and Strategic Warfare," *Institute for Strategic Studies* (June 1965).

Scherer, F., *The Weapons Acquisition Process: Economic Incentives* (Harvard University, 1964).

———, "Measuring Benefits From Government Research and Development Programs" in R. Dorfman (ed.), *Measuring Benefits of Government Investments* (Brookings Institution, 1965).

Schlesinger, J., "Quantitative Analysis and National Security," *World Politics* (January 1963).

Schmookler, J., *Invention and Economic Growth* (Harvard University, 1966).

Tiebout, C., "The Regional Impact of Defense Expenditures: Its Measurement and Problems of Adjustment," in U. S. Congress, Senate Committee on Labor and Public Welfare, *Nation's Manpower Revolution* (Government Printing Office, 1963).

Tybout, R., *Economics of Research and Development* (Ohio State University, 1965).

U.S. Arms Control and Disarmament Agency, *Economic Impacts of Disarmament* (Government Printing Office, 1962).

U.S. Department of Defense, *First Interim Report on Project Hindsight* (October 13, 1966).

U.S. House of Representatives, *The Federal Research and Development Programs: The Decision-Making Process* (House Committee on Government Operations, 1966).

U.S. National Academy of Sciences, *Basic Research and National Goals* (Government Printing Office, March, 1965).

U.S. National Commission on Technology, Automation, and Economic Progress, *Report and 6 Appendix Volumes* (Government Printing Office, 1966).

Yarmolinsky, A., "Science Policy and National Defense," *American Economic Review* (May 1966).

Yovits, M., D. Gilford, R. Wilcox, E. Staveley, and H. Lerner, *Research Program Effectiveness* (Gordon and Breach, 1966).

Zuckerman, S., *Scientists and War* (Harper & Row, 1967).